WHO'S GOING TO READ THIS ANYWAY?

SECOND EDITION

Ray Matthews
&
Gary Webb

NIAGARA
COLLEGE
WELLAND
ONTARIO

Holt, Rinehart and Winston of Canada Limited
Toronto

Copyright © 1983 by Holt, Rinehart and Winston of Canada, Limited.
All rights reserved.

Canadian Cataloguing in Publication Data
Matthews, Ray.
    Who's going to read this, anyway?

Includes index.
ISBN 0-03-921639-X

1. English language — Rhetoric. I. Webb, Gary.
II. Title.

PE1408.M38 1983   808'.042   C82-095276-1

Acquisitions Editor: Anthony Luengo
Managing Editor: Dennis Bockus

Printed in the United States of America
1 2 3 4 5   87 86 85 84 83

*For Judy and Ruth, with thanks
for their patience and support*

Acknowledgements

For Kind permission to reprint copyrighted material, acknowledgement is hereby made to the following:

The Globe and Mail, Toronto for "The Root of Consent" by Susan Cole. *Weekend Magazine* for "Killing Ground" by Patrick O'Flaherty. Patricia Brooks, author of "Pretty Poison." *Weekend Magazine* for "Different Strokes" by Gerry Kopelow. *The Globe and Mail,* Toronto for "Advertising" by Ellen Roseman. Alexander Ross, author of "How To Dress Like a Loser". Brenda Rabkin, author of "A Sin of the Mother Is Visited Upon the Child." Diane Hale, author of "Laser Technology—Straight from *Star Trek*." Dr. Kenneth Walker and W. Gifford-Jones Limited for "Dental X-Rays Shouldn't Be a Matter of Routine" by W. Gifford-Jones, M.D. *Reader's Digest* for "Acid Rain: Scourge from the Skies" by Robert Collins, © 1980 by The Reader's Digest Association (Canada) Ltd. *Weekend Magazine* for "Insane Judgments' by Andreas Schroeder. "Visit to the Enchanted Isles," reprinted by permission from *TIME, The Weekly Newsmagazine;* Copyright Time Inc., 1978. "In the Beginning: God and Science" by Lance Morrow. Reprinted by permission from *TIME, The Weekly Newsmagazine;* Copyright Time Inc., 1979. "Laugh After Laugh" by Dr. Raymond A. Moody, Jr. Copyright ©: 1978 by Dr. Raymond A. Moody, Jr. Reprinted with permission of the publisher. J. L. Granatstein, author of "The Secret Drift To Free Trade With the U.S.: How We Could All End Up as Americans." *Saturday Review* for "Colonizing the Heavens" by Isaac Asimov. "Escape or Reality?" by Burt Prelutsky. Copyright © 1974 *Human Behavior Magazine.* Reprinted by permission. *Newsweek Magazine* for "What TV Does To Kids". Mike Grenby, author of "Cool Nerve Required to Play Commodities." *Harrowsmith Magazine* for "Bio-Engineering Gone Wrong" by Sheila Kulka and Barry Estabrook. *The Globe and Mail,* Toronto for "Good Secretaries Get Harder to Find as Jobs Call for Management Skills" by Peggy McCallum. Elliot Gold, author of "Riding With The Chosen Few". *The Futurist Magazine* for "The Coming of an Information Society" by Edward Cornish. Published by the world Future Society, 4916 St. Elmo Avenue, Washington, DC 20014, April 1981. *Saturday Night Magazine* for "How Telidon May Change Your Life" by Robert Fulford. *The New York Times Magazine* for "Earth's Biggest Blast Felled Trees in 20-Mile Radius" by Walter Sullivan, copyright © 1979 by the New York Times Company. Reprinted by permission. "Winter Camping Can Be Fun" by Berndt Berglund with Jack Batten. Reprinted from *The Review,* Imperial Oil Ltd., 1976, Number 1. "Fiber Optics" A Growing Technology," reproduced from the Maclean-Hunter publication *Design Engineering* by permission of the editor, Royston H. Linnegar. *Reader's Digest Magazine* for "What Do We Really Know About Psychic Phenomena?" by Laile E. Bartlett, © Reader's Digest Magazines Ltd. Reprinted by permission. *Weekend Magazine* for "Reign of Terror" by Jorge Nef, and "The Eyes of God" by Banesh Hoffman. *Psychology Today Magazine* for "Let the Punishment Fit the Crime" by Philip Brickman. Copyright © 1977 Ziff-David Publishing Company. *Report Magazine* for "Sceptics and Optimists Debate Nuclear Power" by John Pepperell. "Heart Attack: Delay Can Be Fatal" by Oscar Roth, M.D. from *Heart Attack! A Question and Answer Book* by Oscar Roth, M.D. with Lawrence Galton (J. B. Lippincott). Copyright © 1978 by Oscar Roth, M.D. Reprinted by permission of Harper & Row, Publishers, Inc. *Popular Science Magazine* for "Coiled Collector" by Katharine Griggs, reprinted with permission © 1978 Times Mirror Magazines, Inc. *The Toronto Star* for "Middle Class Resentment's Base is Envy" by Robert Fulford. George Woodcock, author of "The Liberation of Canada's Writers". "A Better Way of Dying" reprinted by permission from *TIME, The Weekly Newsmagazine;* Copyright Time Inc. 1978. *World Press Review Magazine* for "Japan's Robot Revolution" by Katsukiko Hirano. "Mirror, Mirror on the Wall" by John Leo, reprinted by permission from *TIME, The Weekly Newsmagazine;* Copyright Time Inc. 1978. Andrew Weiner, author of "Unaccustomed As I Am." *Weekend Magazine* for "Lotoland" by David Macfarlane. *Toronto Sun* for "38 Watched Stabbing" by Max Haines, reprinted by permission of Canada Wide Feature Services Limited. Jerry Goodis, author of "Help! There's Sex In My Soup. A Small Plea for an End to Subliminal Silliness." Tabitha M. Powledge, author of "Test Tube Babies." Reprinted from the November, 1978, issue of *Omni.* Andrew Weiner, author of "How To Be a Leader". *Newsweek Magazine* for "The Second Sex" by Susan Cheever Crowley with Betsy Carter.

CONTENTS

Introduction

Anthology

Introduction

For some strange reason, people in school (instructors and students alike) often forget that the real purpose for writing is *to communicate a message to someone.* Whenever this purpose is forgotten, the "in class composition" becomes nothing more than an exercise in creating "in class compositions": students view writing as the search for or repetition of a magic formula for an impersonal grading machine that is only searching for "grammatical correctness", not for what is really being communicated. The instructor, on the other hand, tends to look only for the student's ability to use the language "correctly" within the very narrow limits of the classroom setting. He or she then returns the paper with so few reactions about the message that was actually being conveyed to a real reader that the whole process reinforces the student's assumption that writing is an exercise whose consequences go no further than filling a blank page with words. In the long run, the student comes to view courses in writing as obstacles to be overcome rather than aids to career development.

Yet writing that is done anywhere other than in school always has a real reader and a real purpose that are quite clear and important to the writer. An accountant may be motivated to write in order to convince an employer that some change should be made in the operation of a business; a salesman may want to explain why he acted in a certain way to someone who is going to be judging the value of that action; or a technologist may want to explain how to operate a machine in such a way as to avoid confusion, frustration and perhaps physical injury. In short, in the world outside of the school, the reader suddenly emerges as a "real" person.

Interesting things begin to happen to a person's written communications as soon as he becomes aware of the reader. No longer does the writer think in terms of grammatical errors, but in terms of the message that is really being communicated to the reader: has he explained a task that has to be done clearly enough to be understood by a stranger who has never done this task before? Have any terms been used that might be clear to the writer, but vague to someone else? Is the time sequence clear to the reader? Has the background to the problem at hand been presented clearly enough for the reader to grasp the significance of the recommendations of the report? The questions that the writer begins to ask in these situations go on and on, but they always come back to one central focus: how well will the reader understand what I really mean to say?

Moreover, as the writer struggles to clarify the ideas for the reader, something that at first may be quite surprising begins to happen: the old problems of "grammar" begin to disappear. Mistakes in grammar, it is soon realized, result chiefly from the writer's failure to take into consideration the knowledge that the reader possesses about either the topic being written about or the way in which the writer views that topic. For example, "pronoun reference" errors such as "They do not like me at the college" result from the writer's failure to remember that although he knows who "they" are, the readers may not. When the writer really becomes concerned about the message that he is communicating, choice of words and the order in which they appear, sentence structure and its impact, and all of the other elements that go into good writing suddenly become very important.

Frequently, college students are not fully aware of the importance of good writing in their future careers. The greatest barrier to a student's professional advancement most frequently stems not from an inability to handle the work in his chosen profession, but from an inability to handle the written language that is called for by the job. Reports, memoranda, business correspondence and the many other forms of written communication are vital to success in all professions. Recently we encountered a case in which a college student was refused a job in construction work because his inability to spell correctly would stand in the way of his advancement to a higher position within the company at a later date. Even situations which call for conveying oral instructions or explanations require many of the same skills of audience analysis, organization and word selection that are so important in writing.

On the other hand, many instructors seem to believe that good writing skills can be acquired through the boring process of memorizing "rules of grammar" and doing grammar exercises. Yet all that anyone except an expert learns from doing grammar exercises is how to do grammar exercises. How many times do students encounter a situation in which they register near perfect scores on grammar tests or programmed grammars and then proceed to write an essay that has proven to be virtually incomprehensible to anyone?

In this book, we approach the development of writing skills from the point of view of writing as an act of communication. From this point of view, the key to successful writing lies in fulfilling two prerequisites that are frequently forgotten: i) you must identify clearly for yourself exactly what it is that you want to communicate, and ii) you must identify clearly to whom you wish to say it. Only when you have established these guidelines can you approach your topic in such a way as to achieve effective communication. In the process of clarifying and elaborating your ideas for your reader, you will almost always "correct" your own grammar because *all* that the various rules of grammar do is to provide generally applicable guidelines to the clear, logical presentation of ideas to a reader. If at any time you are in doubt about whether a construction actually conveys the message that you want it to, check it in the Appendices at the back of this book.

The articles that appear in this book have been selected from a wide range of contemporary newspapers and magazines. Not only do they deal with topics which we hope will interest students and stimulate further writing, but each reflects a unique approach to the problem of presenting information and opinions to readers who have different levels of background knowledge about the topic. In other words, each of the authors deals with exactly the same kinds of problems that you are going to be facing whenever you write. The questions which accompany each article are designed to help you see how that particular author has tried to deal with his/her material in such a way as to communicate the message to the reader effectively. The "Thinking and Writing" sections which accompany each article are designed to give *you* an opportunity to do the same things with your ideas on the topic.

The root of consent

by Susan G. Cole

1. The Queen smiles benignly down from a poster-sized photograph flanked by two flags in her place of honor at the front of a Canadian classroom. Beside her a scarlet-clad Mountie sits astride his glossy steed, his flinty gaze intent on the true North, strong and free. Canadians, good citizens most of them, have been brought up under the watchful expressions on authority figures' faces. Unlike their neighbors to the south, who seem to delight in seizing issues and sacred cows and shaking them to their foundations, Canadians are apathetic, content in what Alan Borovoy, general counsel for the Canadian Civil Liberties Association, calls only half-kiddingly "a pleasantly authoritarian state."

2. A Gallup poll reported that 86 per cent of the Canadian populace cheered the application of the War Measures Act in 1970—and in peacetime—and a few years later, when the RCMP was discovered opening our mail for the sake of "national security," Canadians reacted as if police wrongdoing ought to be more or less par for the course. "Middle-class Canadians in particular believed that the police have to do dirty things to protect us," says Peter Russell, a political science professor at the University of Toronto. Russell was research director of the McDonald Commission, which examined police activities, and he and his associates came under fire from the outraged citizenry, who apparently wanted criminals behind bars no matter what the cost to their own rights. "Canadians don't think we should lean on the police too hard, or the RCMP won't get the job done. Critics tended to remark that the commission was naive to think that the police didn't have to break the law to bring criminals to justice.

3. "Unlike other countries," Russell goes on, "we've made our police force into a national symbol. Others make symbols out of the army and the navy. We Canadians have the RCMP."

4. In many ways, the Mountie is to Canada what the cowboy is to the United States. The cowboys roamed the west, staked out their land, settled it, and protected it with guns they were sure they had the right to bear; they didn't call it the Wild West for nothing. The sheriff, usually a local yokel, had little authority except that which the community vested in him, and he appeared on the scene only under the most dire of circumstances.

5. The Mounties, on the other hand, were a veritable fixture on the Canadian landscape. The RCMP settled the Canadian West and was followed by bankers, railways and finally pioneers, who settled into a community with a firmly entrenched infra-structure of law and order. Americans who tried to cross the border from gold-rushing Alaska were met immediately by a Sergeant Steele who divested the prospectors of their guns. Only the Mounties could bear arms in Canada.

6. These and other traditions make it difficult for Canadians to accept information that might sully the reputation of the RCMP. Canadians seem lost in the throes of an unrequited love affair with the forces of law and order.

7. "People believe in their institutions," says civil rights lawyer Clayton Ruby, "but they ignore the facts that show that their trust has been misplaced." Indeed, every once in a while, Toronto erupts with an "our cops are tops" demonstration; and, despite reports of abuse of police privilege in this city, activists are hard-pressed to get Torontonians interested in a civilian review of the local police commission. The love affair is passionate. Making the RCMP a national symbol, as Peter Russell says, "has made it extremely difficult to reform the police force."

8. The American way is very different from the Canadian way when it comes to individual freedoms and rights. The Watergate scandal, which featured shenanigans similar to the RCMP's antics with our mails, forced Nixon out of office and virtually emasculated the CIA for years.

9. Then again, Americans have rights to protect. Their constitution insists that "we the people" run the show and that "inalienable rights" be enforced by the courts and not wrenched away by any authority under any circumstances. Canadian politicians, on the other hand, have just fashioned a constitution that boasts a bill of rights that doesn't insist on much.

10. "One needs to look at the differences between the two countries," says Alan Borovoy when asked why Americans attach so much importance to civil rights while Canadians seem uninterested. "America began as a revolution against authority. In Canada, it was largely a reaction to the American experience. Among the partners in the founding coalition in Canada were the descendants of the finks from the American Revolution, the United Empire Loyalists. So it's not surprising that deep in the Canadian tradition there is a reverence of authority."

11. Just as the British North America Act was in the rough draft stage, Americans were locked in a bitter civil war. One can imagine the founding fathers looking at the situation and deciding that all that high-falutin' talk in the U.S. Constitution led to

violence of the most brutal kind. "The Confederation debates are full of statements saying we should avoid doing what the Americans are doing," says Barry Cooper, professor of political philosophy at the University of Calgary. "It wasn't just the Civil War. They [Canadians] didn't like republics compared with monarchies and a balanced constitution. The Canadians believed that republicanism led to excess. No one admired the Americans, thinking republicanism led to instability."

12. Accordingly, history shows us moving away from Mother England not as a rebellious child but as a rather docile one who still liked to be told what to eat. Keeping the constitution at Westminster was something like going home to Mom and Dad's for dinner once a week. When not viewed as a nation full of truculent souls beating each other over the heads, the Americans were perceived even then as a nation capable of beating other nation states into submission—in the 1800s the threat of an American invasion of Canada was constant. Mother England's skirts would protect us from our everflexing neighbors. Herschel Hardin, in *A Nation Unaware*, explains that the Crown in Parliament was viewed as "the greatest defence against absorption into the continental state."

13. Denigrators of our political forefathers sometimes contend that they were either too drunk or not smart enough to deal in theoretical values, but political economist Abraham Rotstein is a bit more generous. "They certainly weren't the inspired men who wrote 13 volumes on the nature of democracy (as did the American founding fathers in the *The Federalist Papers*)." But then again they were addressing different issues. The Fathers of Confederation were trying to pull together fractious provinces into one federation, which Hardin calls a "marriage of convenience," not one of love. Canadians were never interested in embracing abstract principles but rather signed a contract that dealt with practical questions of resources and who should control them.

14. Since that time when pragmatism was the order of the day, Canada has become the home of waves of immigrants whose concerns for the most part continue to be practical. Novelist Graeme Gibson remarks that "people didn't come to Canada for political freedom; they came for economic freedom; therefore, they don't want to make waves. Canada is such a comfortable country, and there's a place for the new Canadian, a niche he can find."

15. Ceta Ramkhalawasingh, a sociologist and community activist now working for the City of Toronto, feels that immigrants who have come from countries rife with political turbulence especially don't want to tangle with the police. "People who come here from revolutionary situations, whether left or right wing, came here

for stability," she says, "and if the police opening mail is going to maintain law and order, then it's okay."

16. Once in a while a few whispers of dissent are heard, not surprisingly, when an issue involves anything to do with our own turf. "Canadians' self-image is territorially related," says Rotstein, "so that we get exercised by fishing rights, acid rain and, more locally, the extension of the Spadina Expressway. But Canadians don't get turned on by the more abstract issues of civil rights." Ruby puts it more simply. "The most important thing is property rights, and everything else takes second place."

17. Canadians are sure they're doing just fine in the property department. The fact that Canada offers to its inhabitants so many creature comforts in an environment that remains relatively stable explains why Canadians see it as a "pleasantly authoritarian state" and not as a totalitarian state or a police state or any of the terms that are applied to other countries where the government and the police have similar clout.

18. "After the American Revolution," Cooper explains, "the Loyalists came to Canada and the government helped them. The British government subsidized their passage from the former Thirteen Colonies and then, when they got to New Brunswick and Upper Canada, the government made it easy for them to purchase land. So right from the start, the state was viewed as the good guys." Canadians still see government that way. "We see government in terms of the benefits it gives out," says Graeme Gibson. "We believe our government is a concerned one, because it serves up medicare and a host of other social services."

19. If Canadians think of government in terms of what it gives out, Americans think of government in terms of what it might take away. At best, the state for Americans is a necessary evil. While our southerly neighbors are trying to dismantle an unwieldy bureaucracy and have become somewhat obsessed with deregulation, Canadians show no signs of wanting to limit the scope of their government or the powers of the police. Canadians believe that authority deserves our blessings and not our fears.

20. How much longer Canadians will feel grateful to government is another matter; the high standard of living on which Canadian complacency hinges is certainly not built into the Charter of Rights. "All countries that are capitalist and experiencing little or negative growth are going to have difficulties maintaining a society with civil liberties," warns Peter Russell. "There will be strikes, lockouts, violence. Britain is the classic example now. We have to make certain that, in the face of this kind of instability, government and the police respect the civil rights of individuals." Rights may be the only certainty in an uncertain future.

Style and Structure

1. (a) Underline the thesis statement.
    (b) Why does Cole choose to open her article by describing a photograph of the Queen and a Mountie?
    (c) What is the effect of the statement "brought up under the watchful expressions on authority figures' faces" in relation to the reference to the Queen and the Mounties?
    (d) How does this opening prepare the reader for the thesis statement?
2. What aspect of Canadians' contentment with "a pleasantly authoritarian state" does Cole develop in paragraphs 2 to 7? What is the function of paragraphs 3 to 5 in relation to the rest of the section?
3. (a) What aspect of her thesis does the author discuss in paragraphs 8 to 13? What aspect does she deal with in paragraphs 14 to 18?
    (b) Identify in each of these sections the passages that serve the same purpose as paragraphs 3 to 5 in the first section.
4. An author may choose to do a number of things with an article's conclusion. In this essay Cole employs a conclusion of two paragraphs, each of which serves a different, valid purpose.
    (a) How does paragraph 19 serve as a conclusion?
    (b) How does paragraph 20 serve as a conclusion?
5. What attitude toward Canadian complacency and apathy does the writer express in paragraph 20? Underline words, phrases, and quotations in the body of the essay which reflect a similar attitude.
    How does the use of this tone throughout the essay prepare the reader to accept the conclusion presented in paragraph 20?

Thinking and Writing

a. In the essay Cole quotes Peter Russell: "Middle-class Canadians in particular believed that the police have to do dirty things to protect us." Take a survey of 10 people you know to find out whether or not Canadians believe that "police have to do dirty things to protect us". In addition to the general question, ask them about such things as high-speed chases, wire tapping and opening mail. Write a report on your findings.
Audience:
someone who knows nothing about the subject of your survey.

b. Write an essay in which you argue for or against the proposition, "The police should be allowed to commit illegal acts if those acts aid in lowering the crime rate." Use specific examples of such acts to support your view.

Audience:
someone who knows the topic well but holds the opposite opinion to yours.
Send a copy of your essay to your MP or to the public relations department of the RCMP.

Killing ground

by Patrick O'Flaherty

1. Philip Tocque, a 19th-century Newfoundland writer, who spent his life as a teacher, justice of the peace, and minister in the Episcopal Church in the United States, was a lover of dogs. One day in the 1840s he visited a Newfoundland outport and came upon a scene that shocked him. A number of boys were busily engaged in drowning an old dog, whose days of useful toil seemed over. The boys were not following what Tocque called the "general practice" in disposing of a dog in Newfoundland, namely, tying a large rock around its neck and throwing it into the sea, but instead were struggling to drown the creature in a brook where there was hardly enough water to cover its body. Tocque did not describe, but we can imagine for ourselves, the desperate floundering of the animal in its efforts to escape, the splashing water, the frantic activities of the urchins. Tocque protested to the children's father, who saw what was going on and "appeared pleased." Tocque told the man that cruelty to animals was a sin. Instead of allowing his children to drown dogs, he said, the father should be "teaching them not to be thoughtless of the sensations of any thing that has life, and guarding them against any sport or amusement wherein either the larger animals or birds, or even insects, may be treated with cruelty." The outporter, somewhat dumfounded, replied: "I never before heard that it was sinful to drown a dumb animal; if I had thought so, I am very sure I should never have done it." But the dog was saved, and four years later, Tocque rejoiced to learn that it was still living and even working.
2. I have no means of verifying Tocque's account of the episode, and the suspicion lingers that he distorted what he saw for literary reasons. If he did, he was not the first or last local writer to tell lies about his country to make an impression abroad. Although I grew up in an outport close to the one he visited, I never saw a dog treated in the manner described in his book. By the 1940s, in my outport, dogs had long since been replaced by horses as work

animals, and though they still had useful roles to fill, on the whole, they had degenerated into something resembling family pets. But I don't really want to accuse Tocque of being a liar. What he says he saw possibly could have happened.

3. The old outporters were killers, not from deliberate cruelty, but through exigency. The community into which Tocque intruded, lived by unselfconscious brutality toward the animal kingdom, and the play of outport children was influenced by the necessary killing of animals of many kinds. You could not grow up in such a setting — and surely this is also true of life in farming and fishing communities throughout Canada — without seeing animals slaughtered. Lambs, pigs, chickens, cattle, birds, rabbits, goats, fish of all descriptions, and seals (along parts of the coast) were relentlessly butchered before our eyes.

4. I can still recall walking around the corner of a neighbor's house, at the age of 6 or 7, to see the back of an axe descend with enormous force on the forehead of an unknowing cow, peacefully chewing its cud. The axe fell, the chewing stopped, and, horribly, the animal remained standing for what seemed like many seconds. Then slowly it toppled forward, its knees bent to the ground as if it had decided to lie down, and it fell over soundlessly, dying. Such bloody scenes were commonplace, and they had an effect upon the sensibilities of children, who naturally came to view animals with the same kind of impassiveness they saw in their fathers. They picked up from adults the attitudes they needed to succeed in a rough life.

5. I should add that the quality of mind that enabled this killing to go on, year in and year out, coexisted, in many men I knew, with feelings of affection toward housepets, and scrupulous attention to the feeding and care of farm animals. It also did not impair their love for their families or concern for neighbors. The idea that such a life as that provided by the old outport somehow diminished or coarsened a man's moral nature, an idea that Tocque, in one of his most foolish paragraphs, helped to spread, does not stand up to the test of experience. How warmth and compassion could survive in men who had to kill for a living may seem a mystery. Yet such was the case.

6. The story of Tocque and the dog illustrates a clash between two kinds of temperament: one, that of a sensitive, fastidious man of feeling; the other, that of unwitting callousness, exhibited in the behavior of the father and his children. The two men are universes apart. They meet and speak; and sentiment, armed with self-righteousness and Biblical quotations, easily triumphs over instinct. In this quick victory, to my eyes, there may be worrisome implications which shed light on Newfoundland's position within the fabric of North American society.

7. For 30 years, we have been a province of Canada. On the whole, I think, there has been no violent dislocation of life here as a consequence of the union. Some commentators have voiced anxiety about the effects of the new industrial age and the "evil" of consumerism upon our society, but this is mostly ignorant poppycock. Industrialism did not begin in Newfoundland in 1949, nor did we see, for the first time in that year, the delights and advantages of the North American way of life. As the end of the 20th century nears and the shape of past events becomes clear to history, it may well turn out that the impact of the Second World War, on Newfoundland, was of far greater significance than the events of 1948 and 1949. In any event, Newfoundlanders are an old and settled people, and the benefits we have received from union with Canada, such as they are, have been assimilated into our way of life, which, in essence, remains unchanged.

8. Mainland Canadians, I know, have developed a variety of derisive attitudes toward Newfoundland. These attitudes are incessantly displayed in books, newspaper articles, and television shows, but they have, to date, had little if any effect on the tenor of life here, and they have not yet provoked widespread anger or disenchantment toward Canada. I will not discuss all these insults here. One such attitude needs discussion, however, and although it is less a Canadian than a worldwide phenomenon, there may be some point in dealing with it before a Canadian audience. I refer to the annual barrage of mindless abuse that we have to endure, as a people, during the seal hunt.

9. Newfoundlanders have been subjected to harassment over the seal hunt for a number of years, and no sign of slackening is in sight. The arrival of Brian Davies, director of the International Fund for Animal Welfare, together with his chic and muddled entourage, is one of the signs of spring here. The days grow longer, a few birds appear on our bushes and lawns, and the annual flock of jackasses descends on St. Anthony on the Great Northern Peninsula: parlor radicals in jeans, long haired and simple minded; publicity seekers; young starlets with nothing better to do; newspaper men and women with nothing better to do. If you miss seeing some of these fine specimens of humanity in your towns and cities in March and April, you know where they are: down here, blundering idiotically around the ice fields, well fed and well funded.

10. Far from diminishing, the outcry over seals seems to be increasing from year to year, and it is hard to tell how much longer the federal government can resist the international pressure to ban the hunt. Some think the hunt is doomed, for Newfoundlanders are a people small in number, and the forces arrayed against the sealers are strong and unrelenting. It may be that Davies and his crew will

achieve the same kind of quick victory that Tocque won in the outport more than 100 years ago. Mawkishness is hard to beat; armed with money, in a world filled with coddled urbanites, it may be impossible to defeat.

11. As anybody who reads and thinks must know, something has been happening in the world at large which is changing the relationship between human beings and the lower orders of animals. I am no sociologist and can only guess at the reasons for such a change. But one reason, surely, is the growing separation between the kinds of jobs that men and women increasingly have to do and the processes that supply them with the food and the real wealth on which they have to depend.

12. You, my friend — yes, you who are reading this article — what do you do for a living? File index cards, focus a camera, write reports, balance accounts, turn screws on an assembly line, preach, teach, bleach — what? Some urban, limited, narrow, repetitive drudgery, perhaps? Some job in a "service industry?" All right, for eight hours a day you turn a small cog within the vast machinery of a complex society. Good luck to you. But such a cotton wool existence has its perils, and one of them is that it takes us far away from the traditional, vital labors of common people in rural settings, whose hands are dipped daily in ocean, soil and blood.

13. To a growing number of Canadians, the ordinary activities of such people are remote and uncomprehended, and it requires an effort of imagination to sympathize with them or even conceive of them. The killing of animals goes on every minute of every day, and it is invisible. If it is seen, it is seen in circumstances that cannot lead to understanding: on television screens in living rooms at 20°C, where softened urban men and women retreat, after a day's work as functionaries in an office, to view partial images of the world. In this snug setting, a close-up picture of a man killing an animal, any animal, seems gruesome and appalling, and it sears our tender consciences. Little wonder that so many are susceptible to the charlatans who peddle sentiment about dumb animals.

14. Some kind of fundamental adjustment in man's connection with animals is occurring, which is expressing itself in unnatural sentimentality. How else are we to account for such happenings as the favorable reception given to Marian Engel's *Bear*, a book distinguished among recent novels for making the obscene perversion of bestiality into a virtue. Or the spectacle of Brigitte Bardot on the ice floes off Labrador, clutching a savage seal pup to her bosom? Or Farley Mowat, ridiculously communing with whales on the south coast of Newfoundland in the 1960s? Is there not something corrupt in these activities? I think there is.

15. We in Newfoundland are particularly vulnerable to this growing

international wave of sentiment over animals, for a great number of Newfoundlanders still follow the traditional ways of hunting and killing. But this alone does not account for the amount of attention we receive. There are other societies that live by harvesting animals, and the killing of seals is not confined to Newfoundland, so there must be other explanations for the immoderate publicity we get. What are they? We are remote from central Canada and the United States, and therefore we can be attacked without much fear of retaliation. The seal fishery is, though of considerable significance to the local economy, of no great consequence to the Canadian economy as a whole; and so crybabies who contribute to the anti-seal hunt campaign can do so without seeing a threat to their own well being; it won't affect the kind of food they put on their tables. As for journalists, I can see why they would pick the seal hunt as a subject for their stories: a reporter in Winnipeg arouses no resentment if she turns away from writing about such messy local problems as Manitoba's treatment of its native peoples to have a crack at the sealers.

16. But the real reason for Newfoundland's vulnerability is the look of the harp seal pup itself. It is cute. Let's face it, that is why the harp seal, rather than pigs, cows, sheep, moose or deer, has been selected as the focus for international caterwauling over animals. The existence of the harp seal as a species is not threatened. The hunt is supervised, and the killing is as humane as that of other animals. It is an important part of the economy of northern Newfoundland. The seal, when you come right down to it, is in the same position as codfish and flounder, which are harvested annually for profit and food. Except that the seal pup looks cuddly.

17. Here then, it may be, on this frayed edge of the continent, one scene in a symbolic drama is being played out. You may think this a minor episode involving seals. To my mind, it is a conflict between two profoundly different ways of viewing the earth: the traditional, ancient, instinctive way; and that of the new army of sentimentalists, spawned in cities, uprooted from the land, and alien to its demands. Not one Tocque, but a multitude of them, have come to inflict their queasiness upon the living outports of Newfoundland. What the future holds, who can tell? If the hunting of seals ends, what new animal will be selected as a target for monied sentimentality? What would be the next species seen to be threatened? Salmon? Cod? Lobster? You see why we are a little bit worried. Depend upon it, there is no end in sight to this movement, for emotion cannot be refuted with logic. This is no argument to be decided by statistics, but rather a test of belief. Take your stand: are you with Brigitte Bardot fondling the seal pup, or the sealer clubbing it? No compromise is possible. You are friend or foe.

14

18. I don't want to give you the impression that we want to break our union with Canada. On the contrary. After three decades as Canadians, Newfoundlanders have formed an attachment to this great country, and the next 30 years may well see the province take its place as a full partner within Confederation. But note this. Our destiny is not to become assimilated into some melting pot. It is instead, if we can judge from our experience so far, to go on in our own way and build on what we have, using all our resources on land and sea. In our fisheries, our offshore oil and gas, and our hydro and mineral potential in Labrador, we see rich possibilities for the future. We'll stick with you, if you make an effort to stick with us. Sticking with us requires a greater effort of intellect and empathy than I have seen displayed in some recent journalism.

19. The cornerstone of our economy was, is, and must remain, the killing of animals. This is a natural, human activity. It links us with our ancestors on this rock, and ensures a vitality and wholesomeness in our race.

> I'se the b'y that builds the boat,
> I'se the b'y that sails her,
> I'se the b'y that catches the fish,
> And brings 'em home to Lizer.

20. What mastery there is in this traditional ballad! What pride and power! And, in the last line, what homely tenderness! Whatever the singer of that song may have lacked, he did not lack a sense of his own worth, a feeling of manly fulfilment and independence. Nor was he afflicted with the neuroses of pavement dwellers. At its best, this was what the old outport offered: a chance at victory over the elemental forces of nature, an opportunity for a man, through his own nerve and brawn, to provide for his family. So it was; if we are to be true to ourselves, so it must remain. Newfoundlanders are fish and seal killers yet. With the singer of "I'se the b'y," we raise our bloody hands in pride together.

Style and Structure

1. To whom is this article directed, city dwellers or Newfoundlanders? Cite evidence from the article to substantiate your answer.
2. What emotion does the writer try to arouse in paragraph 1? In view of his thesis, why does he try to elicit this reaction?
3. What is the relationship of the material in paragraphs 2 to 5 to that in paragraph 1?
4. Underline the thesis statements. Why does the writer not state them earlier?
5. What is the writer's attitude toward Newfoundland? Illustrate your answer with quotations from the text.

6. What is the writer's attitude toward Brian Davies and the other seal hunt protestors? Illustrate your answer with quotations from the text.

7. "They meet and speak; and sentiment, armed with self-righteousness and Biblical quotations, easily triumphs over instinct."
   This quotation from paragraph 6 sounds a lot like another sentence in paragraph 10. Identify the sentence in paragraph 10 and comment on the implied comparison the writer is making.

8. In paragraph 12 the writer employs the 2nd person singular, "you". Rewrite the paragraph in the third person. (See for example, paragraph 13.) Why is one more effective than the other?

9. In the conclusion, how does the writer use the seal hunt to promote national unity and multiculturalism and vice versa? Is this a logical argument to make, in the face of the evidence presented in the body of the article?

10. Compile a list of the writer's arguments. Indicate which are logical and which are manipulative. (Manipulative arguments are based on emotion rather than logic.)

Thinking and Writing

a. Research and write an essay on one of the following topics:
   (a) the methods used to hunt the harp seal;
   (b) the methods used to slaughter cattle and calves, sheep and lambs and other "domestic" animals;
   (c) the methods used for capturing and slaughtering other fur-bearing animals;
   (d) the effects of hunting upon the North Atlantic seal herd populations;
   (e) the effect upon the ecology of stopping the seal hunt;
   (f) the theory and practice of "cropping" in wildlife management;
   (g) the importance of the seal hunt to the economy of Newfoundland and the inhabitants of the "Northern Peninsula";
   (h) the objections of the Greenpeace Organization and its allies to the seal hunt;
   (i) the attitude of the rural population to killing and to the methods of killing animals for food, furs, and population control;
   (j) the attitude of the urban population to killing and to the methods of killing animals for food, furs, and population control.

Base your work upon concrete evidence and not upon what you imagine to be the case. You may, in the case of topics (i) and (j), have to interview people.

Audience:

an average newspaper reader who knows nothing at all about your chosen topic.

b. Write an essay in which you support or oppose the seal hunt in Newfoundland. Try to anticipate the objections of those who might disagree with your point of view.

Audience:

someone who is relatively well informed about the Newfoundland seal hunt and whose opinion about it is completely different from yours.

Send a copy of your paper to the Greenpeace Organization (if you support the seal hunt), or the premier of Newfoundland (if you oppose the seal hunt).

Pretty poison

by Patricia Brooks

1. Last spring, when four-year-old Sarah Carroll became violently nauseous and dizzy, her mother became so alarmed she called the nearest poison center. Her instincts were right. Sarah had been poisoned, but not by gulping medicine, furniture polish or detergent. Mrs. Carroll wisely kept these household hazards locked away from her child's curious hands. Rather, Sarah was a victim of a daffodil. Yes, daffodil.

2. Each year in this country alone, there are thousands of cases of accidental, plant-caused poisonings. Some are fatal and most of the victims are children, especially susceptible because of their size and inexperience. An adult might, for instance, pick a wild baneberry, pop it into his or her mouth, then spit it out because of its bitter taste. A child, however, is likely to swallow it. While that same berry would cause only discomfort to an adult, it could produce serious effects in a youngster.

3. No one knows the exact number of plant fatalities, but a recent medical study revealed that plant ingestion by children has increased at an alarming rate. The poisons attack in a variety of ways: by striking the nerves, muscles, blood or all three.

4. Aside from dermatological irritants like poison ivy, when we think of harmful plants, the deadly nightshade or poison hemlock spring

to mind. But these are just two of the 700-plus species in the United States and Canada that are, in whole or part, poisonous. The list is probably incomplete. Only ten years ago wisteria was discovered to have poisonous properties.

5. Take the daffodil. Or rather, *don't* take the daffodil — internally, at least. Pretty and commonplace as it may be, it has a dangerous bulb, as do the narcissus and jonquil. Once the bulb is planted, its hazards are not a problem. But Sarah found a basket full of bulbs. To her they looked no different from the garlic and onions in her mother's kitchen. So she plunked one in her mouth.

6. Such is often the case when children mimic adult or even animal behavior. Billy Tatum watched his mother snip dandelion greens to wash and toss into a salad. So one afternoon he went into the garden to snip, too. But instead of the tartly delicious dandelion, Billy nibbled some lily-of-the-valley leaves, which contain properties similar to, though less toxic than, those found in foxglove, one of the deadliest of garden plants.

7. Both Sarah and Billy survived. Their local poison centers advised their frantic mothers to induce vomiting with ipecac, a liquid medication that in most states can be bought in small quantities without prescription.

8. But the problem of plant poisonings remains a complex one. Some of the most innocent-looking plants harbor the most toxic elements, and a single plant sometimes hosts as many as six separate types of poisonous materials.

9. Among the surprisingly dangerous garden plants are some of nature's loveliest. Beware of the iris root, the larkspur leaf and seed, the wisteria pod. All the parts of the buttercup, azalea, and rhododendron are toxic. And the graceful mountain laurel is so potentially lethal that the Delaware Indians called it their "suicide plant."

10. To compound the confusion, some otherwise edible plants have deadly parts. For example, delicious as the cooked rhubarb stalk may be, its leaves can make you fatally ill. If taken in sufficient quantities, they contain enough oxalic acid to cause massive hemorrhaging.

11. Even familiar fruit trees can be toxic. The apple has a bitter seed and the peach, plum, cherry, and almond have danger lurking in their seeds, leaves and bark. Such kitchen staples as the tomato and potato are members of the solanaceous family — relatives of the stealthy nightshade, tobacco, and petunia — and their vines secrete toxic solanine. Castor oil is a mild and harmless laxative, but the bean from which it is derived is one of the deadliest of all poisonous plants. Chewing one bean can kill an adult.

12. Not every problem plant is beyond your doorstep. The ubiquitous

philodendron has toxic properties in its leaf and stem, as do the caladium, dieffenbachia and star-of-Bethlehem. Likewise, the red fruit of the Jerusalem cherry is the plant's prettiest, and most menacing, component and a magnet for munching tots.

13. Children are not the only victims of plant poisoning. The back-to-nature movement has given rise to a high incidence of poisonings among adults as well. Anxious to add zest at little or no cost to their diet, many adventurers set forth, baskets in hand, to collect wild roots, flowers, mushrooms, and edible grasses. It is an admirable idea, but not without possible peril. Unfortunately, there are many look-alikes in the forest. Poison hemlock, for example, is a double for wild carrot. Toxic mountain laurel is a mirror-image of the harmless wintergreen. And so on.

14. Books advocating the stalking of wild greens are often illustrated with imprecise drawings that fail to delineate the safe from the dangerous. If you are determined to gather fiddlehead ferns and other nourishing wild greenery, be sure to equip yourself with a book that includes both clear and specific photographs and detailed descriptions of every plant you pick. When you return from your foraging, wash your hands and face and any other exposed body parts, and change into fresh clothing; you may have brushed unknowingly against shrubbery whose toxic properties could cause skin irritation or worse.

15. At the first symptom of plant poisoning, call the nearest poison center. There are approximately 450 centers in the United States today, some with 24-hour service. If there isn't one in your area, try phoning your doctor. If that fails, call the emergency room of your local hospital. If the symptoms are violent and increasingly severe, don't call — rush the victim to a hospital.

16. Induced vomiting is the usual treatment for a mild case of poisoning. But it isn't the best solution for *all* plant poisoning. If the victim is unconscious or convulsing, vomiting is never induced. In any event, avoid home remedies and seek immediate professional advice. You may easily complicate an easy-to-correct situation by introducing an improper treatment.

17. Knowing these basics, how can a parent best prevent plant poisoning? With greenery almost everywhere, coping may seem difficult indeed. But there are safeguards you can and should take, especially with children.

    • Try to keep your house and garden poison-proofed. Do not buy plants with known toxic elements until your children are old enough not to nibble.

    • If you live in an older neighborhood where plantings are well established, identify the possible danger zones yourself, and then instruct your children that such plants are off limits.

• Do not let young children wander unsupervised in any wooded area.

• Before planting, keep bulbs and seeds carefully locked away from curious hands; treat them like the dangerous weapons they could be.

• After instructing your children not to eat plants, keep reminding them. Explain that the blueberries you eat come from the grocery store — berries on garden bushes may look pretty, but can be poisonous.

18. Although you don't want to make your children fearful of nature, counseling is nonetheless essential. "Look but don't lick, admire but don't pick" is a rhyme one mother made up to help her little girls keep their distance from the lethal lovelies lurking in the woods behind their house. It might not win any poetry contests but, as advice, it's a lifesaver.

Style and Structure

1. Why does the writer choose to open her article with a specific illustration? To what type of reader would this opening particularly appeal?
2. Underline the parts of the article that complete Sarah's story, begun in paragraph 1. Why would Brooks bother to break the story into three parts instead of completing it in the opening paragraph?
3. Underline the thesis statement and list the three main points into which the writer divides her essay.
4. In paragraph 17 the writer chooses to present her recommendations in list form. Why is a list form more effective than a paragraph form in this situation?
5. What is the writer attempting to do in the last paragraph? How effectively does this paragraph act as a conclusion for the essay as a whole?

Thinking and Writing

a. Select a toxic plant or fungus which is commonly found in the homes and gardens of Canadians. Write an essay, in the form of a newspaper article, informing the reader of the dangers of your plant. Try to include information about such things as the history of the plant, or anecdotes, to help make the article interesting and drive home your point. Dieffenbachia, for example, got the name "Dumb Cane" because rebellious slaves in the West Indies were forced to eat the plant which caused constrictions of the vocal cords that made them unable to speak. In addition, try to advise the reader of what emergency measures to take to counteract the effects of the plant you have chosen.

Your library should have information that will be readily available in such books as *Medical Botany* and in magazine articles which you can locate through the *Reader's Guide to Periodical Literature,* and the *Canadian Index.*

Audience:

the "average" homeowner who enjoys having plants in the home but does not know anything about plant poison. Send a copy of your paper to the editor of a newspaper in your area.

b. Write an essay in which you examine the potential for accidental poisoning which exists in every home. (Do not restrict yourself to plants in this essay; try to include other dangers that you find in every room of the house.)

Audience:

a reader who possesses an average level of awareness about the subject.

Different strokes

by Gerry Kopelow

1. When I finally sat down to talk with Hoken Kristiansen in Winnipeg, he took away my glasses. Kristiansen, the president of K-Cycle Engines, kindly polished my lenses with a liquid identified only as "something aeronautical." This small gesture illustrates the approach of the man who is now perfecting a mechanical device that may soon change the world. Precisely and cheerfully, he cleaned my glasses; precisely and cheerfully he offers the world an energy-efficient automotive power plant.

2. To appreciate Kristiansen's invention, the K-cycle engine, you must understand that the conventional internal combustion engine is a mechanical abortion. Only the dedication of engineers and capitalists over the last 100 years has enabled the thing to function at all. Essentially unchanged since its invention in 1859, the gas-eating monster in your car turns 75 percent of the energy in every gallon of fuel into waste heat, noise, and assorted poisons. Banging away in a super hot, mechanically stressful environment, are hundreds of moving parts, all dedicated to the notion of turning the up-and-down motion of the pistons into the rotary motion required to propel a vehicle.

3. Automobile engines have not changed much in efficiency because all heat engines work to an irrefutable law, called a thermodynamic cycle, which governs the process whereby heat is converted into usable power. In the case of the common internal combustion engine, this cycle is the Otto cycle. Here the up-and-down motion of a piston in its cylinder is governed by a connecting rod linked to a revolving crankshaft. When the crankshaft turns, it pulls down the piston and draws vaporized gasoline and air into the cylinder. As the crankshaft continues to turn it forces the piston upward. This compresses the gas-air mixture, which becomes hot. When the piston has moved upward as far as it can, the volatile mixture is ignited with an electrical spark. The resulting burning—the violent expansion of hot gases—forces the piston back down. This transfers mechanical power to the crankshaft and causes it to turn. The next upward motion of the piston expels the waste products of the combustion process. Such engines are called four-stroke engines because the piston performs four operations: intake, compression, power, and exhaust.

4. Our beloved automobiles run as well as they do mostly because of the tremendous potential energy concealed within even a thimbleful of gasoline. The maximum theoretical efficiency of the Otto cycle is less than 30 percent. In practice it averages around 20 percent. A poorly tuned engine can reduce efficiency to 15 percent or less. Poor efficiency is built right into the Otto cycle: a great deal of energy is lost because it is exhausted at quite high pressure, hence the exhaust noise and the need to muffle it. By a stroke of engineering genius, Kristiansen has reclaimed a great deal of this wasted energy.

5. Hoken Kristiansen, 50, has made the study of engines his life's work. He was born in Kristiansand, Norway, one of five children of a meat-packing plant president. "As a child, I was fascinated by all things mechanical," he recalls in his bright corner office at K-Cycle's new headquarters. Before long he was dismantling and repairing the engine of his parents' boat. As a teenager during the Second World War he was a mechanic for the Norwegian underground: "I just kept things running." Later he studied aeronautical engineering at Gotenbörg, Sweden. After emigrating to Canada in 1952, he worked for MacDonald Aircraft in Winnipeg, then moved on to Transair to become head of that airline's technical operations.

6. In a lilting Norwegian accent Kristiansen describes his early days in the aircraft business. Briefly and brightly I am led through the history of the jet engine, from its cranky infancy in the 1930s to its development as the reliable commercial performer we now trust with our lives. Kristiansen was the source of a number of innovations now commonplace in aeronautical technology. As he

describes problems solved by the application of the scientific method, one feels that there's still hope for this creaky planet. "Sound engineering always works," he says. "I have no doubts about the practical confirmation of my theoretical designs."

7. Kristiansen's working methods have always combined theoretical homework with the greasy manual labor of mechanical problem-solving. He recalls one time when an obscure mechanical fault was repeatedly causing engine failure in flight. Kristiansen worked out on paper what was causing the problem, but no one would believe him until he made his point in a scene that must have looked like something right out of *Dr. Strangelove.* "To get to the core of the matter, I climbed up and straddled the engine while it was running full throttle in the field. I wish I had a picture of that."

8. "For years," he continues, "I was greatly disturbed by the basic and inescapable inefficiency of both piston and jet engines." They functioned admirably enough during an era when fuel was cheap and it was possible to surround each machine with a team of mechanical nursemaids. But as head of Transair's technical department, Kristiansen felt the squeeze of rising fuel and skilled labor costs, and the frustration of having to coddle machines in which the basis of operation was self-limiting.

9. So Kristiansen took these problems home with him and wrestled with them in the evenings and on weekends. In the technical literature, most other engineers agreed that the common internal combustion engine had been developed to its limit: it was compact and reliable, but inappropriate for widespread future use. The diesel cycle engine is not much better. It has the same basic limitations as its more popular cousin; the only real difference is that it does away with a fussy electrical ignition system because the greater heat of compression in the diesel allows self-ignition.

10. Other thermodynamic cycles offer greater power with less waste. In the Brayton cycle, which governs the function of jet and turbine engines, the expansion of burning gas works directly against a kind of fan blade, thereby creating rotary power. Unfortunately, engines using the Brayton cycle require internal parts capable of withstanding ferociously high temperatures for long periods of time. Since no known metal can endure such treatment, Brayton cycle engines operate at significantly lower than optimum temperature. "The jet engine looks fancy," says Kristiansen, shifting his six-foot frame in an easy chair, "but it's very limited. In fact, jet engines are in widespread use today only because they work better at high altitudes, where oxygen starvation becomes a problem for piston engines."

11. Two other thermodynamic cycles suggested engines with possible application in automobiles. The Rankin cycle, which governs the

function of the steam engine, is basically unchanged since its invention at the beginning of the Industrial Revolution. The steam engine can use low-pollution external combustion to create superheated steam to operate a piston or turbine. "The problem with steam is time," says Kristiansen. "Would you wait half an hour for your car's boiler to heat up?" Such a system is also too big and clumsy to be suitable for a vehicle. The same is true of the potentially efficient Stirling cycle engine, a complicated machine too big and costly to use in a car.

12. When Felix Wankel invented his rotary engine in 1955, it appeared to be a marked improvement. But that engine, which works to the Otto cycle and is now used in Mazda automobiles, has severe limitations. "The Wankel engine is a problem energy-wise," says Kristiansen, "simply because of geometry." The Wankel eliminates many of the moving parts in Otto cycle engines, but it exhibits low compression and superhot exhaust, demonstrating efficiencies far below what ordinary engines can produce.

13. "It took me years to thoroughly investigate all the possibilities," says Kristiansen, "but when the oil embargo hit, I figured now I *have* to do it." On paper he tried various mechanical hybrids, but no permutation of the available technologies yielded a promising approach. "I fought against the piston engine," he says, "but in the end, only the Otto cycle engine looked feasible for use in cars." It was reasonably compact in terms of power for weight. It functioned at manageable levels of temperature and mechanical stress, and it was being mass produced at low cost. Yet some radical innovation was needed to raise efficiency. As Kristiansen puts it, "I had to somehow modify the Otto cycle itself, so that the thermodynamic stranglehold could be broken."

14. The answer now looks simple. In the Otto cycle, the compression and power strokes have to be the same length because the crankshaft causes the piston to move up and down the same distance. This means that at the end of every power stroke the piston starts to move upward *into* the exhaust stroke. If, however, the power stroke could be longer than the compression stroke, much more useful energy could be extracted from each charge of fuel. Then the combustive gases would exit from the cylinder, cooler and more quietly. The process would be less polluting as well because the longer stroke would allow a more complete, cleaner burn.

15. This then is the Kristiansen cycle, the only thermodynamic cycle invented this century. Like the Otto cycle, the K-cycle has four strokes: intake, compression, power, and exhaust. Unlike the Otto cycle, the K-cycle has a power stroke considerably longer than the intake and compression strokes. This simple change more than doubles the theoretical efficiency of the engine.

16. It remained for Kristiansen to make the K-cycle work in an actual engine. "I discovered a new cycle," he explains, "then had to design an engine to work to it. However, I was fortunate to be able to employ modern technologies. If the guy who designed the leaning tower of Pisa had known about piles, he wouldn't have had any problems. The K-cycle is a hybrid between the piston and the gas turbine."

17. To understand the spectacular way in which Kristiansen transmuted the physics and the math of the K-cycle into an actual engine, think of a roller coaster on a circular track with two depressions, one deeper than the other. The carriage rolling along represents the piston; the track represents the cam, and it replaces the crankshaft of a normal engine. The variation in the height of the cam determines the length of the four mechanical strokes. The deepest depression results in the elongated power and exhaust strokes.

18. The cartridge cylinder of a six-shooter demonstrates how the motion of the piston is converted to useful work. The gun's cylinder rotates on a central axis; so does the cylinder block in the K-cycle engine. Since there are eight pistons moving along the cam, there are eight holes — or cylinders — in the cylinder block. The cam is fixed to the engine's casing so that downward force on the piston causes the piston to roll sideways along the surface of the cam. As a result, the pistons, which are inside the cylinder block, cause the entire block to rotate. The output shafts are attached directly to the block. *Voilà*. Rotary motion. The K-cycle prototype has two opposed sets of eight pistons and two fixed cams, arranged face to face in a mirror image. This allows perfectly balanced motion with virtually no vibration. So many moving parts are eliminated that this configuration (together with the chemical advantages of the K-cycle) produces twice as much horsepower in a structure half the weight of a normal engine.

19. Combustion takes place continually at one spot between the two sets of cylinders. There is only one sparkplug, and it's needed only for starting. The profile of the cam can be designed so that the engine will run on virtually any fuel from kerosene to peanut oil.

20. The engine is so flexible that hundreds of variations are possible. With pistons the size of pencil erasers, tiny K-cycle power packs could conceivably propel bicycles. Gigantic K-cycles could be created for use as stationary industrial engines and as marine engines. All would exhibit high power-to-weight ratios, cool, quiet exhaust and vibrationless operation.

21. These properties invite military applications as well. Imagine a small, pilotless aircraft flying at very high speed below radar altitude. Powered by a K-cycle engine, such an aircraft would be

extremely quiet. More significantly, because of its cool exhaust it would have what aviation types call a "low infra-red signature" — it would be virtually invisible to the heat-seeking infra-red sensors used to detect conventional missiles.

22. It seems inevitable that the K-cycle engine will become ubiquitous, and that Hoken Kristiansen will one day be mentioned in the same breath as Thomas Edison, Alexander Graham Bell, and James Watt. A major European engine builder has signed a development contract on the basis of test reports on the K-cycle prototype, and talks are progressing with one of the North American engine builders and with a prominent Japanese motorcycle company. This winter, experimental K-cycle engines will be installed in automobiles, and full-scale production will begin as soon as the inevitable kinks are smoothed out.

23. As negotiations continue, though, you can expect to hear less and less about the K-cycle. The Europeans insisted on a contractual promise of complete silence until they are ready for mass production, and the Americans also want a media blackout until their version of the engine is perfected. So the people at K-Cycle aren't saying much these days. But they are doing a lot of smiling.

Style and Structure

1. How does the writer attempt to capture the reader's attention in paragraph 1? Is it a successful device?
2. Underline the thesis statement and draft a plan of the article's organization.
3. What information does Kopelow present in paragraphs 2 to 4? Why does he present this information at this particular point in the article?
4. (a) Why does the author choose to present the specific biographical data that he does in paragraphs 5 to 8?
   (b) What structural purpose does paragraph 8 serve?
5. What is Kristiansen's "problem" that the writer refers to in the opening sentence of paragraph 9? How does the author use Kristiansen's "problem-solving process" to give unity and coherence to paragraphs 9 to 13? Why would the author feel that it is necessary to present the information contained in paragraphs 9 to 13 before introducing the K-cycle engine itself?
6. Kopelow was directing this article at the average newspaper reader rather than at an automotive engineer. Examine his description of how the K-cycle engine works:
   (a) What techniques does he use to help the reader understand the workings of the engine?

(b) Is his choice of words geared to the level of the average newpaper reader? Use specific examples to illustrate your answer.

(c) Do you understand how the K-cycle engine works after having read the description? If not, what qualifications do you think a reader would have to have to understand fully the operation of this engine?

7. What areas does the author explore in the last two paragraphs of his article? Why do these work as an adequate conclusion for the article as a whole?

Thinking and Writing

a. Write an essay in which you explain, in terms that the average non-technical reader can understand, the operation of one type of "propulsion device" commonly in use today (for example, gas turbine, electrical, linear induction, Wankel, steam, and so on).

Audience:
as outlined in the assignment.

b. Write an essay in which you outline the method of propulsion that you feel will probably be most commonly used in the year 2000 in view of the increasing energy shortage. Point out the advantages of this device and try to convince members of the general public that using this device would be practical.

Audience:
as outlined in the assignment.

Give a copy of your essay to a friend or a member of your family; after this person has read the essay, ask the reader whether he or she is convinced that your device is the best alternative. From the reply, try to judge how you could have improved your presentation.

Advertising

by Ellen Roseman

1. What would happen if suddenly, magically, men could menstruate and women could not?

2. "The answer is clear," argues feminist Gloria Steinem in a recent issue of *Ms.* magazine. "Menstruation would become an enviable, boast-worthy, masculine event."

3. Imagine the possibilities, she says. Men would brag about how long and how much. Government would fund a National Institute of Dysmenorrhea to help stamp out monthly discomforts. Sanitary supplies would be federally funded and free.

4. "Of course, some men would still pay for the prestige of commercial brands such as John Wayne Tampons, Muhammad Ali's Rope-a-dope Pads, Joe Namath Jock Shields ("for those light bachelor days") and Robert 'Baretta' Blake Maxi-Pads."

5. Men don't menstruate, but they do dream up sanitary products and write commercials for them on television. And, judging by the response of *Consumer Game* readers, many people find these advertisements offensive.

6. Letter-writers say they're annoyed, and often deeply embarrassed, by feminine hygiene ads invading the privacy of their living rooms and causing discomfort in mixed company.

7. Also, many women are upset by what they feel is a double standard: that intimate feminine products are advertised on TV but rarely any intimate masculine products, such as condoms or jockstraps.

8. Now, don't get me wrong. I'm sympathetic to arguments, made by groups such as the Sex Education and Information Council, that these ads help lift the veil of secrecy from normal, natural bodily functions.

9. But I don't think that advertisers should run ahead of the prevailing levels of public taste. In the five years since the commercials were allowed on the air (the Canadian Broadcasting Corporation still doesn't accept them), the pitches have become more graphic and more explicit.

10. Feminine hygiene manufacturers now spend $4,000,000 a year on TV ads. They offer products for light days, heavy days, and in-between days; mini-pads, maxi-pads, and panty shields; tampons in regular, super, and super-plus sizes; deodorant tampons, which many doctors criticize as unneccessary and possibly hazardous.

11. Because the competition is so hot and heavy, manufacturers who don't use TV are losing sales. *Canadian Tampax Corporation Limited,* in Barrie, started a TV campaign this summer after years of restricting its ads to women's magazines.

12. "We don't like TV and we don't think it's the best way to get the message across," says Canadian president Harry Kelly. "But women don't read magazines as much as they used to. We felt our sales would suffer if we didn't use TV."

13. The industry leader is *Johnson & Johnson Limited,* of Montreal, which manufactures under the *Carefree, Modess,* and *Stayfree* labels. The company spends $1,600,000 a year advertising its products on TV; its research (done two and a half years ago) shows only seven percent of viewers are offended by the ads.

14. *Kimberly-Clark* of Toronto, which sells under the *Kotex, New Freedom,* and *Light Days* labels, also advertises extensively on TV. So does *Playtex Limited* of Toronto, which uses its own brand name. *Scott Paper Limited,* of Vancouver, which makes *Confidets,* dropped its TV ads three years ago when it decided they offended some viewers.

15. The companies say they're re-evaluating the money they spend on TV commercials, but they're reluctant to tone down the ads or pull them off the air. The regulatory authorities are also unwilling to take action, fearing they'll be accused of censorship.

16. "People should direct their complaints to the manufacturers," says a spokesman for the Canadian Radio-Television and Telecommunications Commission, in Ottawa. "We have no mandate to ban commercials for a product that's legally available for sale."

17. But the CRTC is coming under increasing pressure to do something. Two Vancouver newspapers, the *Sun* and the *Province,* ran coupon campaigns urging readers to protest against feminine hygiene advertising on TV; at last count, they had received 24,000 replies. The coupons will be presented to the commissioners when they visit Vancouver this week.

18. If you're upset with graphic sales pitches for feminine products, write to the CRTC at Central Building, 1 Rue Principale, Hull, Quebec, K1A 0N2.

19. You own the airwaves. If you feel the advertisers are refusing to exercise taste and discretion in the messages they broadcast, it's up to you to let the regulatory authorities know.

Style and Structure

1. What techniques does the writer use in the introduction to arrest the reader's attention? Taking into account how the writer feels about advertising sanitary products on TV, how can she justify the first four paragraphs?

2. Underline the thesis statement and draft a plan of the essay's organization.

3. How objective is the author's presentation of the manufacturers' point of view in paragraphs 10 to 15? Cite specific examples to support your answer.

4. Comment on how effectively the writer makes the transition from the manufacturers to the CRTC.

5. How objective is the author's presentation of the CRTC's point of view in paragraphs 16 and 17? Cite specific examples to support your answer.

6. Who, according to the conclusion, should be determining what should or should not be broadcast over TV? How has the author, in the rest of the essay, prepared us to accept this conclusion?

Thinking and Writing

a. Select a TV commercial (or a series of commercials that deal with the same product) to which you object for one reason or another. Write an essay stating and justifying your objections.
   Audience:
   someone responsible for the advertisement to which you object. The person could cause the ad to be discontinued.
   Send a copy of your paper to the president of the company whose product is being advertised.

b. Write an essay in which you attempt to draw up a "code of standards" that advertisers should have to follow. Remember, however, that you must try to avoid the accusation that you are acting as a censor (the advertising industry has a "voluntary code" that you might like to consult before doing this essay).
   Audience:
   a reader who is familiar with the techniques and problems of advertising.
   Send a copy of your paper to the president of an advertising agency.

How to dress like a loser

by Alexander Ross

1. Listen: Elizabeth Storms didn't make the rules, so don't blame her when she tells you that what you're wearing right now isn't doing your career any good. I mean, if you think that your powder-blue leisure suit and your white penny-loafers truly express the Inner You, that's okay with Ms. Storms. All she's saying—and she's paid to say it by companies such as London Life and sober-sided law factories such as Thomson Rogers, in Toronto—is that people who dress like John Turner tend to get treated like former or potential finance ministers, and people who dress like aluminum-siding salesmen tend to get doors slammed in their faces.

2. Ms. Storms is only 23, a University of Toronto psychology dropout who spent two years studying marketing and design in Boston. Also, she's got an entrepreneurial streak. And so, instead of competing with arts graduates for some underpaid job as a proofreader in a publishing house, she formed a company last year called Storms, and hung out her shingle as an "image consultant." Yes, we know it sounds silly. But silly or not, she's now pulling down a good income advising employees of various large companies how to dress.

3. Her first client was a large and stately Toronto law firm, which asked Ms. Storms to talk to the clerical staff. Too many of the women were turning up in jeans and low-cut dresses—dreadfully bad for the corporate image. "I think they hired me because it's so much easier for an outsider to talk to employees about the way they dress," she says. "From the boss, they'd resent it. Coming from me, they listen."

4. Analyzing the accoutrements of everyone from CBC television hosts to legal stenographers has given Ms. Storms a wealth of insight into how and what your clothes communicate to other people. Bow ties communicate dishonesty, for instance; blue pinstripe suits and thin gold watches communicate power.

5. Ms. Storms is thus not only an expert on how to Dress for Success; she's also eloquent on the subject of how *not* to dress. In the interests of accentuating the negative, then, we present on these pages Ms. Storm's choices of the worst things a business person can wear. Read and heed, or prepare yourself for a demotion to the mail room.

The Mafioso Look

6. Pinstripes are fine, but if you push stripes too far, you'll look more like Don Corleone than John Turner. Ms. Storms has seen more than one executive's career short-circuited because his stripes were too wide, or the fabric too black, instead of blue. Accessories can disastrously accentuate the impression. Worst of all is a white tie with a dark shirt; it practically convicts you of international narcotics trafficking. Other ingredients of the Mafioso Look, to be avoided at all costs are tinted glasses indoors, heavyweight jewelry, shoes that are too smooth and shiny, wide-brimmed hats.

The Excessively Busy Look

7. Checks and plaids — indeed, anything with a crisscross pattern — should
   be treated with extreme caution, especially if you're large. The trouble
   arises when you mix patterns: paisley tie, window-pane sports jacket,
   polka-dot shirt, tweed trousers, argyle socks. The effect is *loud*. "You
   see these guys with all these checks," says Ms. Storms, "and it's like a
   battleship coming at you with all guns blazing." The benighted souls
   who mix patterns often compound their error, and wreck their careers,
   by wearing bow ties, which — Pierre Berton, Gordon Sinclair and Lester
   Pearson notwithstanding — tend to make people vaguely distrust you. Or
   they lean toward turtleneck sweaters. That's okay if you're an architect
   or a CBC story editor, but it won't cut much ice at MacMillan Bloedel or
   Massey-Ferguson. Turtlenecks look, well, *arty*.

The Saturday Night Fever Look
(Male and Female Divisions)

8. In the age of Travolta, this look has become increasingly common in Canadian offices, and it's a sure-fire obstacle to being taken seriously by your boss. "The disco look," says Ms. Storms, "suggests that you're more interested in boogieing than you are in getting ahead." God forbid that Canadian office workers should betray an interest in boogieing. For women, some things to avoid are low-cut dresses, skirts with slits that show a flash of thigh; anything that jangles, such as charm bracelets; net stockings; open-toed shoes or excessively high heels and too much makeup.

9. For men, anything that would look right at Regine's will probably look wrong from nine to five: white suits, shirts casually unbuttoned to reveal a hairy chest, neck medallions, trippy shoes and pastel shirts. Sad as it may seem, it all boils down to one simple rule for both sexes: don't look sexy.

The Columbo Look

10. Amazingly enough, most slobs don't know that they're slobs. Some slobs
    think they're merely expressing their individuality. Some just don't care.
    Some slobs actually believe they're quite dapper fellows. But slobbism,
    as vividly portrayed by Peter Falk in the *Columbo* police series, is
    probably the most pervasive transgression against corporate dress codes
    that Ms. Storms encounters in her work.

11. Curing slobbism may involve radical therapy, since it's so deeply
    ingrained in the victim's character. Some people seem to be *born* with
    cigarette ashes on their vest and spots on their tie.

12. To determine whether or not you're a slob, check yourself against
    Ms. Storms' list of dreadful symptoms: unkempt hair; untrimmed beards;
    winter salt stains on your pant cuffs; nicotine-stained fingers; scuffed
    shoes; a dirty-old man raincoat; rumpled clothing; mismatched socks;
    tattletale-grey, smelly shirts, usually short-sleeved, with sweat stains at
    the armpits; too short socks that reveal an unsightly expanse of calf
    when you pull up your pant-leg; a bundle of pens in your breast pocket,
    sometimes accompanied—horrors!—by one of those little plastic pocket
    guards, which reveal you as the perfect man to spend the rest of your
    working life buried in the stockroom.

The Green Suit

13. A suit can be conservatively cut, the accessories can be understated, the shirt can be exactly right. But if the suit's the wrong color, it fairly shrieks of unpromotability. Green, of course, is the worst of all; it's the corporate equivalent of leprosy. But fashion designers come up with equally disastrous shades every season: muted maroons, electric blues, pale peach, and, worst of all, fabrics of any color that have a silvery sheen. It's a truly tragic spectacle, and it saddens Ms. Storms, for she sees it frequently. "All those awful colors," she breathes. "They make men look like parking lot attendants."

The John Turner Look

14. This guy, as you can see, is The Boss. He isn't necessarily any smarter than his colleagues. He just dresses as if he were. The key, to use an overworked but appropriate phrase, is understated elegance. Ms. Storms is a connoisseur of "power symbols" — those silent costume messages that reassure or even intimidate your audience. Our hero has deployed his power symbols shrewdly. The blue pinstripe suit is perfect. The polka dots on his tie are discreet. His black (not brown) wingtip shoes are polished, but not dazzlingly so. But it's the minor touches that make him a man to be reckoned with. His Cartier tank watch ($1,500 and up for solid gold version; only $450 for the gold plate) is an international power signal. So is his gold Cross pen, his Gant button-down shirt, his Dunhill lighter, his signet ring, his leather attaché case — brown, not black. Some of his power symbols are so understated that only fellow cognoscenti can recognize them. The buttons on the sleeves of his suit actually unbutton, for instance. "The amazing thing about these power symbols," says Ms. Storms, "is that they're not really expensive, considering how effective they are."

Style and Structure

1. The tone of a piece of writing refers to the attitude of the writer toward his topic and/or his audience as communicated mainly by his choice of words. Thus a writer might adopt an objective tone in one work, hostile in another, friendly in a third and so on.

   What tone does the writer adopt in this article? How do you as the reader, react to this tone? How is it appropriate (or inappropriate) to the subject and projected audience? Would this tone be appropriate to most business writing?
2. Underline the thesis statement of this essay.
3. Repetition of the same basic point in a variety of ways is a common writing technique. Underline all sentences in which the relationship between dress and job success is made. Comment on whether this is an effective technique or if it is overdone.
4. This article does not contain a formal conclusion. Does it need one? Write a brief conclusion which fits the tone of the article.

Thinking and Writing

a. Assume that you are working for a large corporation that has both office and sales employees. Your supervisor has asked you to investigate Ms. Storms and to write a report upon which he/she can base a decision on whether to retain her service for the corporation. Try to show the positive and negative things that she would offer to your corporation; use examples of her comments in her article to verify your points.

b. There are many people who would take issue with Ms. Storms' contention that people should dress to make an impression on others. There are some who would even argue that by following such rigid dress codes, one is only demonstrating to an employer a lack of initiative and imagination, qualities which, despite a popular misconception, are highly prized by business.
Write an essay in which you outline your personal opinions on the importance of dress in the business world in general or in the specific field that you have chosen to pursue as a career. Use concrete evidence and well thought out arguments to support your opinions.
Audience:
someone who holds a supervisory position and who will therefore have personal experience relating to the subject and an awareness of the dress policies of a number of companies.
Send a copy of your paper to someone who holds a supervisory position in the field which you plan to enter upon graduation (do

not send your paper to a personnel officer, as he/she will be mainly concerned with the personal appearance of job applicants, which is a completely different topic.) or to one of your instructors who has worked for a number of years in the field which you plan to enter.

A sin of the mother is visited upon the child

by Brenda Rabkin

1. Jenny Pike, a 27-year-old Toronto nurse, was pregnant and still smoking a pack of cigarettes a day. She knew vaguely that her smoking might cause her baby to be smaller than average, but was confident that there would be no other significant ill effects on the fetus. Then, in her seventh month, she began attending prenatal classes and found out that her smoking could even kill her unborn child. The guilt and anxiety she felt until the moment she delivered a baby that happily was alive and normal made the last two months of her pregnancy the most unpleasant of her life. And yet she didn't give up smoking: "It made me angry rather than positive about quitting."

2. The experience of Jenny Pike—not her real name—is not unusual. Thousands of Canadian women may be inflicting irrevocable damage on their unborn children for no reason other than ignorance. If nothing else, the case of Jenny Pike clearly illustrates the wall that exists between scientific knowledge and its translation into public information that could prevent disease and disability.

3. While the relation of smoking to cancer and the circulatory diseases has become well known, little has been said publicly about the damage smoking may do to the unborn. Yet medical literature is filled with studies that prove that smoking during pregnancy hurts the development of the fetus. As early as 1957, British obstetrician Dr. Winea Simpson published her original finding that babies born to women who smoke during pregnancy weigh on the average six to eight ounces less at birth than do newborns of nonsmokers—and more alarming reports have followed. According to the *New England Journal of Medicine,* the risk of spontaneous abortion in smoking women is almost double that of nonsmokers and the babies of mothers who smoke throughout pregnancy

are 28 per cent more likely to be stillborn or to die soon after birth. Respiratory illness is more common in newborns of mothers who smoke during pregnancy and congenital malformations have been attributed to smoking as well.

4. The deleterious effects of smoking continue to show up long after birth. Studies conducted in Britain and at the University of British Columbia (involving several thousand cases in Britain and more than 500 in Canada, as reported in the *British Journal of Preventive and Social Medicine* and the *Canadian Journal of Public Health*) followed the development of children born to women who smoked during pregnancy from birth to 11 years. Not only were they a half inch shorter on the average, but they were between three and five months behind in reading, mathematics and general ability, compared with the children of mothers who did not smoke.

5. Scientists, reporting in *The Lancet,* speculate that the two main culprits responsible for stillbirths and neonatal distress are nicotine and carbon monoxide, both part of tobacco smoke. Nicotine can actually reduce fetal breathing movements, in addition to causing the death of cells around the edges of the placenta. The placenta may then break away from the uterine wall, cutting off the baby's supply of food and oxygen. *Abruptio placentae,* as the phenomenon is known, is the second leading cause of death of unborn and newborn infants in Canada. Carbon monoxide is no less destructive. Since it combines with the mother's red blood cells 200 times more readily than does oxygen, the amount of oxygenated blood to the fetus is seriously diminished — by as much as 40 per cent if the mother smokes two packs of cigarettes a day.

6. The hazards of such disruptions of prenatal development can only be assessed alongside the smoking habits of Canadian women of childbearing age. Approximately one-third of all women 15 to 44 years of age now smoke — and the percentage is climbing. There has been an increase in smoking among girls 15 to 19, from 18 per cent in 1965 to almost 30 per cent in 1974. Two years later a survey conducted in Metropolitan Toronto showed that 48 per cent of teen-aged girls were smokers, as well as almost 42 per cent of adult women.

7. Until last year no campaign was ever mounted in Canada to warn women of the special dangers of smoking while pregnant. According to the *British Journal of Preventive and Social Medicine,* it is now believed that even if women stop smoking by the 20th week of pregnancy they can circumvent some of the ill effects. A $52,000 smoking and prenatal education study, funded by Health and Welfare Canada, is now being conducted by the department of health administration at the University of Toronto. Its aim is to reach women attending prenatal courses. As indicated by nurse

Jenny Pike, who stubbornly refused to quit smoking even when told it might hurt her child, the study has found that its task is much more complex than merely conveying information. Health-care professionals are often reluctant to confront the smoking issue with women already in their seventh month when they begin to attend prenatal classes. Sharon Tripp, who has instructed over 500 public health nurses and prenatal education teachers on the subject, says, "They're so used to reassuring and giving support to expectant mothers that telling them they are doing something that might harm their baby is out of character — they feel very uncomfortable."

8. Half the women surveyed in the new program said that at an even more crucial time, the beginnings of pregnancy, their doctors hadn't asked them if they smoked. "It's not that doctors aren't concerned," says Dr. Robert Langford, associate professor of community health at U of T, "but they have to be thinking about so many other things: conveying information about proper nutrition, monitoring weight gain, warning about the harm of taking drugs and alcohol. It's easy to understand why a doctor might think, 'I wouldn't be able to influence this woman's smoking behavior; I'll just make her anxious.' "

9. Some idea as to why it is so difficult to persuade even pregnant women to stop smoking has been suggested by a 1976 study conducted in England by scientists at the University of York during a wide-scale campaign against smoking during pregnancy. A cigarette is more than just a smoke it turned out: women use cigarettes to take a break from everything that is going on around them. The study also revealed that women don't put much store by what they learn from such impersonal sources as mass media and prenatal clinics. Information received from friends or relatives was much more readily accepted. Said one mother, "Well I smoke and they say you shouldn't. But our Paul was eight and a half pounds and he's never backward. If they could definitely prove it then I'd do something. But it's just facts, no one has proved it." To such opinions Sharon Tripp answers, "You were lucky."

Style and Structure

1. Instead of opening with a thesis statement the writer first attempts to get the attention of the reader. What device does she use? Rewrite the introduction, placing the thesis statement first. Give reasons why one approach is more effective than the other.
2. What strikes us as surprising, illogical or even shocking about the account of Jenny Pike's experience? How does her reaction fit into the thesis of the article?

3. Underline the thesis statement(s) and draw up a plan of the essay organization.

4. What form of proof does the writer present to support her thesis that smoking during pregnancy is dangerous? Given the nature of the topic, suggest other types of evidence that the writer could have used (e.g. other specific case histories). Which is more effective?

5. In her opening illustration, the writer shows us that even women with considerable medical knowledge do not stop smoking during pregnancy. Why, then, does she include paragraphs 7 and 8?

6. What does the author suggest is the real reason that pregnant women refuse to stop smoking? What does she show to be the real barriers which the medical profession must overcome to convince pregnant women not to smoke? Give reasons why this is or is not an effective way to conclude her article?

Thinking and Writing

a. Write an essay from one of the following points of view:

1. A public health professional who is trying to persuade a smoker to quit.

2. An addicted smoker defending his habit to a health professional.

Try to anticipate your reader's arguments and meet them in advance.

Audience:

as indicated in the topic.

b. Write an essay in which you take a stand for or against the topic "All tobacco smoking should be banned in any places that people congregate (other than a private home)." Research the topic well and try to anticipate and meet in advance the arguments of someone who would oppose your stand.

Audience:

someone who is in a position to make changes in the laws affecting smoking in public places.

Send a copy of your paper to a member of your local municipal council.

Laser technology — straight from *Star Trek*

by Dianne Rafalik Hales

1. The nurse dims the overhead lights in the operating room. The small body of a two-year-old child lies still on the table, his head tilted back, a tube called a bronchoscope placed deep in his throat. The otolaryngologist (ear, nose and throat specialist), Herbert Dedo, MD, of the University of California at San Francisco, peers through an operating microscope to get a three-dimensional, enlarged view of the clusters of white grapelike growths, called papillomas, that cover the boy's vocal cords, making it impossible for air to pass through. Because of these growths, the little boy has never spoken a word.

2. Dr. Dedo sights his target with a tiny red dot of light. Stepping on a release pedal, he fires tightly focused beams of intense light from a specially designed carbon-dioxide laser. With each split-second "hit," the tissue is vaporized in a puff of smoke. Moreover, since the laser cauterizes as it vaporizes, it leaves an almost bloodless path, with comparatively little swelling and scarring.

3. As the laser blasts away at the blob-like growths, normal vocal cords begin to appear. "I feel like Michelangelo sculpting," says Dedo, "but when you hear the zap of the laser beam and think of the precision and power of this light, it seems more like the twenty-first century and *Star Wars* than anything else."

4. The laser beam may never replace the scalpel, since the light that must travel a direct path into the body has a limited range. Yet, in certain types of surgery, light is now proving to be mightier than metal.

5. A hundred years ago, for example, children with growths in their throats choked to death. And even until very recently, a surgeon's best option was clamping a cup forceps around one of the polyps and tearing it free. It was a crude and difficult approach, as Dedo recalls: "I had to go by feel and instinct. Blood would pool up and block whatever view I had. I'd do fifty or seventy-five procedures under general anesthesia on a single patient, and the papillomas kept coming back, like warts on the skin."

6. In adults, laser surgery is becoming the most attractive approach for removing small cancers in the mouth and throat. "With the laser, we remove the tumor in a few hours, and the patient has

nothing more than a sore mouth for a couple of days," says Dedo. New instruments may even extend the laser's range into the larynx by using mirrors to reflect the light.

7. Most otolaryngologists started using lasers to operate on the tiny bones of the inner ear. But the real pioneers in this futuristic field were ophthalmologists, who now use lasers almost routinely to prevent and correct certain forms of blindness. In one office procedure, these eye doctors fire a laser thousands of times, covering the retina and the back of the eye with a tiny checkerboard of burns so precisely spaced that the victim's vision is not impaired. This "pattern bombing" is effective in halting diabetic retinopathy, a proliferation of abnormal blood vessels that can lead to retinal detachment and blindness.

8. Ophthalmologists use an argon laser, or one that emits a wave length of light that will cut through only red tissue, such as blood vessels. Other specialists now use carbon dioxide as their laser light source; this kind can cut through any tissue containing water (90 percent of your body tissue is H_2O). Gynecologists are experimenting with lasers to remove cervical cysts and superficial lesions; gastroenterologists may be able to cauterize bleeding ulcers with lasers. Plastic surgeons use lasers to remove unsightly birth marks, such as port-wine stains.

9. "This approach is still in its infancy," says Dedo frankly. "We can't even estimate what its eventual potential will be."

Style and Structure

1. Draw up a plan of the article's organization and underline the thesis statement.
2. What are the advantages of opening the essay with the scenario in paragraphs 1 to 3?
3. What image or impression does the writer create in paragraph 5? How does this contrast with the image or impression created in paragraphs 1 to 3? Why does the writer choose to emphasize this contrast?
4. For what purpose does Hales use parentheses in this article? Find one or two other devices that she uses for the same purpose. What type of reader does the use of such techniques suggest?
5. How does paragraph 9 serve as a conclusion to the article?

Thinking and Writing

a. New technological developments, such as laser surgery, present a difficulty to a writer. Without proper assistance, many readers tend to think of such developments as something to be frightened of (e.g. computers) or as "science fiction" (e.g. lasers). Select a technological development with which you are familiar and write an essay that subtly convinces the reader of the advance's positive values, just as Hales has done in her article on laser surgery. Consider such topics as solar energy, wind-generated energy, microwave ovens, heat exchangers, test tube babies and pedal powered cars. (If you do not feel qualified to discuss new developments, take the stance of a person living in 1900 and present the airplane, radio or telephone.)

Audience:

someone who knows very little about the development and who tends to be skeptical of "brave new worlds".

b. Some new technological developments (e.g. microwave ovens, convection ovens and television) achieve more general acceptance among the public than others that appear to have just as much value (e.g. solar heating and wind powered generators). Write an essay explaining why people behave in this way.

Audience:

someone who is familiar with marketing new technological devices.

Send a copy of your essay to the public relations department of a major electrical corporation or another corporation that is attempting to market new technological devices.

Dental X-rays shouldn't be a matter of routine

by W. Gifford-Jones, M.D.

1. Some dental offices should be in the travel business. They know more about the Caribbean sun than about X-ray dosages. But dentists are not alone. Too many radiologists, doctors, chiropractors and patients have developed X-rayitis. It's high time that Canadians learned to protect themselves and their families from needless radiation.

2. First of all, be a little skeptical about a new concept which is becoming routine dentistry. Many offices insist on taking batteries of X-rays even before the dentist sees the patient. They state these are required to detect decay in difficult locations and that this procedure constitutes sound dental practice.

3. Others would strongly disagree. For example, a report on radiological protection condemns this approach as one of the largest abuses of X-rays in dentistry. It stressed that films should only be taken when they're likely to provide significant information. I couldn't agree more.

4. But I was repeatedly given the same sales pitch when I called dental offices for appointments. I was told not to worry about these routine X-rays. After all, a full set of films was "just the same as spending a week in the Caribbean sun". The dentist would see me after they had been examined. And not a single dental assistant asked me when my last set of X-rays had been taken.

5. Not one could tell me about how many milliroentgens I'd received from these X-rays. Or how much radiation I was allowed during my lifetime. Most had never heard of a roentgen unit that measures the amount of radiation. But they all knew it would cost me approximately $30.

6. Examining X-rays before seeing a patient borders on malpractice, particularly when dealing with young people. Parents should refuse to accept this routine. Visual inspection is adequate for most children's and teen-age teeth, and some older people.

7. A study a few years ago found that dental X-rays seemed to be directly related to a person's income. People have simply been sold a bill of goods by the dental profession. I can imagine the hue and cry if physicians insisted on X-rays prior to physical examination, or ran up a bill of $70 for X-rays and dental hygiene even before facing the patient. Patients should allow the dentist to take selective X-rays, but I think the taking of a full mouth of films is an unconscionable act. No member of my family will again be subjected to it.

8. Dental X-rays are not without danger. The lens of the eye receives 50 milliroentgens from 15 films. The thyroid gland similarly gets about the same amount of scatter radiation. And some highly respected scientists argue that repeated low-dose radiation is hazardous.

9. Two previous studies on this subject also showed that faulty hospital machines are giving patients 60 times more radiation than other X-ray units. Dental and chiropractic offices are not immune to this trouble.

10. In 1976 the journal of the Canadian Medical Association focused attention on chiropractic offices. One article stated that reliable authorities believe that the 14 x 36 full-trunk X-ray, so beloved by the chiropractor, presents one of the greater radiation hazards and published figures show that chiropractors subject 90 per cent of their patients to this type of exposure.

11. The chiropractors I questioned were no more knowledgeable than

other professionals about radiation doses. Like everyone else, they had forgotten about safe dosages. Most said they knew the figures in college but couldn't remember them now, although some had graduated within the past year.

12. The journal of the American Medical Association raised this warning in 1977. It found that X-ray machines in private offices gave patients twice the radiation of hospital units.

13. Canadians have only one choice when faced with such a calamitous situation. Use every trick to side-step dangerous radiation. Remember that your body will tolerate only so many X-rays in a lifetime. So never say, "Couldn't you take an X-ray, doctor?" It doesn't take too much X-rayitis to use up the 40 allowable roentgens, even using excellent X-ray machines.

14. Don't forget that tincture of time will cure most aches and pains; that antacids should be tried for an upset stomach before resorting to X-rays; that you should shy away from X-rays during pregnancy at all costs; that you should insist on lead shielding for the gonads whenever films are taken; that you should take dental X-rays with you if you change dentists; that mobile X-ray units are best avoided. And don't label your doctor old-fashioned if he fails to order X-rays.

15. This is a good time to start your own radiation card. Show it to the doctor before he orders additional X-rays. By expressing concern about radiation, you can circumvent some X-rays. Start asking if the X-ray is really needed. And try to find a dentist who is more concerned about radiation hazards than the danger of a week in the Caribbean sun.

Style and Structure

1. What is the effect of the first two sentences on the reader?
2. Underline the thesis statement and draft a plan of the essay's organization.
3. Underline all references to the Caribbean sun. At what point does the relationship between dental offices and the Caribbean sun become clear? How do these references help the writer unify his essay?
4. What types of argument does the writer use to convince us that we should not allow medical professionals to take routine x-rays?
5. Why is the use of parallel structure particularly effective in paragraph 14?
6. How does the writer's conclusion (paragraphs 13-15) build upon his observations in the body of the article?
7. Why does the writer refer, once again, in his final sentence to the Caribbean sun?

Thinking and Writing

a. Assume that you have been asked to sit on a committee whose purpose is to select a board of directors for a comprehensive neighbourhood health care clinic. Write an essay in which you outline whom you would select to be on the board and what special contributions your selections would make to a complete and humane health service. Limit your selections to five or six individuals (e.g. one doctor, one dentist, one business man and three labourers).

Audience:
an average member of the community who would be using your recommendations to aid him/her in deciding how to vote in the election of board members.

b. Ivan Illich, in a book entitled *Limits to Medicine,* maintains that "the medical establishment has become a major threat to health. The disabling impact of professional control over medicine has reached the proportions of an epidemic." Among his specific charges against the "medical establishment", Illich claims that the medical profession causes more physical and mental damage to patients than it provides benefits, and that the medical profession takes away the individual's ability to determine his/her own health treatment and environment. It would appear that Dr. Gifford-Jones provides examples of both such "threats to health" in his article. Your own personal experience, the experiences of people that you know, and information that you have acquired in your reading will provide you with other examples that either verify or challenge Illich's charges.

On the basis of the above-mentioned sources, write an essay defending or refuting Illich's charges against the medical profession. Use specific examples and well reasoned arguments to support your position.

Audience:
someone who is very familiar with the medical profession.
Send a copy of your paper to a member of the medical profession.

Acid rain: scourge from the skies

by Robert Collins

1. Lumsden Lake, on the north shore of Ontario's Georgian Bay, twinkles like a sapphire in a setting of verdant forest and sparkling quartz. Blue, incredibly clear and seemingly pure, just 20 years ago it abounded in fish.
2. But now this exquisite lake is dead, its fish wiped out, the other creatures and plants in its aquatic food chain dead or dying. Like hundreds of other lakes and rivers in North America, Lumsden has been ravaged by acid from the sky.
3. From the smokestacks of power plants, smelters and factories across eastern Canada and the United States, and from vehicle exhausts in major cities, invisible clouds of sulfur dioxide and nitrogen oxide gases soar across provincial, state and international boundaries. They settle, sometimes 1500 kilometres from their sources, as acid rain, acid snow or dry particles that mingle with surface water to become acidic. The fallout erodes building surfaces and automobiles, may harm trees, crops and soils and could pose a threat to human health.
4. Already 140 Ontario lakes are dead or dying. An additional 48,000 are sensitive to acid rain because of the natural acidity of surrounding soil. In Nova Scotia, acid rain has killed all the salmon in seven rivers, threatening a $2-million-a-year salmon fishing industry. In New York State's Adirondacks region, more than 150 lakes are fishless. Acid rain, concludes an intensive study by a committee of the Ontario legislature, is "a national emergency." Says John Fraser, former federal minister of the environment, "It is the most serious environmental problem now facing Canada."
5. Approximately one third of the acid falling from North American skies is nitric, mostly from motor vehicle combustion; about two thirds is sulfur and produced mainly from coal-burning plants and nonferrous smelting. In Canada, the International Nickel (Inco) and Falconbridge smelters near Sudbury, and the Noranda Mines smelter at Noranda, Que., are notable offenders. Inco, the largest single source in North America, accounts for 20 percent of the sulfur dioxide emitted in Canada and one percent of known sulfur dioxide emissions in the world. In the United States, two thirds of sulfuric acid rain comes from power-generating plants,

particularly those burning high-sulfur coal. Each year the eastern United States belches forth 48 million metric tons of sulfur
dioxide and nitrogen oxides; Canada emits seven million tons.

6. North Americans have been smelting ore and burning fossil fuels
for generations. In the past the gases went up ordinary chimneys
or small smokestacks, to descend upon nearby areas and pollute
them. In time, governments and industries opted for taller smokestacks, and Inco's 350-metre one near Sudbury, the tallest in North
America, was one such vain attempt to disperse pollution harm-
lessly into the atmosphere. Instead, these gases may ride the winds
for days—time enough for critical chemical reactions to take place.
Within three days aloft, for example, half of a sulfur dioxide (SO_2)
emission will oxidize into sulfate particles (SO_4). A rainstorm or
snowfall, settling through these particles, produces sulfuric acid
(H_2SO_4), which falls to the ground, usually far from the source.

7. Nitric oxides similarly turn into nitric acid, but the chemical
reaction is more complex and the pollutant more difficult to
"track." Environment Canada's atmospheric environment service,
feeding twice-daily weather reports from a North American network into computers, can track an acid storm fairly accurately
back to its point of origin. We know that each year about two
million tons of sulfur come drifting across the border into Canada
aboard prevailing winds that in summer sweep north up through
the United States from the Gulf of Mexico, then curl in an easterly direction over Ontario, Quebec and the Maritimes. In the
meantime, winds carry half a million tons a year of Canada's
pollution into the eastern United States.

8. The lethal fallout is measured on a "pH" scale (referring to the
concentration of hydrogen ions), wherein O is acid, 14 is alkaline
and 7 is neutral. But because the pH scale is logarithmic, a pH of
5 is 10 times more acidic than a pH of 6. The *mean* pH rainfall in
Ontario's Muskoka-Haliburton lake country ranges between 3.95
and 4.38, about 40 times more acidic than normal rainfall, while
storms in Pennsylvania have registered 2.8—almost as acidic as
vinegar.

9. Some lands and waters, according to their natural acidity, are
particularly susceptible. Lake Ontario is safe with a pH8 reading.
Southern Ontario's farmland, much of the central United States
and Canada's prairies have well-buffered soils. But environmentalists worry that vast Athabasca oil sands developments will acidi-
fy sensitive northern Albertan and Saskatchewan lakes. Most of
the Precambrian shield, including large portions of Quebec, are
of a bedrock geology, low on alkalinity and easily harmed. Although damage reports from Quebec are scarce, federal scientists
fear that Quebec is *at least* as badly off as Ontario.

10. New York State's beautiful Adirondack Mountains region, says park agency commissioner Anne La Bastille, has become "an atmospheric cesspool." It receives large amounts of rain and snow, much of it acidic, because it is the first easterly mountain range to be hit by prevailing winds from the Midwest. As a result, half of the Adirondack lakes 600 metres or more above sea level are no longer able to support fish.

11. From studies of dying North American lakes and thousands of already-dead Scandinavian lakes, scientists know acid rain kills aquatic life by direct action on fish, by releasing toxic metals and by depleting aquatic foods. In Canada some species, such as lake trout, fail to reproduce below pH6. Scores of lakes on our continent fit into this killer category. Harold Harvey, University of Toronto zoologist and one of Canada's foremost experts on acid rain, can tick off the tragic life-and-death history of such lakes by name: "Tyson Lake was pH7.4 in 1955 and 4.9 by 1971, a horrendous change. . . . George Lake: 8 species left out of 13. . . . O.S.A. Lake: all fish extinct. . . ."

12. Below pH5.5, nearly all shrimplike organisms, essential diet for certain fish, disappear. Frogs and aquatic insects may be dying off, too. Part of the slaughter is caused by metal poisoning; aluminum, manganese and possibly other metals are released by chemical action from lake beds or surrounding soils. Inevitably, the deadly chain reaction touches other wildlife: fish-eating ducks, loons, ospreys, otter and mink.

13. Paradoxically, a trace of acid rain can actually improve the growth of certain plants in some soils, providing nitrate or sulfate nutrients. But rains of between pH4 and 3 damage the foliage of almost all plants and reduce the yields of carrots, radishes, beets and broccoli. Acid rain leaches calcium and potassium from plant tissues and erodes the waxy coating that protects their leaves from disease.

14. On the ground, acid rain leaches essential calcium, magnesium, potassium and sodium from the soil. It also prevents the decay of vegetation, depriving the soil of valuable nutrients. It kills earthworms, encourages unwanted fungus, prevents some seeds from germinating and releases toxic quantities of metal to be absorbed by roots.

15. More alarmingly, authorities fear acid rain in municipal water systems dissolves particles of copper or lead from pipes into drinking water. In one area of the Adirondacks, says park commissioner La Bastille, residents are advised to let their taps run five minutes every morning to flush out water that may have become toxic overnight.

16. What should be done? North America has been slow to recognize

the problem and scientists across the continent deplore the lack of research funds. Scandinavia spends about 50 cents per capita on research compared to ten cents in North America. "Acid rain is not a 'jazzy' problem," complains David Schindler of the federal Freshwater Institute in Manitoba. "Unfortunately," says Minnesota Congressman James L. Oberstar, "it's easier to get $2 billion for a nuclear aircraft carrier than $6 million to protect the environment." Scores of studies *are* underway, but new technologies must be applied, existing laws and controls tightened and a Canada–U.S. agreement reached.

17. If acid rain is not to get the upper hand, we will have to apply the best available technology, with all the political will we can muster. The U.S. Environmental Protection Agency (EPA) is experimenting with a burner assembly for pulverized-coal boilers that could reduce nitrogen oxide emissions by 80 percent.

18. Technology for reasonable control of sulfur dioxide already exists, says EPA's David Hawkins. "All we have to do is to apply it." Basically it consists of washing coal before combustion or cleaning emissions during combustion. Grinding coal and putting it through a liquid bath can remove as much as a third of the sulfur, says Lowell Smith of EPA. Yet about half of the high-sulfur coal presently used in the eastern states is not washed. Ontario Hydro, one of the largest coal users in Canada, buys washed coal but admits it would be improved by a further washing.

19. Of several techniques to remove pollution during industrial coal combustion, perhaps the most effective is "scrubbing," in which the gases are washed in a desulfurizing bath before going into the atmosphere. Scrubbers can remove at least 90 percent of sulfur dioxide. Yet only the *newest* coal-burning plants in the United States, and *none* of the major Canadian utility plants is so equipped. To remove a further 12 million tons of SO_2 by fitting scrubbers to some eastern U.S. power plants would cost $3 to $4 billion a year, says Lowell Smith.

20. Many new processes are under study in both Canada and the United States. But will they be used any more than the existing pollution-removal devices? Industries tend to put off such expensive items until they are pushed by government. Governments, hectored by industrial lobbies or by regions whose economy depends on mining, tend to drag their feet until the public demands action.

21. "We must not give up on acid rain," says Tom Brydges, supervisor of limnology and toxicity with the Ontario Ministry of the Environment. "We must not be bamboozled by six-figure clean-up costs. If industries and utilities are pressed, they often find solutions that are better for the ecology and more efficient for them. We

citizens must look these industries in the eye and say *'This won't do!'* "

22. An international agreement which serves as the framework for national, provincial and state standards is essential. Canada and the United States are now inching toward it, but action is unlikely in the near future. The core of such an agreement would be *enforced* reduction of emissions in both countries.

23. "We must at least get an agreement for huge cutbacks in emissions, maybe by state or province," suggests Ontario's Brydges. But Ron Reid, staff environmentalist with the Federation of Ontario Naturalists (FON), is one of many who sees enormous difficulties in reaching international accord: "The United States seems to be going in the opposite direction, in its trend to coal usage and the demands in some parts of the country for *relaxed* emission standards. Yet the American *people* seem sympathetic whenever they hear about what's happening to Canadian lakes."

24. Both in Canada and the United States, laws governing emissions are often ineffective and ambiguous. Whether a community in one country could sue a polluter in the other, for instance, causes jurists to shudder. In Canada, pollution control laws are primarily a provincial matter. Thus, Canada's federal Clean Air Act is of very little direct benefit, says John Swaigen of the Canadian Environmental Law Association. The federal government can set emission standards where emissions would clearly endanger human health or violate an international agreement, but for acid rain there is yet no international agreement, nor is the threat to human health fully documented. Nevertheless, says Ray Robinson, assistant deputy minister at Environment Canada, this country could cope with acid rain without changes in the laws, given the cooperation of the provinces.

25. The U.S. federal Clean Air Act of 1970 and a subsequent amendment do lay a firm hand on all new coal-burning plants. Utilities will have to invest several billion dollars to remove 70 to 90 percent of the sulfur from coal. They will be required to reduce SO_2 emissions by 55 percent and nitrogen oxide emissions by 20 percent over the current standard.

26. The trouble is, the new standards do not apply to existing plants. They are exempted on the premise that the stiff new regulations, requiring additional multimillion-dollar equipment, would impose a crushing financial burden on the companies and their customers. Yet by 1995 these older plants will still account for 73 percent of all SO_2 emissions from coal-fired utilities in the United States. Unless new rules are applied to existing plants, they will continue to pour acid rain on Canada and the eastern United States for the remainder of this century.

27. Canada wants the United States to amend its Clean Air Act. In the United States, Robert Rauch, staff attorney with the nonprofit Environmental Defense Fund, wants EPA to get tougher by implementing a provision in the Clean Air Act which would prohibit interstate pollution and allow injured states to sue polluters and by refusing to relax state limits. Lax application of the Ohio standard, he says, enables 10 or 12 large coal-burning plants to legally emit five to ten times as much SO_2 as new plants would be permitted to do. "EPA may have to be given the flexibility to regulate particular coal-burning facilities," adds Gus Speth of the President's Council on Environmental Quality.

28. The annual cost of curbing emissions until the end of this century has been estimated at $350 to $500 million in Canada and $5 to $7 billion in the United States. But the cost of not cleaning up is surely worse. "We're not talking about the damage to date," says Harold Harvey, "but about the potential loss if nothing is done now—and that is truly horrendous!"

29. Who can assess the value of a living lake, the splash of trout, the croak of frogs or the cry of an osprey? These are lost forever already in some lakes. Yet, as Minnesota Congressman Oberstar says, "We have a rare opportunity to see a disaster coming." We have had a taste of it in the Adirondacks and we can learn from Sweden and Norway where, without any international controls, 15,000 lakes have been denuded by acid rain. There is time to stop it here, if enough citizens in *both* countries care enough to insist on quick decisive action.

30. Says Ontario's Tom Brydges: "It would be a crime to pass on to our grandchildren 50,000 lakes without fish, without loons, without fish-eating ducks. Dammitall, we're *not* going to let the environment go down the tube!"

Style and Structure

1. (a) What image of Lumsden Lake does the writer present in paragraph 1? Which specific words and phrases create this image? How does this description fit the reader's expectations of a northern lake?
   (b) What image of Lumsden Lake does the writer present in paragraph 2? Which specific words and phrases create this image? How does this description fit the reader's expectations of a northern lake?
   (c) Why does the writer keep paragraphs 1 and 2 separate instead of combining them?
2. The appeal to the reader in paragraphs 1 and 2 is mainly emotional. On what level does the writer appeal in paragraphs 3 and 4?

3. Assuming that the thesis statement comes at the end of paragraph 4, what purpose do paragraphs 1 to 3 and the first half of paragraph 4 serve?

4. What information is contained in paragraphs 5 to 8? Why does the writer choose to include this information at this point in the essay? What does this organizational strategy indicate about the intended reader of the article?

5. What information is contained in paragraphs 9 to 15? How does the writer give the problem of acid rain impact for a reader who may not be very concerned about wildlife and the ecology?

6. What information is contained in paragraphs 17 to 28? How does paragraph 16 help prepare the reader for this long section?

7. In paragraphs 17 to 28 the writer presents three things that "should be done" about acid rain. Do you detect any parallels in the way in which he develops these sections? (Pay particular attention to transitional words such as "but" and "yet".)

8. How do the final two paragraphs of the essay act as an appropriate conclusion? Why does the author use quotations?

Thinking and Writing

a. Environmentalists frequently criticize industrialists for not doing enough to clean up pollution. Research the industrialists' point of view on acid rain, and write an essay in which you present their arguments sympathetically.
   Audience:
   an average citizen who has a minimal knowledge of the problems of acid rain.

b. Write an essay in which you argue for or against new measures to control acid rain.
   Audience:
   a legislator or business executive in a position to do something about the problem.
   Send a copy of this essay to your representative in the provincial parliament or to the president of your local or provincial hydro company.

Insane judgments

by Andreas Schroeder

1. On February 17, 1976, Renée and Dennis Carlton (pseudonyms) of Toronto became embroiled in a heated marital spat. As a result, Renée developed a splitting headache for which she took several codeine tablets and a tranquilizer, but the headache refused to subside. Finally her husband impatiently bundled her off to a nearby hospital, where he explained what had happened and mentioned as well that Renée had become hysterical on a similar previous occasion. Then he left.

2. The emergency ward staff gave Renée another tranquilizer and put her to bed. The next day a psychiatrist visited her briefly, and she described her fairly routine marital difficulties to him. The psychiatrist patted her hand and suggested that a few days of rest would solve the whole problem. That was the last Renée saw of him.

3. Two later days Renée felt revived, rested and ready to leave. Her request for her clothes, however, simply produced the head nurse, who demurred. "Just stay over the weekend," she urged. "Then we'll let you go." Renée agreed, but when she requested her clothes on the following Monday the intern shook his head. "You're not going anywhere, lady," he shrugged. "You've been certified."

4. Renée's protest went totally unheeded. The psychiatrist who had taken her case was nowhere to be found; he was, she was told, on holidays. Renée waited for three more days, hoping this misunderstanding would be cleared up. Nothing happened. Finally she lost patience, gathered her possessions, and headed for the hospital door.

5. She didn't get far. An off-duty nurse recognized her and alerted the interns. Renée was taken back up to her ward, stripped and forced to take a dose of tranquilizers, despite the fact that she had not resisted her captors in any way. Before they left, a nurse gave Renée an additional syringeful of a drug which knocked her out for most of two full days. When she finally regained her senses, Renée contacted her lawyer who advised her to file an appeal with the provincial mental health appeal board. "If you do that," the head nurse warned her, "they'll just send you to a stiffer institution." By now thoroughly cowed, Renée waived an appeal. Thirty days later she was suddenly released, without warning and without explanation.

6. The story of Renée Carlton's brush with the Mental Health Act of Ontario is not only alarming but also distressingly common. The regularity with which journalists, lawyers and civil libertarians are turning up similar cases from every province suggests that we are committing people to mental institutions with an unseemly eagerness these days.

7. Mental health acts vary from province to province, of course, as do the precise procedures by which a person may be involuntarily committed, but the similarities outweigh the differences. In all provinces, any person deemed to be suffering from a mental disorder which might endanger his or someone else's safety may be forcibly detained for emergency examination, without appeal, *on the initiative of one person*. In some provinces this person must be an official—a justice of the peace, a police officer, psychiatrist, psychologist, physician, nurse or social worker, for instance—but often it can be a relative or friend. Emergency commitment ranges from 24 to 72 hours (again, it varies from province to province), which seems safe enough until one considers this: in most provinces these periods of "emergency" commitment can be renewed almost indefinitely at the discretion of the attending psychiatrist, unless he is overruled by the institution's staff or a consulting doctor.

8. Beyond "emergency" commitment, there is what might loosely be called "regular" commitment, and regulations governing it also vary. The signature of *a single physician* (even one without a background in psychiatry) can put you away for a month in Ontario, New Brunswick and Prince Edward Island, and in Manitoba for 21 days, without any appeal whatsoever. The remaining provinces require two signatures, from either two physicians or two psychiatrists or one of each, and periods of commitment range from 14 to 30 days, also without any appeal. These periods too can be renewed at the discretion of the attending psychiatrist. It should be kept in mind that even persons arrested for the most heinous crimes have a legal right to question their confinement; persons detained by civil commitment, on the other hand, have no such right, despite the fact that they have probably committed no criminal offense.

9. "The plain truth of the matter is that the deck is so stacked against a civilly committed person in Canada, and particularly in British Columbia," an exasperated British Columbia lawyer told me, "that he couldn't win the game if he had a royal flush up each sleeve and four aces in his hand." The same complaints are heard across the country: newly committed persons are not told about the review boards (a review board generally consists of two psychia-

trists, one lawyer and one layman), or they are actively discouraged from filing an appeal. Hospital staff are accused of trying to convince patients that they're more sick than they really are. Patients are refused access to their commitment and medical papers and are forced to undergo both drug and group therapy on pain of negative, damaging notations on their records. Failure to cooperate in any way is deemed instant proof of the psychiatrist's original diagnosis. Often patients are tranquilized so routinely and so extensively that their mental deterioration is virtually guaranteed, regardless of their original state of mind.

10. Alan Borovoy of the Canadian Civil Liberties Association cautions that complaints like these shouldn't be considered an assault on psychiatrists. "I'm sure that doctors are doing the best they can in the best interests of their patients," he says. "But their good intentions are small consolation to the person held involuntarily." Toronto lawyer Edward Greenspan is more outspoken. "The extraordinary influence psychiatrists exert in the determination of who shall be involuntarily hospitalized is disturbing," he states. "This must be changed." He insists that there is no empirical support for the belief that psychiatrists can predict dangerous behavior with any degree of certainty.

11. Toronto psychiatrist John Richmond flatly disagrees. "We may not be perfect" he argues, "but we are certainly more competent than non-psychiatrists in these matters. And the notion that psychiatrists can't recognize potential violence is nonsense. Such recognition is implicit in a psychiatrist's entire training. . . . The point is, *anyone* could commit murder under certain circumstances, and *everybody* has at some time in his life experienced an impulse of murderous rage. Psychiatrists are concerned with the point at which that impulse becomes irresistible."

12. An impressive array of medical studies, however, has begun to support Greenspan's rather than Richmond's view. In a massive document entitled *Psychiatry and the Presumption of Expertise*, Bruce Ennis and Thomas Litwack analyze dozens of experiments conducted in both Europe and North America over the past decade. Among other things, they conclude that psychiatrists are prone to overprediction of psychosis; that no one, not even highly trained psychiatrists, can predict dangerous behavior in an individual with no history of it; and that the chance of two psychiatrists agreeing on a diagnosis is rarely better than 50-50.

13. A study of 200 certificates of commitment made by two Toronto law firms for the Canadian Civil Liberties Association (which recently presented a brief to the Ontario health minister outlining its proposals for changes in Ontario's Mental Health Act) proved

that more than 70 percent of the certificates examined violated even the minimum safeguards of that province's act. There is little reason to believe the situation is very different elsewhere in Canada. The reasons given by some of the doctors or psychiatrists for forcibly detaining their patients were little short of appalling. For instance, in the space allotted for *Facts indicating mental disorder as observed by physician*, one doctor wrote, "Shouting obscenities—very disturbed." Another wrote, "Patient very paranoid; no insight." And another reported, "Patient crying on phone." Under *Facts indicating mental disorder communicated to physician by others* were such comments as, "Unable to stop drinking," "Wife reports she doesn't want him back," "Speech incoherent and suspicious." Under *Reasons why no measure short of hospitalization is appropriate*: "Dangerous to himself: will not follow diet," "Leaves hospital," "Unpredictable—disturbed."

14. Harry Bowlen (pseudonym), a forensic psychiatrist in Edmonton, urges that such studies and complaints be put into perspective. "People attack the psychiatric profession from the safety of hindsight," he says. "I mean, put yourself in my place: a woman comes in screaming that she's going to commit suicide, or a man threatens to put a match to his house. The fact that neither person carries out the threat makes the problem simple for you, but you didn't have to deal with it from the start, when the threat really did sound convincing. We simply make the best possible assessment we can, with as much information as we can get our hands on at the time."

15. However, there is a consensus that changes in Canada's mental health acts are necessary and a basic agreement as to what these changes should include: the definition of committable mental disorders must be made far more precise; there should be a limit of 72 hours to any initial commitment, after which a review should be mandatory; mental institutions should be legally required to give a patient a complete explanation of his or her rights, and friends or relatives should be notified promptly. Review boards, which in most provinces meet in camera, generally keep no records of their proceedings and often don't permit patients to represent their cases, should be forced to operate more openly. Alan Borovoy says, "Any extension of the original commitment should be adjudicated by an independent tribunal, judge or psychiatrist—not by the same doctor or psychiatric facility that initiated commitment. And the patient should be given the opportunity to challenge the evidence against him in open court, with legal counsel available." Edward Greenspan says, "Commitment should be expressly disallowed where the physician's conclusions are based

entirely on information communicated to him by others." And Harry Bowlen says, "I'd like to see more community-based, informal facilities, so that we're not always faced with sending a patient either into the streets or into a large mental institution, neither of which is desirable. If more options were available, many people could be dealt with without being committed at all."

16. It might be possible to squint past the potential misapplications of our present laws if their effect was demonstrably restricted to committing only the raving lunatics among us. Unfortunately, the more one digs, the more one finds that people temporarily upset over domestic difficulties, persons of unusual religions or philosophic persuasions, and people who seem "different" but who are hardly dangerous or insane are being institutionalized alongside unpredictable psychopaths. Often they are detained in environments where any possible benefits that might accrue from rest and therapy promptly evaporate in a disorienting and debasing milieu, in numbing routine, endless tranquilizers, or more extreme measures like shock therapy.

17. "Under the present mental health acts," Edward Greenspan says, "virtually everyone I know has been certifiable at one time or another." People like you and me.

Style and Structure

1. How does the writer get the reader's attention and empathy in the introduction of the essay? To what kind of reader is Schroder directing his article?
2. Underline the thesis statement.
3. What information does the writer present in paragraphs 7 and 8? Given the reader identified in question 1, why must the author include this information?
4. Paragraphs 9 to 14 are structured much like a debate. Identify the resolution (the statement of the topic for debate). Draw up a plan of paragraphs 9 to 14 in which you list the arguments made for and against this resolution.
5. What aspect of Canadian mental health acts does the author consider their major weakness? How does his presentation and organization of the "debate" material emphasize this weakness?
6. How does paragraph 15 function in relation to the "debate" in paragraphs 9 to 14?
7. Many conclusions present a summary of the main point of the essay. What does Schroeder choose to present in his conclusion (paragraphs 16 to 17)? What effect does he wish to have on the reader?

Thinking and Writing

a. Imagine yourself faced with the following situation. A family member has walked out on her husband and two pre-school children and is living on welfare in a teepee in the woods. Every time anyone tries to convince her to return to family responsibilities, she goes into a rage, screams obscenities, and threatens suicide. At all other times she lives quietly and produces enough food to survive, but she refuses to visit with anyone. The family has given you the task of deciding what should be done about her.

Write an essay in which you recommend whether or not this person should be committed to a mental institution.

Audience:

the members of the family. Remember that the situation is quite emotional.

b. There is a very fine line between being concerned for the mental health of another person and meddling with other people's affairs to make them fit your concept of "normal". Write an essay in which you try to define where that line should be drawn.

Audience:

someone who knows the field of mental health and the problems of commitment well.

Send a copy of your essay to a local mental health organization.

Visit to the enchanted isles

1. *Lying astride the equator in the Pacific Ocean some 600 miles off the coast of South America, the Galapagos Islands are a fabled natural wonderland—of giant tortoises, dragon-like iguanas and birds so fearless that they ignore the approach of a human. Old Spanish explorers called them* Las Islas Encantadas *(the bewitched or enchanted islands). It was here, among the exotic flora and fauna of the isolated islands, notably their startlingly varied finches, that the young Charles Darwin found the key evidence for his theory of evolution. Yet these unique biological enclaves, long despoiled by*

pirates and passing sailors, are still under attack. Thousands of peering, prodding, picture-taking tourists now visit the Galapagos annually, at considerable risk to the islands' frail ecology. To assess the damage already done to this irreplaceable showcase of evolution, a UNESCO team visited the islands this month. TIME Associate Editor Frederic Golden was with the group and sent this report:

2. Our guide was quite firm. "Please don't annoy her too much," he said as we approached a blue-footed booby that had decided to nest directly in our path. But even the guide, a serious young Australian biologist named Bob Close, could not resist the temptation, along with the rest of us, to poke a camera right in the face of the comic bird with the garishly colored webbed feet. The booby blithely continued to sit on her two eggs while the cameras clicked away. Said Close: "You would think that after having hundreds of tourists parade by them they would have learned to pick a more secluded place to nest. But they really seem to like the ground when it is all scuffed up by our feet."

3. Other creatures on the islands do not always take so kindly to human intrusion. When we moved toward a well-worn rock that had long ago been staked out by sea lions, a huge bull came huffing toward us and made it all too plain that he wanted us off his favorite perch. Our retreat was a prudent move: a few weeks earlier, a German tourist who insisted on holding his ground lost a leg to another enraged bull. The visitors can also inflict damage, even when they have the best of intentions. Biologists on Santa Cruz, one of the 13 major islands in the archipelago, were mystified recently when some of the iguanas they were studying stopped producing offspring. A little investigation provided the explanation: handouts from kindly tourists at a dock were drawing so many iguanas to the site that breeding territories were being broken up.

4. It is to protect animals and tourists alike from just such mishaps that Ecuadorian authorities have begun to impose strict regulations under the legislation that has turned most of the 3,000-sq.-mi. territory into a national park. Before visitors arrive from the mainland by boat or the twice-weekly plane, they must now get their proposed itineraries approved by park authorities. Once they are on the islands, they must stick closely to the marked paths laid out for visitors, always be accompanied by a trained guide and never touch, feed or molest the animals. Explains the park system's dedicated 26-year-old director, Miguel Cifuentes: "There is a place for humans in the Galapagos, but they must be integrated into the natural system without being permitted to overwhelm it."

5. Unfortunately, the islands have a long history of being overwhelmed. For centuries, passing ships freely helped themselves to

the resident *galapagos* (Spanish for tortoises). Stacked in a ship's hold, these great beasts, which often weigh more than 500 lbs. and live for a century or more, can survive for a year without food or water. Thus in the days before refrigeration, they were an ideal source of fresh meat aboard ship. At least partly because of the sailors' depredations, three or four subspecies of tortoises were wiped out and still others threatened with extinction. In the late 19th century, the slaughter was extended to seals and sea lions, highly valued for their skins and furs. Even the chubby little Galapagos doves did not escape the carnage, since they were easy to catch and provided a tasty free meal.

6. More recently the killing has been done in the name of science. As late as the 1930s, zoos, museums and other institutions were carrying off shiploads of endangered species, many of which wound up as stuffed skins inside display cabinets. World War II also took its toll. Largely out of boredom, the U.S. servicemen who built and manned the airstrip on Baltra took potshots at iguanas, eventually making them extinct on that island. Some of the other assaults on Galapagos fauna and flora have also come through man's thoughtlessness.

7. Built up from the ocean floor millions of years ago, the islands are little more than volcanic rocks—"heaps of cinders dumped here and there," wrote Herman Melville. Despite the desolate appearance of the Galapagos, their isolation and the severe shortage of fresh water, intrepid colonizers have been trying to settle on the islands since the 19th century. The results were usually unsuccessful, and the settlers perished or fled. Even so, some of their animal companions—goats, cats, dogs, donkeys, pigs and, of course, the ubiquitous rat—remained behind to thrive, compete with and prey on the native wildlife.

8. Lately, humans too have secured a permanent foothold. A handful of the homesteaders are Americans and Europeans who were drawn by the dream of a simple, Gauguin-like life away from civilization. Most, however, are Ecuadorians from the mainland who engage in cattle raising or other types of farming. Even though these settlers are largely limited to the three islands with some fertile areas—Santa Cruz, San Cristobal and Floreana— they now number more than 5,000, including several hundred Ecuadorian navy and air force personnel.

9. This population explosion has complicated the job of Cifuentes and his 50 park wardens. Some residents have angrily objected to the shooting of pillaging goats; they insist that the animals are part of their food supply. Indeed, one embattled fisherman secretly planted several goats back on an island after Cifuentes' marksmen had finally managed to eliminate these animals there. No less

exasperating is the effort to keep residents from bringing in new grasses and trees for grazing land and timber. For example, balsa trees, introduced by settlers, are crowding out the more fragile — and uniquely local — native plants within the parklands. Rats have also become stubborn pests. Only on the small island of Bartolomé have traps and poisons made any real inroads against the durable rodents.

10. In the past, Ecuador lacked the inclination, the money or the manpower to do much about its priceless island territory, except to establish occasional penal colonies there. But in 1962 it got some badly needed international assistance with the opening of the Charles Darwin Research Station near Puerto Ayora on Santa Cruz. Staffed by resident and visiting scientists, largely from the U.S. and Europe, the station has conducted intensive investigations into the ecology of the islands and is now waging a major campaign, in collaboration with the Ecuadorians, to save endangered species. Darwin scientists have begun a tortoise-breeding program, raising them until the age of six or seven. By then the animals are large enough to fend for themselves against dogs and other predators and are released into the wild. Howard Snell, a young Smithsonian Peace Corps volunteer from San Diego, Calif., is conducting a similar iguana-rearing project.

11. Impressed by these activities, officials in the far-off Ecuadorian capital of Quito are showing a growing new pride in their island possession. Schoolchildren from the mainland are now regularly shuttled over on tours, during which they are told about the special place of the Galapagos in the history of biology. The Galapagans, too, are becoming less blasé about their heritage; the main street in Puerto Ayora is named Avenida Charles Darwin. Cifuentes, meanwhile, is making plans to extend the park area to the teeming coastal waters around the islands, which are chilled and fertilized by the cold Humboldt Current. Indeed, he sees the Galapagos as a kind of laboratory for the future in which man and beast harmoniously share the same wild habitat. Says Cifuentes: "Humans can live in the Galapagos, but they must do it in a boldly different way — without pollution, without despoliation, without any of the dreadful mistakes of the past."

Style and Structure

1. Without the section in italics would the introduction of the article be sound? What difficulties would the omission cause the reader?
2. Underline the sentence in italics which best states the thesis of the article. If the italicized paragraphs were omitted, where would you find another suitable thesis statement?

64

3. The tone of the italicized section is quite different from the tone of the rest of the essay. Describe how they differ and comment on whether you find this abrupt change of tone effective or distracting.
4. The article begins with three illustrations of the effect of tourists on the ecology and vice versa. It is not until paragraph 4 that the writer introduces the regulations designed to prevent abuses. What would the impact on the article be if the order of the paragraphs were reversed *i.e.* 4, 2, 3?
5. What is the author's purpose in repeating the word "overwhelm" in paragraphs 4 and 5?
6. The writer deals with one main point in paragraphs 5 and 6; then he moves on to another main point in paragraphs 7, 8 and 9. Is this transition smoothly accomplished? If not, rewrite the opening section of paragraph 7 to achieve this end.
7. Throughout the article, the writer makes use of direct quotation. Rewrite the final sentence of the article, changing the direct quotation into an indirect quotation. How does this change affect the impact of the conclusion?

Thinking and Writing

a. Write an essay from the point of view of *one* of the various inhabitants of the Galopagos Islands outlining the direction that the future development of the islands should take. Some of the inhabitants are homesteading farmers, town councillors, naval and air force representatives, the governor, representatives of the tourist industry, officials attempting to establish a national park, visiting scientists who wish to study an "undisturbed ecology", and tourists.
Audience:
other inhabitants of the islands who do not see the problems of the islands from the same point of view as you do and who want future development to take a different form than you do.

b. Cifuentes is quoted at the end of the article as saying, "Humans can live on the Galapagos, but they must do it in a boldly different way—without pollution, without despoliation, without any of the dreadful mistakes of the past."
Write an essay in which you outline your own personal point of view on how the problems faced by the Galapagos Islands and Cifuentes' proposed solution to these problems relate to the situation faced by the world as a whole.
Audience:
someone who, though he/she knows the implications of "pollution...," despoliation..., [and] the dreadful mistakes of the

past", is involved in one way or another with allowing or producing further problems, even though this person is in a position to effect substantial changes in the situation.

Send a copy of your paper to the public relations officer of a firm that is a major polluter in your community.

In the beginning: God and science

by Lance Morrow

1. Sometime after the Enlightenment, science and religion came to a gentleman's agreement. Science was for the real world: machines, manufactured things, medicines, guns, moon rockets. Religion was for everything else, the immeasurable: morals, sacraments, poetry, insanity, death and some residual forms of politics and statesmanship. Religion became, in both senses of the word, immaterial. Science and religion were apples and oranges. So the pact said: render unto apples the things that are Caesar's, and unto oranges the things that are God's. Just as the Maya kept two calendars, one profane and one priestly, so Western science and religion fell into two different conceptions of the universe, two different vocabularies.

2. This hostile distinction between religion and science has softened in the last third of the 20th century. Both religion and science have become self-consciously aware of their excesses, even of their capacity for evil. Now they find themselves jostled into a strange metaphysical intimacy. Perhaps the most extraordinary sign of that intimacy is what appears to be an agreement between religion and science about certain facts concerning the creation of the universe. It is the equivalent of the Montagues and Capulets collaborating on a baby shower.

3. According to the *Book of Genesis,* the universe began in a single, flashing act of creation; the divine intellect willed all into being, *ex nihilo.* It is not surprising that scientists have generally stayed clear of the question of ultimate authorship, of the final "uncaused cause." In years past, in fact, they held to the Aristotelian idea of a universe that was "ungenerated and indestructible," with an infinite past and an infinite future. This was known as the Steady State theory.

4. That absolute expanse might be difficult, even unbearable, to contemplate, like an infinite snow field of time, but the conception at least carried with it the serenity of the eternal. In recent decades, however, the Steady State model of the universe has yielded in the scientific mind to an even more difficult idea, full of cosmic violence. Most astronomers now accept the theory that the universe had an instant of creation, that it came to be in a vast fireball explosion 15 or 20 billion years ago. The shrapnel created by that explosion is still flying outward from the focus of the blast. One of the fragments is the galaxy we call the Milky Way — one of whose hundreds of billions of stars is the earth's sun, with its tiny orbiting grains of planets. The so-called Big Bang theory makes some astronomers acutely uncomfortable, even while it ignites in many religious minds a small thrill of confirmation. Reason: the Big Bang theory sounds very much like the story that the Old Testament has been telling all along.

5. Science arrived at the Big Bang theory through its admirably painstaking and ideologically disinterested process of hypothesis and verification — and, sometimes, happy accident. In 1913, Astronomer Vesto Melvin Slipher of the Lowell Observatory in Flagstaff, Ariz., discovered galaxies that were receding from the earth at extraordinarily high speeds, up to 2 million m.p.h. In 1929, the American astronomer Edwin Hubble developed Slipher's findings to formulate his law of an expanding universe, which presupposes a single primordial explosion. Meantime, Albert Einstein, without benefit of observation, concocted his general theory of relativity, which overthrew Newton and contained in its apparatus the idea of the expanding universe. The Steady State idea still held many astronomers, however, until 1965, when two scientists at Bell Telephone Laboratories, Arno Penzias and Robert Wilson, using sophisticated electronic equipment, picked up the noise made by background radiation coming from all parts of the sky. What they were hearing, as it turned out, were the reverberations left over from the first explosion, the hissing echoes of creation. In the past dozen years, most astronomers have come around to operating on the assumption that there was indeed a big bang.

6. The Big Bang theory has subversive possiblities. At any rate, in a century of Einstein's relativity, of Heisenberg's uncertainty principle (the very act of observing nature disturbs and alters it), of the enigmatic black holes ("Of the God who was painted as a glittering eye, there is nothing now left but a black socket," wrote the German Romantic Jean Paul), science is not the cool Palladian temple of rationality that it was in the Enlightenment. It begins to seem more like Prospero's island as experienced by Caliban. Some

astronomers even talk of leftover starlight from a future universe, its time flowing in the opposite direction from ours. A silicon-chip agnosticism can be shaken by many puzzles besides the creation. Almost as mysterious are the circumstances that led, billions of years ago, to the creation of the first molecule that could reproduce itself. That step made possible the development of all the forms of life that spread over the earth. Why did it occur just then?

7. A religious enthusiasm for the apparent convergence of science and theology in the Big Bang cosmology is understandable. Since the Enlightenment, the scriptural versions of creation or of other "events," like the fall of man or the miracles of Jesus Christ, have suffered the condescension of science; they were regarded as mere myth, superstition. Now the faithful are tempted to believe that science has performed a laborious validation of at least one biblical "myth": that of creation.

8. But has any such confirmation occurred? Robert Jastrow, director of NASA's Goddard Institute for Space Studies, has published a small and curious book called *God and the Astronomers,* in which he suggests that the Bible was right after all, and that people of his own kind, scientists and agnostics, by his description, now find themselves confounded. Jastrow blows phantom kisses like neutrinos across the chasm between science and religion, seeming almost wistful to make a connection. Biblical fundamentalists may be happier with Jastrow's books than are his fellow scientists. He writes operatically: "For the scientist who has lived by his faith in the power of reason, the story ends like a bad dream. He has scaled the mountains of ignorance; he is about to conquer the highest peak; as he pulls himself over the final rock, he is greeted by a band of theologians who have been sitting there for centuries."

9. Isaac Asimov, the prodigious popularizer of science, reacts hotly to the Jastrow book. "Science and religion proceed by different methods," he says. "Science works by persuasive reason. Outside of science, the method is intuitional, which is not very persuasive. In science, it is possible to say we were wrong, based on data." Science is provisional; it progresses from one hypothesis to another, always testing, rejecting the ideas that do not work, that are contradicted by new evidence. "Faith," said St. Augustine, "is to believe, on the word of God, what we do not see." Faith defies proof; science demands it. If new information should require modification of the Big Bang theory, that modification could be accomplished without the entire temple of knowledge collapsing. Observes Harvard University Historian-Astronomer Owen Gingerich: "*Genesis* is not a book of science. It is accidental if some things agree in detail. I believe the heavens declare the glory of God only to people who've made a religious commitment."

10. A number of theologians concur that the apparent convergence of religious and scientific versions of the creation is a coincidence from which no profound meaning can be extracted. "If the last evidence for God occurred 20 billion years ago," asks Methodist W. Paul Jones of Missouri's St. Paul School of Theology, "do we not at best have the palest of deisms?" Jesuit Philosopher Bernard Lonergan goes further: "Science has nothing to say about creation, because that's going outside the empirical. The whole idea of empirical science is that you have data. Theologians have no data on God." There comes a point, somewhere short of God, at which all computers have no data either. With the Big Bang theory, says Jastrow, "science has proved that the world came into being as a result of forces that seem forever beyond the power of scientific description. This bothers science because it clashes with scientific religion—the religion of cause and effect, the belief that every effect has a cause. Now we find that the biggest effect of all, the birth of the universe, violates this article of faith."

11. Some scientists matter-of-factly dismiss the problem of creation. Says Harvey Tananbaum, an X-ray astronomer at the Harvard-Smithsonian Astrophysical Laboratory: "That first instant of creation is not relevant as long as we do not have the laws to begin to understand it. It is a question for philosophers and religionists, not for scientists." Adds Geoffrey Burbidge, director of Kitt Peak National Observatory: "Principles and concepts cannot be measured. A question like 'Who imposed the order?' is metaphysical." Still, virtually everyone—both scientists and laymen—is taken by the sheer unthinkable opacity of the creation and what preceded it. Says Jastrow: "The question of what came before the Big Bang is the most interesting question of all."

12. One immense problem is that the primordial fireball destroyed all the evidence; the temperature of the universe in the first seconds of its existence was many trillion degrees. The blast obliterated all that went before. The universe was shrouded in a dense fog of radiation, which only cleared after 1 million years, leaving the transparent spangled space we see in the night sky now. The first million years are as concealed from us as God's face. There are many forms of knowing: science, experience, intuition, faith. Science proceeds on the theory that there is method in all mysteries, and that it is discoverable. It obeys, reasonably, what is called the "first law of wingwalking": "Never leave hold of what you've got until you've got hold of something else." Faith, by definition, is a leap. It must await its verification in another world.

13. If it has done nothing else, however, the new coincidence of scientific and theological versions of creation seems to have opened up a conversation that has been neglected for centuries. Roman

Catholic Theologian Hans Küng detects the beginning of a new period, which he calls "pro-existence," of mutual assistance between theologians and natural scientists. People capable of genetic engineering and nuclear fission obviously require all the spiritual and ethical guidance they can get. As for theologians, the interchange between physics and metaphysics will inevitably enlarge their ideas and give them a more complex grounding in the physically observed universe. The theory of the Big Bang is surely not the last idea of creation that will be conceived; it does suggest that there remain immense territories of mystery that both the theologian and the scientist should approach with becoming awe.

Style and Structure

1. What device does the writer use in paragraph 1 to create controversy? How is the overall organization of the article reflected in the first paragraph?
2. Isolate the sentences in paragraph 2 which most effectively state the thesis of the essay.
3. The writer combines two expressions in the following quotation: "Render unto apples the things that are Caesar's, and unto oranges the things that are God's".
   How does this marriage of sayings relate to the thesis?
4. Examine the body of the essay (paragraphs 3-12) and plot out its development paragraph by paragraph. How does the order in which the writer presents his main points impart a logical development to his thesis?
5. How does the author emphasize that most scientists and theologians feel that the premise stated at the conclusion of paragraph 7 is superficial.
6. How does the author use his conclusion to propose a real as opposed to a superficial reconciliation between science and religion? In what ways is this type of conclusion more satisfactory than a simple recapitulation of the thesis?

Thinking and Writing

a. In his article, the writer states the following opinions:
   "Science was for the real world: machines, manufactured things, medicines, guns, moon rockets. Religion was for everything else, the immeasurable: morals, sacraments, poetry, insanity, death and some residual forms of politics and statesmanship."
   "People capable of genetic engineering and nuclear fission obviously require all the spiritual and ethical guidance they can get."
   "Science and religion proceed by different methods. Science

works by persuasive reason. Outside of science, the method is intuitional, which is not very persuasive. In science, it is possible to say we were wrong."

Write an essay in which you support *or* refute *one* of the quotations.

Audience:
a layperson who is not directly involved with the sciences.

b. Write an essay on your personal view of what the ideal relationship between science and religion should be in the future.

Audience:
someone who has strong religious convictions and is involved in trying to help others come to grips with religious doubts caused by their perception of science.

Send a copy of your paper to a member of the clergy that you know.

Laugh after laugh: the link between humor and health

by Dr. Raymond Moody

1. This article is about the medical implications and uses of laughter and the sense of humor, about laughter and humor as they bear upon questions of health and disease. Now, at first thought it may seem strange that someone should think about putting these two apparently incongruous concepts—humor and medicine— together. So perhaps I should indicate briefly how, as a physician, my attention was drawn to this subject.

2. First of all, I have always been a repressed humorist, and as a child one of the very first things I ever wanted to become when I grew up was a professional comedian. Humor has always played a big part in my life and in my response to people and situations. I am an inveterate practical joker and punster, and I love to laugh. Naturally, I carried these tendencies along with me into medical school when I entered training.

3. Second, over the years I have encountered a surprising number of instances in which, to all appearances, patients have laughed

themselves back to health, or at least have used their sense of humor as a very positive and adaptive response to their illnesses. These remarkable recoveries, some of which will be detailed here, have suggested to me the possibility that there may indeed be something therapeutic about humor, just as folk belief has long assured us.

4. Third, a significant insight gradually dawned on me as I continued my studies in medical school. I was told during my training that I should try to find out about each patient's appetite, sexual functioning, habits of sleep, nutrition, and elimination. I was carefully instructed to take note of any peculiarities of language, appearance, complexion, posture, and gait. Great emphasis was placed on how essential it was to record carefully on hospital charts, and various other forms, the patient's age, occupation, marital status, general level of intelligence, weight, blood pressure, heart rate, respiration rate, and a host of other parameters, evaluating each as to whether it was normal or abnormal. In fact, at one time or other I was explicitly directed to take note of almost every kind of information about my patients that one can imagine. However, not once in all those years of training do I remember anyone reminding me to probe into an individual's sense of humor or to observe and to record how willing a person was to smile or laugh. Yet, as time has gone on, I have come to feel that a human being's ability to laugh and to appreciate funny material is just as important a fact, and just as valuable and valid an indicator of the state of a person's health, as are all those other things.

5. Furthermore, as I began to learn by experience how valuable an aid humor is in assessing the state of someone's physical and emotional health, it became apparent—little by little—that humor and health are not unrelated notions at all. Indeed, the connection between laughter and health is drawn almost universally, by laymen and medical professionals alike, in ancient writings as well as in the most up-to-date medical journals. In all probability, one reason why the relationship was never explicitly pointed out to me in medical school or in subsequent training is simply that it is so obvious. The ability to laugh is one of the most characteristic and deep-seated features of man. Many psychologists and philosophers have even argued that man is the only creature who laughs or has a sense of humor; some have taken this so far as to suggest that man might be defined as "the risible animal," the animal who can laugh. Accordingly, a person's sense of humor is such an important aspect of him or her that it is something which others notice almost automatically, without thinking much about it. It is only in cases in which there is something extreme or inappropriate about someone's laughter or

sense of humor that it is likely to enter another's conscious awareness. Otherwise, it probably wouldn't seem worthy of notice at all.

6. No doubt, then, doctors have probably always noted—even if only preconsciously—their patients' senses of humor. Nonetheless, probably in part because of its obvious and almost unconsciously appreciated significance, the role of humor in health is one which hardly ever is openly and explicitly discussed. To my knowledge, no medical schools offer courses or lecture series on the topic, and—even in our paper-oriented society—there is probably not a single health form on which there is a space for checking off whether or not the patient's sense of humor seems normal.

7. The automatic, unconscious nature of our recognition of another person's sense of humor, however, may be only part of the explanation for the dearth of open discussion of the subject. It is possible that another factor lies in what the psychologist Gordon Allport has called the "tenderness taboo." He has pointed out that academicians seem as a group to be more comfortable investigating negative mental states and emotions—hostility, aggression, anger, greed, depression, anxiety—than they are studying positive ones—love, elation, altruism, sympathy, generosity, understanding, humor. At times, indeed, it appears that as an institution, professional psychology is somewhat embarrassed to dwell upon these more happy states.

8. There are reasons in the present instance, though, for going on and breaking the taboo, and for articulating the obvious. In the first place, as a society we appear to have become obsessed with the notion that there ought to be a pill or an operation or a machine to treat each illness. We tend to think that the doctor should be able to cure us—instantaneously, preferably—of any ailment, with a minimum of effort or cooperation on our own part. Such magical attitudes about the efficacy of modern technological medicine have led to a neglect of the very real factors of emotion and mental outlook which may precipitate disease, and affect its course, duration, and outcome. Focusing for a while on the relationship between humor and health may help to correct this imbalance, at least to some degree.

9. As to the instances of apparent healing by humor, it is true they are somewhat puzzling and, taken by themselves, seem difficult to explain. In fact, a natural response for a person trained in modern medicine to make to these reports would be: "But this is just anecdotal. There are no experimental controls," or "But these people probably would have gotten better anyway!" Such objections are valid and are to be taken seriously.

10. My only point, for the present, is that observations of this type, coupled with the longstanding folk belief in the value of laughter

as a remedy, at least suggest that there may be something here which is worth looking into.

Healing by humor: some examples

11. We'll begin with a personal example, whose circumstances may be far from your life.

12. At one time during my medical training, I was treating a middle-aged man who was suffering from chronic depression. He had almost constant headaches and complained, as depressed persons so often do, of insomnia — of awakening in the early morning hours and being unable to get back to sleep. He was chronically unable to say no to other people who made unreasonable demands on him. This man had essentially no formal education and for that reason was unable to get a satisfactory job. At that time, he was working in an intolerable setting, in a cookie factory.

13. As I talked with this fellow during our first few psychotherapeutic sessions, he consistently maintained a gloomy countenance. For week after week, he kept coming to me, never once smiling, with tale after tale of his troubles, while I tried unsuccessfully to steer him into the public education which was available to him at no cost. I felt that there was a strong situational component to his depression, and that further training would give him more self-confidence and enable him to get a better job, thus improving his life situation. However, he had been steadfastly resisting my efforts.

14. One day, when he came in for his appointment, he related in a most woebegone fashion that a new foreman had come to work in the factory. The new boss had expressed dissatisfaction with the rate of cookie production, and had talked of an increase. My patient had weakly protested that the wrapping machine just would not function any more quickly, but to no avail. The decision was made, the order was given, and the cookie production was speeded up. True to my patient's prediction, the wrapping machine went haywire, and soon an avalanche of cookies was spewing all over everything. Helpless before the onslaught of cookies, my patient had stood there while the boss railed at him — the only person who had challenged the scheme in the first place.

15. Sitting there as he related the story to me, I conjured up an image of it in my mind. As I contemplated the scene, try as I did to prevent myself, I did something which I had been constantly told that I should never do. Despite the fact that I was biting the inside of my cheeks, I felt the corners of my mouth begin to form a smile. Amazingly, my patient, responding, began to smile, and then he burst out into peals of laughter.

16. It is interesting that this event started the therapeutic relation-

ship between us anew. From that point on, I believe that he got better. I think that in that moment, standing back from his life situation and seeing it from a comic—even perhaps cosmic—perspective, he realized that he had been playing a game with himself. It really was up to him to get himself out of his troubling life situation. He resolved to do something about it. He went into a training program so that he could obtain more gratifying employment.

17. There are reports, both in the professional literature and in the context of anecdote and folk belief, of persons who have been cured, or at least eased, in medical and/or psychological conditions, by the use of laughter and humor.

18. One of the most remarkable of these is an account published in the conservative *New England Journal of Medicine,* one of the most respected medical journals in the world. In it, Mr. Norman Cousins, editor of *The Saturday Review,* detailed his remarkable recovery from a grave and potentially life-threatening illness. Following a stressful incident at the end of an emotionally and physically draining trip abroad, Mr. Cousins noted the onset of a fever and feelings of achiness and malaise during his flight home to the United States. His illness progressed, and soon after his return he was admitted to the hospital, where clinical and laboratory findings indicated that he was suffering from a serious collagen disease. Collagen is a substance found in the connective tissue of the body which is essential in holding the cells and larger structures of the body together. Mr. Cousins soon experienced great difficulty and pain in moving his joints, and he was told that his prospects for recovery were in no way favorable.

19. He refused to accept this grim prognosis, and—with the sympathetic understanding of his physician—he decided to take charge of his own treatment. He remembered reading of the role of the endocrine system in fighting disease, and of the adverse impact of negative emotional states on the chemical balance of the body. He reasoned that, if negative emotions played any part in predisposing him to the illness, then perhaps positive emotions could restore the balance and aid in his recovery.

20. He already was gifted with a vigorous will to live, and he resolved to help it along by the use of mirth. He obtained some funny movies — specifically, some old "Candid Camera" segments — and had them shown to him by his nurse. He noted that laughter was a powerful analgesic; one ten-minute interlude of laughter would yield two hours of painless sleep. In addition, and even more remarkably, it was found that an important medical test for inflammation, made before and after each session of laughter, showed cumulative improvement.

21. Mr. Cousins's self-prescribed regimen included other components

as well. Disgruntled with the non-nutritious hospital food and with what he perceived as an unwarranted and too-frequent invasion of his veins for blood samples, he checked himself out of the hospital and into the more cheerful (and less expensive) environment of a hotel. Here, he continued his humor therapy, relieved of the concern that his laughing would disturb fellow patients. He continued to improve, and at the time he wrote his account, over a decade later, was still at a vigorous level of functioning, despite realistic and informed medical predictions to the contrary.

22. One could always offer the objection that Mr. Cousins would have recovered anyway, even without the laughter. Or one could say, with some justice, that the results were not scientifically significant, since they represent observations of a single case. Still, it is clear that Mr. Cousins himself believes that laughter played an important part in his recovery. Personally, on grounds other than scientific ones, I haven't any qualms about concurring with him.

23. One of the most fascinating uses of humor in healing has never, to my knowledge, been recorded in medical literature. In fact, had I not seen it with my own eyes and gathered many reports of it, I would be rather hesitant to mention it myself. It is that sometimes, through their antics, clowns can bring people back from severely withdrawn and unresponsive states even after all attempts by their doctors and nurses have failed. It is not at all unusual for clowns to be fully aware of this; everyone I know who has been a clown for a respectable period, and who makes it his practice to visit hospitals while dressed up and "in face," has his own stories of this to tell. Doctors, as a group, are not cognizant of it.

24. One clown, whose face is known to most American children, related to me how, as he was walking through a large hospital, he saw a little girl with a doll of his likeness lying beside her in bed as she was being fed by a nurse. As the clown walked in, the child said his name, whereupon the nurse threw down the spoon and dashed off to call the physician. For the child—diagnosed, he said, as catatonic—had been *unresponsive* for six months. The doctor was able to get her to follow up this first communication with other responses, and the child progressively improved following this breakthrough.

25. In another case, a ninety-five-year-old man was admitted to the hospital with severe depression. He had not eaten for several days, and for the same period had not said a word to anyone. His physicians were alarmed; they were concerned that he would soon die. A clown entered his hospital room and within thirty minutes had succeeded in getting the elderly man to talk, to laugh, and to eat. The man lived for several more years and the clown maintained communication with him during this time.

26. I have looked on as an internationally famous clown strolled the

floors of pediatric wards in hospitals. In one room, we found a three-year-old boy who was so frightened and distressed at being in the hospital that he hadn't talked to anyone — the doctors, the nurses, or even his mother or father — for three weeks. He immediately responded verbally to the clown's overtures, and told us good-by as we left. Afterward, this child, too, continued to communicate.

27. Some doctors will react with a good, healthy skepticism to my claim that clowns may occasionally bring a patient out of a prolonged state of withdrawal. All I would suggest is that any doubting physician invite a professional clown to visit the wards, follow along, watch, and then decide.

28. There are certain medical conditions in which humor, though not specifically curative, is widely recognized as an important, healthy, and desirable response. This is strikingly evident in the case of several kinds of stigmatizing medical conditions — among them, severe facial deformities.

29. One of the very worst psychological catastrophes that can befall a human being is to receive a disfiguring injury to the face. I am impressed that all of those patients I have seen who have adapted most successfully to such injuries seem to have a good sense of humor. They have fallen back on humor in two ways. First, they have used it to help them develop an outlook from which their horrendous misfortune seems more bearable. Second, they employ humor successfully to solve a complicated problem in interpersonal communications which is inherent in their situation. We all depend heavily upon facial expression in regulating our communications with others, in figuring out how they feel and what they are thinking about. If someone's face is distorted and frozen by an injury, other people have a hard time comfortably talking with her.

30. Obviously, then, the stigmatized patients are faced with the problem of learning to put others at ease in social situations. The patients I am talking about — those who adapt favorably — solve this dilemma in communications by coming up with a repertoire of one-liners to introduce themselves. They have discovered that they can defuse the mounting tension in an awkward social situation by opening the conversation with a funny remark alluding to their condition. The ability of humor to aid those who must bear this kind of burden surely makes it among the greatest gifts of the human spirit.

31. The possible role of humor in dealing with another important medical problem should not be neglected. Mr. Cousins mentioned the anesthetic effect of laughter in recounting the story of his illness, and there are other indications of an inverse relationship

between humor and pain. One well-known anthropological study compared the different styles of conceiving of and dealing with pain among patients of various ethnic backgrounds. The researchers discovered that among members of what they called the Old American population, it is widely believed that keeping one's sense of humor is an indispensable aid to coping with chronic pain. A physician I know would agree; he is often able to cure his patients' tension headaches simply by getting them to laugh!

32. Finally, the sense of humor has been linked — by longstanding tradition — with longevity. A doctor acquaintance of mine whose specialty is geriatric medicine has concluded that one thing which almost all his very healthy elderly patients seem to have in common is a good sense of humor. Obviously, one must avoid drawing any inferences from such observations, for there are many unsolved mysteries about the aging process. Until they are unraveled, however, it remains a possibility that the mental attitude reflected in a lively sense of humor is an important factor predisposing some people toward long life.

Why humor works

33. Why are humor and laughter sometimes therapeutic?

I have already suggested that one meaning of "having a good sense of humor" is being able to acquire a cosmic perspective on one's problems. This seems to me to have been an important factor in the case of my patient whose severe depression seemed to improve after he was able to laugh at a stressful incident which took place in the cookie factory where he worked. I believe that a real breakthrough for him came during that particular therapeutic session because, at that time, he could view his actions, attitudes, and behavior from a somewhat detached and comic perspective, and could use this insight to gain the determination to make the needed changes in his life.

34. How are we to explain the unusual instances in which clowns appear to have brought people out of withdrawn states? Perhaps at least the beginning of an explanation lies in considering a factor which humor and withdrawn states share: regression. People who are withdrawn have, in one respect, returned to the helpless state of the infant: They are unable to take care of their basic needs, including taking the initiative in establishing communication with others. From the psychological point of view, there are reasons for characterizing humor as a kind of joint, playful regression. Clowns seem to have a special license to engage in regressive behavior; professional clowns frequently comment on the exhilarating feeling of freedom from customary social restraints which they experience while made up and costumed.

35. It is not inconceivable that if a person is withdrawn, it may help to regress back to her level to retrieve her. To express this point in the simple form of a spatial metaphor, it is as though the clown were saying to the withdrawn person: "If you cannot or will not come out of your shell, then I will go into it with you and lead you back out."

36. Humor and laughter may have a more multifaceted role in pain control. Response to pain has been found to have very significant social-cultural determinants, as do humor and the response to it. The importance of one's general outlook — including that of persons with a laughing attitude toward life — in pain sensitivity and tolerance is still a relatively neglected, but fertile, area of research.

37. Also, it is possible that in certain cases the anesthetic effect of mirth resides in a different psychological mechanism. Some aches and pains can be made worse by the very act of paying attention to them. Laughter can take one away from oneself, one's worries. For at least a moment, a person who laughs can forget her troubles. Perhaps humor sometimes works just by withdrawing attention from pain.

38. Certain kinds of pain are caused, or made worse, by muscle tension which the person is producing herself, although she may not be consciously aware that she is doing so. For example, if a person becomes aware of a minor pain in a small area of her body and begins to concentrate on it, she may unconsciously tighten up the muscles around that spot. As a consequence, the pain will worsen as the taut muscles themselves begin to ache. Another example of a pain syndrome which is self-generated is the muscle-tension headache. Someone becomes anxious or depressed and, without realizing it, begins to tighten the muscles at the back of her head and neck; soon, she has a headache.

39. It is interesting to speculate, therefore, about whether some of the alleged anesthetic benefits of laughter could be related to the decrease in muscle tone which is one of the demonstrable physiological effects of laughter. In that case the sequence of events would be this: Unconsciously produced tension in the muscles increases, or causes, a headache. The person is presented with humorous stimulus. She laughs, the tension of her muscles in the affected area decreases, and the pain is relieved.

40. Another basis for the therapeutic effect of humor may lie in its efficacy in establishing or restoring communication between the doctor and his or her patient. In medicine, maintaining communication is necessary not only as a social amenity, but also because of the importance of securing the patient's cooperation and understanding in both diagnosing and treating the person's condition.

41. As a good social lubricant, humor may well aid in getting communication established. As I began to practice medicine, one way I

naturally began to use humor to advantage was to poke fun at the strange instruments doctors use. The gadgetry of modern medicine looks awesome and frightening to people who are not familiar with it (and sometimes even more awesome and frightening to doctors who *are* familiar with it). Patients who are uneasy and apprehensive when they are about to be probed with an infernal-looking machine can often be put more at ease if the doctor will make a joke about the apparatus.

42. One final therapeutic effect of humor is conceivably the most important of all. The will to live is a force which is very hard to define, or to specify precisely; nonetheless, it must be reckoned with in medicine. It sometimes happens that a patient will come into the hospital for a minor ailment or surgical procedure and assert that she is going to die, that she will never get out of the hospital alive. Despite thorough physical examination and laboratory measurements which indicate that the patient is healthy, she does die during her hospital stay. Many physicians have learned to take such remarks by patients very seriously.

43. The opposite phenomenon takes place, too. Sometimes a patient comes into the hospital and is given a grim prognosis by his or her physicians. The person is told that she has only a few weeks or months of life remaining, that it is inconceivable that she will be able to live much longer in her condition. The patient believes otherwise. She asserts that she is not going to die, that she will overcome the condition; and, contrary to prediction, she does live. Some such patients have outlived by decades the doctors who delivered the pronouncements.

44. All this is an expression, I feel, of factors which we do not as yet understand. At most, of course, the will to live is something which only holds the balance of power in a certain range of cases. Obviously, it cannot make anyone immortal. Nonetheless, despite its ambiguous and at present rather mysterious nature, it may be that there are some cases in which mobilizing the patient's will to live is one of the most important things a physician can do.

45. There is a link between the will to live and the sense of humor. Sigmund Freud put this very well:
Like wit and the comic, humour has in it a *liberating* element. But it has also something fine and elevating...the ego's victorious assertion of its own invulnerability. It refuses to be hurt by the arrows of reality or to be compelled to suffer. It insists that it is impervious to wounds dealt by the outside world; in fact, that these are merely occasions for affording it pleasure. This last trait is a fundamental characteristic of humour.

46. Perhaps ultimately, and in the deepest sense, humor works by rallying, and by being a manifestation of, the will to live. One of the most hopeful responses I have received on this subject came

from a professional comedian who attended one of my presentations on the medical aspects of mirth. Afterward, he came up and told me that before, on those occasions on which he had really made his audience laugh, he had always told his wife, "I killed them tonight!" Now, he said, he is going to tell her, "I helped them live!"

Style and Structure

1. The article opens with the words. "This article is about. . . ." Give the reasons why the opening sentence would be of more interest to a health professional than to the general public. Rewrite the introduction to make it more appealing to the general public.
2. Underline the sentence which best states the topic of the article.
3. The author does not present any examples of the effect of humour on healing until paragraph 11. For what purposes does he include paragraphs 2 to 10?
4. Why does the writer present the reader with specific illustrations of healing by humour (paragraphs 11-32) instead of developing abstract arguments?
5. In paragraphs 33-43 the writer theorizes on how humour heals. List the points he makes and demonstrate how he builds them upon his specific illustrations in the previous section.
6. What purpose does the writer's conclusion (paragraphs 44-46) serve? Why is the final quotation effective?

Thinking and Writing

a. Write a precis of this article (a precis is an essay that summarizes the ideas of a longer work down to approximately one-third of the length of the original while still accurately conveying the main ideas and logical development of the original).
   Audience:
   someone who is not employed in the health sciences.

b. Write an essay in which you use your own experience or the experiences of others to support *or* refute Dr. Moody's contention that laughter is the key to the "Will to live". Pay special attention to his statement that laughter achieves this end by giving a "cosmic perspective on one's problems".
   Audience:
   someone who is in a position that brings him/her into close contact with the sick and the dying.
   Send a copy of your paper to your family doctor; or any person that you know who is employed in the health services field.

A soft focus on erotica, a hard line on violence

by Mark Czarnecki

1. "Something is rotten in the state of Denmark" must be what Danish under-12s are thinking these days when they find out they're forbidden by law to see *Star Wars* and its successor, *The Empire Strikes Back*. But it really does not matter; they can always move on to the theatre next door and enjoy a thoroughly explicit nonviolent homosexual film. In setting age restrictions for juvenile viewing, Denmark gives carte blanche to loving sex but prohibits entry to films that might desensitize children to violence and suffering.

2. The wisdom of Denmark's ways has been confirmed in two separate psychological studies conducted by the University of Wisconsin's Edward Donnerstein and by Neil Malamuth and James Check of the University of Manitoba. Both studies showed that, while nonviolent erotica had no significant effect on antisocial behavior, non-erotic depictions of violence increased aggressive behavior by both sexes against both sexes. They also demonstrated for the first time that films fusing sex and violence triggered even more aggressive attitudes and behavior toward women in normal male subjects than did violence alone.

3. In the Manitoba study, involving 271 students, one group was sent to see non-violent erotic films (*A Man and a Woman* and *Hooper*) while another went to "aggressive-erotic" films (*Swept Away* and *The Getaway*) in which violence against women was "justified" by an eventual relationship between the women and their assailants. A carefully worded 104-item questionnaire completed a week later showed that men in the second group were more willing to accept interpersonal violence against women, a finding paralleled by more aggressive behavior (also prompted by films) in Donnerstein's male subjects.

4. The fact that such studies are being done at all is in itself significant. Ever since the U.S. President's Commission on Obscenity and Pornography concluded in 1970 that there is "no evidence to date that exposure to explicit sexual materials plays a significant role in the causation of delinquent or criminal behavior among youth or adults," researchers have tended to ignore the subject, even though the commission's findings were disputed, especially

by feminists. In explaining the apparent contradictions between the commission's findings and their own, Donnerstein and Malamuth point out that erotica, both hard-core and soft-core, has become increasingly violent since the commission's study, which examined relatively mild material.

5. The Manitoba study is particularly interesting because it was not conducted in a laboratory setting and tried to assess the effects of mass media stimuli over an extended period of time. If other studies confirm the applicability of these findings to daily life, there should be further implications for censorship. University of Toronto professor Lorenne Clark, coauthor of an influential book on the legal aspects of rape, asks: "What more do you have to show to get sadomasochistic and child pornography banned? If men learn to associate sex with violence they will act upon it." In answer to men who argue that aggressive thoughts do not a rapist make, Malamuth has conducted another study in which men were asked whether they might commit rape if there was no chance of being caught—and an astonishing 40 per cent said yes. Concludes Malamuth, "In the general male population, a sizable minority shows the arousal/behavioral pattern of rapists."

6. However, interviews with convicted rapists rarely reveal a direct link between violent erotica and a particular act of rape. Says Dr. Barry Boyd, retired superintendent and medical director of Ontario's Penetanguishene Mental Health Centre: "There's very little evidence that violent erotica has a direct effect on the behavior of sexual offenders. I've talked to dozens of them, and more often than not it seems to have kept them from committing a crime by providing a sexual outlet at the fantasy level." Of far more relevance in determining the bases for rapists' behavior is their exposure to sex in childhood and adolescence. In a book on the effects of pornography on sexual deviance, University of California psychologist Michael Goldstein reports that offenders had much less exposure to sex education or erotica during adolescence and when caught by their parents reading erotica were invariably punished whereas only 20 percent of non-offenders caught were reprimanded. Interviews with offenders have shown that as adolescents they felt guilty about masturbation and normal sexual fantasies and were unable to translate desires and fantasies into healthy sexual relationships in later life.

7. Some psychiatrists believe that suppressing erotica entirely is impossible and may even be harmful: adolescent exposure to sex education or erotica (for most people their only sex education) may "immunize" juveniles against the overwhelming emphasis on sexuality in modern Western culture. Encouraging evidence for this idea comes from Donnerstein's study and several others

demonstrating that exposure to mild erotica such as *Playboy* in fact reduces aggressive male tendencies toward women. If such erotica could be controlled so that its content did not degrade women, it might play a useful part in adolescent socialization: since North American society has traditionally made sexual relations difficult for youths, they would learn to mitigate the desires prompted by erotica and, if necessary, develop defence mechanisms such as sublimation, repression, postponement and self-control. Sex offenders who have had little exposure to erotica may not have had the chance to develop these capabilities.

8. Researchers agree that the most widespread and dangerous factor in criminal behavior is the violence permeating modern culture and impinging upon young minds in acceptable contexts (contact sports, $500 billion a year spent on armaments, the evening news). Dr. Robert McCaldon, a psychiatrist working at Kingston Penitentiary, states in the recently published book *Why Men Rape*, "In our whole culture, whether it's in television or magazines or other media, violence both as a way to achieve some kind of domination and as a means of problem-solving has been portrayed as laudable." Violence against women in particular is built into Western civilization and to a large extent approved. Says Clark, "Men are misogynists because they see women as the hoarders of an attractive commodity which they desperately desire." Citing his rape attitude survey, Malamuth comments, "Rape is really an extension of normal socialization." Many rapists are surprised when convicted because they genuinely believe they have done no wrong; after all, the "art of seduction" assumes that the woman initially always says no but really means yes and that the man applies pressure until she yields. Only physical pressure is illegal, and Clark believes that in punishing rapists the law is in effect only penalizing those male seducers with a limited repertoire.

9. With all this evidence exonerating sex and condemning violence, why aren't North Americans denying their children the Force too? Possibly because the Danish experiment hasn't been around long enough; when the children now undergoing comprehensive sex education and violence deprivation mature, there will be more statistics and much more analysis. Research is needed in every aspect of the problem, and the subject is so volatile that objective evaluation is at a premium. But most important is the fact that what a society allows its members, especially its children, to experience expresses that society's values. Changes grow from within, not without.

Style and Structure

1. What is the average North American reader's initial reaction

to paragraph 1? How does the phrase "loving sex" modify this reaction? Why does the author choose to begin his article with this paragraph?

2. An adequate introduction should contain a thesis statement and a clear indication of how the body of the essay will be developed. How well does paragraph 2 meet these criteria?

3. (a) What main points about violent and non-violent erotica does the writer make in paragraphs 3 to 5?

   (b) What points about violent and non-violent erotica does the writer make in paragraphs 6 and 7?

4. What relationship between socialization on the one hand and violent and sexual offenses on the other does the writer express in paragraph 8?

5. The writer assumes that North Americans have a prejudice that is reflected in their toleration of violence and their censorship of sex. Why does he choose to deal with the topics presented in paragraphs 3 to 8. Why does he present them in that order?

6. How do the ideas in the concluding paragraph relate to the introductory paragraph? How does the author's choice of references tie the conclusion to the introduction? Why does he use these devices?

Thinking and Writing

a. Before your next class, watch a selection of television shows. For each show, make a list of how many times each of the following occurs: (i) violence alone; (ii) sex associated with violence.

   On the basis of your observations, write an essay in which you argue for or against Czarnecki's statement that "violence [is] permeating modern culture and impinging upon young minds in acceptable contexts (contact sports, $500 billion a year spent on armaments, the evening news)."

   Audience:

   a North American who has never thought of this problem before.

b. Write an essay outlining your opinion of the role that a provincial censorship board should play in determining which movies are shown in your community. Support your stand with concrete evidence and well reasoned arguments.

   Audience:

   someone who knows the subject of censorship relatively well and is in a position to act upon your suggestions.

   Send a copy of your paper to the censorship board in your province or to your representative in the provincial parliament.

The secret drift to free trade with the U.S. How we could all end up as Americans

by J.L. Granatstein

1. Quietly—almost secretly—there's growing pressure in Canada for free trade with the United States. To many Canadian nationalists, it represents nothing less than the most sinister threat yet to the continued existence of Canada. But to many others—including businessmen, bankers and industrialists—the trend to even closer links with the U.S. is our one hope of survival as a major economic power.

2. There's nothing new about cries for free trade—or reciprocity—with the U.S. "No truck or trade with the Yankees" was the battle cry with which Robert Borden and his Conservative party crushed the government of Sir Wilfrid Laurier in 1911. Laurier's Liberals had struck a deal with the United States for reciprocity, or free trade, in a substantial list of largely natural products; but to the manufacturers in Canada, protected by high tariff walls from foreign competition, that reciprocity agreement was the thin edge of the wedge that spelled an end to their protected industries.

3. Reciprocity had to be defeated and industrialists and politicians pulled out all the stops. The Americans and their "Manifest Destiny" were denounced; the British tie was pulled ever tighter, and Laurier was cursed as a French Canadian who was soft on the Empire. And it worked brilliantly. Laurier was defeated; Borden was in power, and reciprocity was dead. Victory for British Canada. Victory for Canadian industry. Defeat to the grasping Yankees.

4. We all know that it didn't work out that way—that Canada's trade with the United States grew and grew as our trade with Britain and the rest of the world declined drastically. Today, approximately 70 percent of Canada's exports go to the United States, much of it in raw materials, and 70 percent of our imports, most of it in manufactured goods, come from the south. With just 10 percent of the population of western Europe, we buy as much from the U.S. as does all of western Europe and more than twice as much as Japan. The links are close—and growing closer all the time.

5. There are two main bodies in Ottawa leading the still-building crusade for free trade. One is the Economic Council of Canada, a

creation of the federal government with a certain degree of independence, but one that reflects the overwhelming belief of Canadian professional economists that free trade would be a good thing because economic theory says it would. More important perhaps is the Senate standing committee on foreign affairs, and its report last fall on "Canada's Trade Relations with the United States." The Senate committee is important not because it is a Senate committee (the only thing less important than a Senate committee in Ottawa these days is a House of Commons committee), but because the senators represent in and of themselves the economic elite of Canada. They are the businessmen and bankers and industrialists — the movers and shakers in the corporate board rooms. And if they now want free trade, that is important.

6. And they do. The senators report that Canada is facing a difficult future as far as trade is concerned. The European Common Market is a tough nut to crack, increasingly sure of its own strength and interested in Canada only as a supplier of raw materials, not of manufactured goods. The Japanese are much the same; and both Japan and the Common Market are hustling around the rest of the world selling their own manufactured products, often at terms that relatively inefficient Canadian firms cannot match. Times are tough and getting tougher, for Canada and the United States, too.

7. In the committee's view, this throws Ottawa and Washington together, two victims of the booming power of the rest of the world; but two victims who together can survive very well, thank you. And the senators point to the Canada-U.S. Auto Pact, signed by Lester Pearson and Lyndon Johnson in the mid-1960s, as a perfect example of how free trade can benefit both countries.

8. Of course, there are problems for Canada in such an arrangement. The Senate committee readily admits that Canada's trade deficit under the Auto Pact is increasing — we are selling far less in value of auto parts to the U.S. than we are buying. That is a concern. So, too, is the lower technological content and less skilled labor component in the Canadian industry. In other words, Canada gets the easier jobs in the North American auto industry, presumably because these are the only ones that the head offices of Ford, General Motors and American Motors believe can be done here in the backward north. Worse still, as the committee notes, almost all the research and development for the auto industry is done in the U.S. Cars still cost more in Canada than in the United States; and since 1970, the big automakers have been investing less of their money in Canada than they should be.

9. Those are the problems in *one* industry. They seem serious enough to give anyone pause before recommending that free trade be sought across the whole spectrum of Canadian-American manu-

facturing. But there is more bad news yet to come. The Senate committee also notes that free trade would pose risks for Canada, because of the number of branch plants of American corporations located here. "How would they react in a free-trade situation? The optimum would be if companies were to opt for specialization on a North American basis, with the Canadian plants supplying particular products to the combined market of the two countries. However," the Senate committee goes on, "there are a number of factors—overcapacity in U.S. plants in low periods of the business cycle, the pull of the larger (i.e. U.S.) market, a perceived change in the reliability or stability of the Canadian political base, and a natural tendency to reinvest at home rather than in a foreign jurisdiction—all of which might cause repatriation of production to the United States."

10. What all that means is that if Canada had free trade, the American branch plants might be closed down, their production lines moved to Arkansas or Georgia or New York. Canadian nationalists would probably be delighted that the American control of Canadian industry had disappeared at last—until the unemployment rolls reached about half the work force. In other words, free trade just might mean that much of Canadian industry would disappear. And still the senators are in favor of it.

11. Even more incredible, the Senate committee fails to consider the political impact of free trade. Could Canada and its separate North American nationality survive the inevitable dislocation that free trade would bring? Or would Canadians finally say that the game was no longer worth the effort and throw in the towel? If what has happened to the auto industry occurred in every major industry in Canada, what would be left here except the soup kitchen and the welfare office? If the concerns forseen (but dismissed) by the Senate committee took place and industries relocated, would not our people try to follow them south?

12. What would be left? Only raw materials, largely non-renewable, such as oil, coal, minerals and metals. We have a market for most of these materials now in the U.S., in Europe and in Japan. But what happens when they're gone—and when Canadian industry has been eliminated as well? What happens, in brief, is that Canada will be no more. Our children will have become Americans, our country will have been swallowed up.

13. Nor is this just an Ontario concern. At one time it might have been, but no longer. The government of Alberta seems to have become aware of the need to build an industrial base before its vast, but still limited, oil supplies are depleted. That is why Premier Lougheed has bargained so toughly with Ottawa and the other provinces, trying to get his province an industrial and manufactur-

ing base before the oil reserves have been drained. And that is significant for another reason, too, for Alberta and the other western provinces have historically been the bastions of free-trade sentiment in Canada. They have paid more for their goods because of the tariff that was designed to protect central Canada's industries. And now, just when Alberta is at last starting to become industrialized, some Ottawa politicos start thinking of changing the rules again.

14. No, free trade with the United States is not the answer. In an ideal world it might be; in an economist's computer model it might make some sense; in a senator's daydream world in the Red Chamber, removed from the stresses of daily living, it might sound good. But Canadians want to keep their country going, growing, and independent. Canadians want to maximize trade with all countries, not just the United States. And Canadians want to be sure there are jobs in Canada for themselves and their children. If that *is* what we want, we will all have to deliver a message to Ottawa and to politicians in all parties, and soon. Otherwise we might find that events have moved too far and too fast for us to reverse the trend.

Style and Structure

1. Underline the thesis statement. Do you detect any words or phrases which give away the writer's attitude to the question of free trade?

2. How does the organization of paragraph 1 prepare the reader for the organization of the body of the essay? How does the use of the device in the introduction help the reader?

3. In paragraph 3 the writer makes use of parallel structures. Underline the parallel structures and comment on their effectiveness in this context.

4. If the writer is concerned with our present trade relations with the United States, why does he include paragraphs 2 to 4?

5. In paragraphs 5 to 13 Granatstein presents the arguments for and against free trade with the United States. What role does paragraph 8 play in this presentation?

6. In paragraph 11 the writer asks a series of questions for which he does not provide answers. Rewrite the paragraph changing the questions to statements. Why is one technique more effective than the other?

7. What emotional appeals does Granatstein employ in his conclusion? Illustrate your answer from the text. In the body of the article how does the writer prepare the reader to accept the emotional appeal of the conclusion?

Thinking and Writing

a. Write an essay in which you argue for or against the proposition that "Canada should form a political union with the United States." Such a union if it were to take place would affect all aspects of Canadian life, cultural, political, economic, nationalistic, etc.; however, for the sake of this essay, you might be wise to limit your discussion to the effect of the union on just one aspect of our lives.
Audience:
an "average" newspaper reader who knows very little about the issues involved with the topic, but nevertheless, for some emotional reason, holds an opinion on the topic that is opposite to yours.

b. Write an essay in which you either endorse *or* oppose free trade with the United States. Use as much concrete evidence as possible in your essay.
Audience:
someone who has at least some insight into the history of Canadian/U.S. trade and is in a position to help implement your proposals.
Send a copy of your essay to your MP.

Colonizing the heavens

by Isaac Asimov

1. The population bomb ticks on steadily...
2. We are 4 billion now, in 1975. Barring catastrophes, we shall be 5 billion in 1986 and 6 billion in 1995 and 7 billion in 2002 and 8 billion in...What do we do with all of ourselves when already, with our puny 4 billion, we find that the effort to feed and power the population is destroying the planet that feeds and powers us? We must reduce the birthrate and lower the population, but that will take time. What do we do meanwhile?
3. One answer is that we do as we have done before. We must take up the trek again and move on to new lands. Since there are no new lands on earth worth the taking, we must move to new worlds and colonize the heavens.
4. No, not the moon. Prof. Gerard O'Neill of the physics department of Princeton University suggests two other places to begin with—

places as far from earth as the moon is, but not the moon. Imagine the moon at zenith, exactly overhead. Trace a line due eastward from the moon down to the horizon. Two-thirds of the way along that line, one-third of the way up from the horizon, is one of those places. Trace another line westward from the moon down to the horizon. Two-thirds of the way along that line, one-third of the way up from the horizon, is another of those places.

5. Put an object in either place, and it will form an equilateral triangle with the moon and earth. It is 237,000 miles from earth to the moon. It is also 237,000 miles from earth to that place, and from the moon to that place.

6. What is so special about those places? Back in 1772 the astronomer Joseph Louis Lagrange showed that in those places any object remained stationary with respect to the moon. As the moon moved about the earth, any object in either of those places would also move about the earth in such a way as to keep perfect step with the moon. The competing gravities of earth and the moon would keep it where it was. If anything happened to push it out of place, it would promptly move back, wobbling back and forth a bit ("librating") as it did so. The two places ideally are merely points in space and are called "Lagrangian points," or "libration points."

7. Lagrange discovered five such points altogether, but three of them are of no importance because they don't represent stable conditions. An object in those three points, once pushed out of place, would continue to drift outward and would never return. The two points in which an object remains stable are called "L4" and "L5." L4 is the one that lies toward the eastern horizon, and L5 the one that lies toward the western.

8. Professor O'Neill wants to take advantage of that gravitational lock and suggests the building of space colonies there, colonies that would become permanent parts of the earth-moon system. He envisions long cylinders designed to hold human beings plus a complex life-support system, facilities for growing food, maintaining atmospheres, recycling wastes, and so on.

9. Such concepts have been used in science fiction. The most memorable example is Robert A. Heinlein's story "Universe," published in 1941, in which a large ship, supporting thousands of people through indefinite numbers of generations, is making its slow way to the stars. The men aboard have forgotten the original purpose of the voyage and consider the ship to be the entire universe (hence the title). A lineal descendant of the story, translated to television, was the recent ill-fated series, "The Starlost."

10. In science fiction, though, such enormous, self-contained ships are *ships*, thickly spaced with decks, utterly enclosed with walls — the equivalent of many-layered caverns. O'Neill's vision is of another

kind. He sees hollow cylinders with human beings living on the inner surface, a surface that is designed and contoured into a familiar world with all the accoutrements and accompaniments of earth. The cylinder would be composed of long, alternating strips of opaque and transparent material — aluminum and tough plastic. Sunshine, reflected by long mirrors, would enter and illuminate the cylinder and turn what would otherwise be a cave into a daylit world. The entry of light could be controlled by mirror-shifting to allow for alternating day and night.

11. The inner surface of the opaque portions of the cylinder would be spread with soil, which could be used for agriculture and, eventually, animal husbandry. All the artificial works of man — his buildings and machines — would be there, too.

12. What makes this concept plausible and lifts the vision out of the realm of science fiction is the careful manner in which O'Neill has analyzed the masses of material necessary, the details of design, the thicknesses and strengths of materials required, the manner of lifting and assembly, and the cost of it all. The conclusion is that the establishment of such space colonies is possible and even practical in terms of present-day technology.

13. It would be expensive, of course, and getting the process started would require an input equivalent to that spent on the Apollo program. But O'Neill demonstrates clearly that the expense would decline rapidly after that. As the colonies increase in number, they could be expected to grow larger and more elaborate, too. O'Neill conceives the first space colonies (Model 1) to be only as large as is required to be workable — two spinning cylinders, each 3,280 feet long and 328 feet wide, supporting a total of 10,000 people.

14. The two cylinders, each spinning about its long axis, would turn in opposite directions. When they were held together, the total system would have virtually no spin and the cylinders could be designed in such a way as to have one end of the structure point constantly toward the sun in the course of the orbit about the earth.

15. It is from the sun that the colony would obtain its energy — a copious, endless, easily handled, non-polluting form of energy. It would be used to smelt the ores, power the factories, grow the food, recycle the wastes. It would serve to start the cylinders spinning and increase the rate of spin to the point where there would be a centrifugal effect sufficient to hold everything within to all parts of the inner surface with the apparent pull of normal gravity. For a cylinder 328 feet wide, this would require a spin of three revolutions a minute.

16. O'Neill envisions larger cylinder-pairs, too, and has calculated the requirements for some as large as 20 miles long and 2 miles wide

(Model 4), spinning once in two minutes. Each cylinder of a pair like that would be as wide as Manhattan and half again as long, would have a total inner surface 10 times as great as that of Manhattan, and could support up to 20 million people if it were exploited to the full, though 5 to 10 million might be a more comfortable population.

17. With so great a width, the cylinder would have a sufficient depth of air within to allow a blue sky and to support clouds. In a Model 4 colony the end caps of the cylinders could be modeled into mountainous territory — full-sized mountains, not just bas-reliefs.

18. But where are we to get all the material for the construction of these space colonies? Our groaning planet, sagging under its weight of humanity, with its supply of key resources sputtering and giving out, couldn't possibly afford to give up the colossal quantities of supplies needed for it all. (Over half a million tons of construction is needed for each Model 1, probably a thousand times as much for a Model 4.)

19. But earth is lucky, for virtually none of the material need come from our planet. As it happens, we are supplied with a moon, an empty and dead world that is one-eightieth the size of the earth. It is close enough for us to reach — we have already reached it over and over — and it is free to be used as a quarry. Lunar material will yield the aluminum, glass, concrete, and other substances needed for constructing the colony. Lunar soil will be spread over the interior surface, and on it agriculture will be practised. Not only is all that material present on the moon in virtually unlimited quantities, but lifting it off the moon against that body's weak gravity would require only one-twentieth the effort necessary for lifting it off earth. All the smelting and other chemical work would, of course, be done in space. But the lunar material is not perfectly adapted to human needs. It is low in volatile elements, those that vaporize easily when heated. The most serious lack is the volatile element hydrogen (an essential component of water).

20. O'Neill calculates that setting up a Model 1 colony would require some 5,400 metric tons of liquid hydrogen, and that would have to come from earth. Fortunately, earth can spare that much. We can get it from sea water, and there is an embarrassing oversupply of sea water on earth. We live in comfort only because so much of the earth's water supply is tied up in the ice caps of Greenland and Antarctica. If these ever melt, the sea level will rise 200 feet and drown our population-packed coastal areas. Extracting hydrogen from a little of our oversupply and giving it away will do us no harm.

21. As colonies multiply, of course, the quantity of hydrogen we would have to give up could become a little painful. Once space coloniza-

tion swings into high gear, however, hydrogen and other volatile elements of which the moon has insufficient supply can be obtained from further out. They can come from some of the asteroids or from the occasional comet that blunders past the earth-moon system on its way to wheel about the sun.

22. The first space colony would be by far the most expensive, even if it were small, for we would have to supply not only the advanced equipment, the machinery, the various life forms, the basic food supply and energy, but even some 2 percent of the raw materials. After that, there would be leapfrogging. Each space colony would help to build up the next, while the facilities for mining, smelting, shipping, and constructing would be ever improving. In the end, new colonies might be formed with no more trouble than it now takes to put up a new row of houses in the suburbs.

23. O'Neill thinks that if all were to go optimally, the first space colony could be floating in space by the late Eighties and that several hundred more elaborate colonies would be there by the mid-twenty-first century. These would be comfortable worlds, not, like earth, taken as found, but carefully designed to meet human needs. The temperature and weather would be controlled; energy would be free and non-polluting; weeds, vermin, and pathogenic bacteria would be left back on earth.

24. Dangers? Difficulties? Yes, some.
The possibility of a meteor strike exists, but that is not very strong. The space of the earth-moon system is full of meteoric dust, which is not likely to be bothersome, and pinhead meteors may pit the aluminum and graze the plastic, but that would be a minor annoyance. A meteorite large enough to cause serious damage to a colony is so rare that the time between strikes could be counted in the millions of years per colony. As the colonies grow more numerous, the chances that *one* will be hit increases — but mankind can live with that. We now live with the knowledge that there is a finite chance that at any moment a large meteorite, or a major earthquake, may strike and demolish a city of earth.

25. Energetic solar radiation is dangerous but would not be a problem in a cylinder protected by aluminum, plastic, and soil. Cosmic rays are much more serious. They are ever present and ever dangerous and very penetrating. There is some question as to whether O'Neill's original design offered sufficient protection. At the most recent scientific conference held on the subject (at Princeton on May 7 — 9, 1975) this subject was among those discussed.

26. Then, too, the centrifugal effect of the cylinder spin does not perfectly duplicate earth's gravitation. On earth the gravitational pull is not perceptibly altered as we rise from the surface. Inside a spinning cylinder the effect weakens rapidly as one rises from the

inner surface, falling to zero at the long axis. Is a fluctuating gravitational effect dangerous to the human body in the long run? We have no way of knowing as yet, but if not, a gravitational pull that lessens with height can have its advantages.

27. The small distances on the space colonies would make it unnecessary to use high-energy systems for transportation. Bicycles would be ideal for the ground, and with the lowering gravity, gliders would be perfect for air transport — and amusement.

28. Mountain climbing on the larger colonies would have comforts unknown on earth. As one climbed higher, the downward pull would weaken, it would become easier to climb farther, and, of course, the air would grow neither thinner nor colder. In carefully enclosed areas on the mountaintops, people could fly by their own muscle power when they were outfitted with plastic wings on light frames. Shades of Icarus!

29. As the space colonies increased in number, the room available for human beings would increase, too, and at an exponential rate. Within a century there could be room for a billion people on the space colonies, and by 2150, perhaps, there would be more people in space than on earth.

30. This prospect does not obviate the need to lower our birthrate in the long run, for if human beings continue to multiply at their present rate, the total mass of flesh and blood will equal the total mass of the known universe in 6,700 years. Long before then the building of space colonies would not be able to keep up under any conceivable conditions.

31. The colonies could act as a safety valve, however, that would give humanity a somewhat longer time to accomplish the turnabout without absolute disaster.

Style and Structure

1. What techniques does Asimov use in paragraphs 1 and 2 to catch the interest of the average reader?
2. Underline the thesis statement.
3. Asimov uses as his basic organizational principle the questions how, when, where, and why as they relate to colonizing the heavens. Identify the "paragraph groups" which deal with each of these questions.
4. What kind of argument is Asimov presenting, logical or emotional? Substantiate your answer with reference to (a) his choice of words and (b) the types of data he presents.
5. (a) How does Asimov anticipate the objections of his opponents?
   (b) Why does Asimov position the "dangers and difficulties" section (paragraphs 23—25) where he does?

(c) How do paragraphs 26 to 28 relate to the "dangers and difficulties" outlined in paragraphs 23 to 25?

6. How does the conclusion (paragraphs 29 and 30) relate to the introduction and to the material presented in the body of the essay?

Thinking and Writing

a. In an age of increasing specialization such as the present, the role of people like Asimov who "interpret" specialized fields for the general public has become very important. To see how difficult it is to do this type of writing without falling into the traps of using specialized "jargon" or making unwarranted assumptions about a reader's knowledge (even when it deals with apparently simple subjects), do the following exercise.

1. Select a task that seems relatively simple to you; the task may be one involved in a specialized area of study or one taken from everyday activities (a horticulturalist might, for example, choose "how to prune a rose bush"; a photographer might select "how to load film in a camera"; a "non-specialist" topic might be "how to change a tire", "how to tie a shoelace", or "how to open and close a door").

2. Write an essay in which you explain to someone who is completely unfamiliar with the task how to do it.

b. 1. Either from the knowledge that you already possess or from reading an account in a magazine or book aimed at professionals in your specialized subject area, select a topic on a process that will be of interest to the general public but will be unfamiliar to most people outside of the field. Write an essay on the selected topic in which you both capture the interest of the "average" reader and give him/her a good understanding of the topic.

Audience:

someone who knows very little about either the topic chosen or the subject matter of your subject area.

Send a copy of your essay to someone who is not enrolled in your program, or to a newspaper in your area (to be used as an article).

The comics:
escape or reality?

by Burt Prelutsky

1. There are any number of reasons that people will give for buying newspapers, but the section they most often turn to first is the comics. The question is — why? What is it that we seek in those four-panel microcosms? I, for one, am delighted to find that academia is finally getting around to paying proper attention to the comics and to the influence they've had on our lives.

2. There are those elitists who look down on us readers of comic strips, dismissing us as escapists from reality. They contend that comic strips are a waste of time and, what's more, aren't even funny. They miss the point; comics aren't supposed to be amusing. For a strip to succeed, it must fulfill at least one of two basic needs, as I see it. First, a large number of people must be able to identify with the plight of its characters, and/or, second of all, the comics must satisfy our fantasies.

3. Little Orphan Annie does both, for she represents nothing less than America's vision of itself. As symbolized by her blank eyes, she is naïve and trusting. As indicated by her faithful dog, Sandy — who is always clean and well fed, although she may be starving and clothed in tatters — Annie is considerate, responsible and compassionate. And, best of all, if anyone messes with her, Daddy Warbucks, the Avenging Angel of Capitalism, with his business associates Punjab and Asp (who could easily be mistaken for the CIA and the U.S. Marines), shows up in the nick of time to clean their clocks.

4. Like America, Annie is forever trying to help others less fortunate than herself, whether they want to be helped or not. She is constantly trying to uplift the downtrodden and bring economic and social salvation to the misguided. And heaven help them if they had other plans. Society may write off the old bum and the unwed mother, but not Annie. Where other mortals see only human derelicts, she can envision the GM board chairman and the happily married carhop of tomorrow. Of course, there are always those, human nature being what it is, who don't appreciate a 50-year-old midget meddling in their private affairs. In such cases, Annie has no option but to call in reinforcements who see to it that her more recalcitrant adversaries disappear in the fog or get fed to the crocodiles.

5. What, though, do our other favorite comic strips tell us about ourselves, our dreams, our fears and our aspirations? The enduring appeal of Mary Worth strongly suggests to me that America is, at heart, a matriarchy (or even, as feminists contend, that God is a She). Mary is an elderly woman who is welcome wherever she goes; however, she is never confronted with the problems other people her age have to face. Judging by her clothes, her hair and her robust figure, if she's making do on a fixed income, it was fixed at about $100,000 per year. Of course, she hasn't had to fork up the rent or pay for a meal in 30 years. She is constantly being invited home by strangers and she is constantly accepting. Nobody, to the best of my recollection, has ever asked her for a reference. And it's just as well. By now she would have a few thousand, and an old lady could hurt herself carting them around.

6. Mary's stock-in-trade is curing neuroses with good old-fashioned horse sense and patching up broken marriages with timely proverbs. In her lilac-scented wake, alcoholics become teetotalers, philanderers turn into homebodies and psychosomatic invalids throw away their crutches and dance a jig. Not only is she a combination of Henry Kissinger, Kathryn Kuhlman and Dr. Spock; she can also cook, baby-sit and give a first-rate massage.

7. In terms of longevity, few strips can compare with Dick Tracy, Brenda Starr, Li'l Abner and Rex Morgan, M.D. What they all have in common is a strong fantasy element. Dick Tracy, for instance, offers us, in this day and age, an incorruptible cop. He exists in a black-and-white world where none of those nuisance grays can muck up the reality of law enforcement. His foes aren't merely criminals; they're evil incarnate. They all look as if they had just tunneled out of Hades. And God help the witness who has to go downtown for a typical Tracy lineup. A good memory is less essential than a strong stomach. "What do you mean," one can hear Tracy shouting, "you're not sure? Take another look. Now, once and for all, was it the dwarf with the two heads, the guy who looks like a frog or the icky one on the end with all the flies on his face?"

8. Brenda Starr has long served as a female-role model. And no wonder. She's glamorous, goes to chichi parties, never worries about dieting and is self-supporting as a widely acclaimed journalist. While she has never wanted for male attention, she has spent her life waiting for the return of the one-eyed mysterious stranger. To the extent that life imitates art, we may someday wake up to hear that Gloria Steinem and Moshe Dayan are an item.

9. Li'l Abner has, regrettably, fallen on hard times. At some point, Al Capp got it into his noggin that folk singers posed a greater threat to America than politicians, and Dogpatch hasn't been the same

place since. However, in its prime, that locale gave us the shmoo, the Yokums and an obnoxious U.S. senator whose platform consisted of reminding his constituents that, if elected, he would go back to Washington for another six years — but, if defeated, he'd be moving back to town for good. As a result, even his opponent voted for him.

10. Long before Marcus Welby hung out his shingle, Dr. Morgan was cashing in on America's greatest fantasy of them all. Namely, a doctor who not only made house calls but suffered intermittently from a form of amnesia that prevented his remembering to mail out bills at the end of the month.

11. In recent years, there have been a swarm of successful new comic strips. These include Andy Capp, Doonesbury, Peanuts, Momma, B.C. and, of course, The Wizard of Id. Id is a domain in which all the lawyers look and sound like W. C. Fields and are less concerned with anything faintly resembling justice than in collecting their fees and keeping themselves out of the slammer. The king hates the media, cheats on his income taxes and uses the national census as his enemies list. He is a two-foot tall, power-mad paranoiac who locks people in the dungeon if they commit such *faux pas* as trying to make a long story *short*, offering to give him the *low*-down or describing his royal presence as *down*-to-earth.

12. What do these contemporary strips that deal with ale-swilling adulterers, pot-smoking hippies, 5¢-an-hour know-it-all psychiatrists, guilt-dispensing mothers and sociopathic chiefs of state tell us about our society? Forty years hence, someone may better be able to tell us. But, in the meantime, is it any wonder that we comic strip aficionados regard the front page news stories and the fire-and-brimstone editorials as escapist fare fit only for the consumption of the chicken-hearted amongst us?

Style and Structure

1. What does the opening expression "There are any number of reasons that people will give for buying newspapers, but..." imply? Why is this an effective opening sentence?

2. What effect does the writer's use of pronouns in paragraphs one and two have upon the reader?

3. Why does the writer employ such diction as "proper attention" "elitists" and "escapists"?

4. Underline the thesis statement and draft a plan of the essay's organization.

5. What tone does the writer employ when describing individual comic strips? Does this tone enhance or detract from his argument? Why?

6. What is the function of the first sentence in paragraphs 7 and 11? How do they help the reader?

7. In the last sentence of his article the writer employs paradox (an apparent contradiction of reality). This statement is an inversion of a charge that he deals with in the introduction. Underline the sentence in the introduction and comment on why this is an effective way of concluding this essay?

Thinking and Writing

a. Select a comic strip and write an essay in which you demonstrate how it fits into the two "basic needs", just as Prelutsky did with "Little Orphan Annie".
Audience:
someone who consistently reads your chosen comic strips in the newspaper but has never thought of why that strip has such general popularity.

b. Sometimes cartoons, especially political cartoons, come too close to reality for comfort. Recently in British Columbia a provincial cabinet minister took a cartoonist to court as the result of a political cartoon that showed the cabinet minister pulling the wings off flies.
Write an essay in which you outline your stance on the degree of censorship that should be imposed upon political cartoonists. Use specific examples of political cartoons to prove your point.
Audience:
someone who is very familiar with political cartoons, may occasionally be the target of such cartoons, and is in a position to influence the legislation that relates to the freedom allowed to political cartoonists.
Send a copy of your essay to your MP or your representative in the provincial parliament.

What TV does to kids

1. His first polysyllabic utterance was "Bradybunch." He learned to spell Sugar Smacks before his own name. Recently, he tried to karate-chop his younger sister after she broke his Six Million Dollar Man bionic transport station (she retaliated by bashing him with her Cher doll). His nursery-school teacher reports that he is passive, noncreative, and has almost no attention span; in short, he is very much like his classmates. This fall, he will officially reach the age of reason and begin his formal education. His parents

are beginning to discuss their apprehensions—when they are not too busy watching television.

2. It is only in recent years—with the first TV generation already grown up—that social scientists, psychologists, pediatricians and educators have begun serious study of the impact of television on the young. According to television survey-taker A. C. Nielsen, children under five watch an average of 23.5 hours of TV a week. Today's typical high-school graduate has logged at least 15,000 hours before the small screen—more time than he has spent on any other activity except sleep. At present levels of advertising and mayhem, he will have been exposed to 350,000 commercials and vicariously participated in 18,000 killings. The conclusion is inescapable: After parents, television has become perhaps the most potent influence on the beliefs, values and behavior of the young.

3. Unquestionably, the plug-in picture window has transmitted some benefits. In general, the children of TV enjoy a more sophisticated knowledge of a far larger world. They are likely to possess richer vocabularies, albeit with only a superficial comprehension of what the words mean. Research on the impact of "Sesame Street" has established measurable gains in the cognitive skills of many pre-schoolers.

4. Nonetheless, the overwhelming body of evidence—drawn from more than 2,300 studies and reports—is decidedly negative. Michael Rothenberg, a child psychiatrist at the University of Washington, has reviewed the 50 most comprehensive studies involving 10,000 children from every possible background. Most showed that viewing violence tends to produce aggressive behavior among the young. "The time is long past due for a major, organized cry of protest from the medical profession," concludes Rothenberg.

5. An unexpected salvo was sounded last winter when the normally cautious American Medical Association asked ten major corporations to review their policies about sponsoring excessively gory shows. "TV violence is both a mental-health problem and an environmental issue," explained Dr. Richard E. Palmer, president of the AMA. In defense, broadcasting officials maintain that the jury is still out on whether video violence is guilty of producing aggressive behavior. And network schedulers say they are actively reducing the violence dosage.

6. But televised mayhem is only part of TV's impact. TV has at the very least preempted the traditional development of childhood itself. The time kids spend sitting catatonic before the set has been exacted from such salutary pursuits as reading, outdoor play, even simple, contemplative solitude. Few parents can cope with its

tyrannical allure. Recently, Dr. Benjamin Spock took his step-daughter and granddaughter to New York to see a concert and a Broadway show. But the man who has the prescription for everything from diaper rash to bedwetting had no easy solution for dislodging the kids from their hotel room. "Of all the attractions in New York," recalls Spock, "they seemed to find the TV set the most fascinating."

7. Small wonder that television has been called "the flickering blue parent." The after-school and early-evening hours used to be a time for "what-did-you-do-today" dialogue. Now, the electronic box does most of the talking. Dr. David Pearl of the U.S. National Institute of Mental Health suspects that the tube "has displaced many of the normal interactional processes between parents and children which are essential for maximum development."

8. Even more worrisome is what television has done to, rather than denied, the tube-weaned population. A series of studies has shown that addiction to TV stifles creative imagination. For example, a University of Southern California research team exposed 250 elementary students to three weeks of intensive viewing. Tests found a marked drop in all forms of creative abilities except verbal skill. Some teachers are encountering children who cannot understand a simple story without visual illustrations. Nursery-school teachers who have observed the pre-TV generation contend that juvenile play is far less imaginative and spontaneous than in the past. "You don't see kids making their own toys out of crummy things like we used to," says University of Virginia psychology professor Stephen Worchel. "You don't see them playing hopscotch, or making up their own games. Everything is suggested to them by television."

9. Too much TV too early may also instill an attitude of spectatorship, a withdrawal from direct involvement in real-life experiences. "What television basically teaches children is passivity," says Stanford University researcher Paul Kaufman. "It creates the illusion of having been somewhere and done something and seen something, when in fact they've been sitting at home."

10. Conditioned to see all problems resolved in 30 or 60 minutes, the offspring of TV exhibit a low tolerance for the frustration of learning. Grade-schoolers are quickly turned off by any activity that promises less than instant gratification. "You introduce a new skill, and right away, if it looks hard, they dissolve into tears," laments one first-grade teacher. "They want everything to be easy — like watching the tube."

11. The debate over the link between TV violence and agressive behavior in society has had a longer run than "Gunsmoke." Today, however, even zealous network apologists concede that some

children, under certain conditions, will imitate antisocial acts seen on the tube. Indeed a study of 100 juvenile offenders commissioned by ABC found that no fewer than 22 confessed to having copied criminal techniques from TV. Behavioral sleuths are also uncovering evidence that the tide of TV carnage increases children's tolerance of violent behavior in others, because they have been conditioned to think of violence as an everyday thing.

12. And now a word about the sponsors. The hottest battle in this area involves the impact of child-directed commercials on their audience's eating habits. Many of the ads on Saturday and Sunday morning "kidvid" peddle sugarcoated cereals, candy and chewing gum, hooking children on poor eating habits long before they develop the mental defenses to resist. "This is the most massive educational program to eat junk food in history," charges Sid Wolinsky, an attorney for a San Francisco public-interest group. According to a study by Columbia University psychology professor Thomas Bever, misleading TV ads may also be "permanently distorting children's views of morality, society and business." From in-depth interviews with 48 youngsters between the ages of 5 and 12, Bever concluded that by the time they reach 12 many find it easier to decide that all commercials lie than to try to determine which are telling the truth.

13. A few daring parents have counterattacked by simply pulling the plug. Charles Frye, a San Francisco nursery-school teacher and the father of five boys, decided he would not replace his set after it conked out in 1972. Frye's brood rebelled at first, but today 14-year-old Mark fills his afternoon hours with tapdancing lessons, scout meetings and work in a gas station. Kirk, his 13-year-old brother, plays a lot of basketball and football and recently finished *Watership Down* and all four of the Tolkien hobbit books.

14. Short of such a draconian measure, some parents are exercising a greater degree of home rule. Two years ago, the administrators of New York's Horace Mann nursery school became distressed over an upsurge of violence in their students' play. Deciding that television was to blame, they dispatched a letter to all parents urging them to curb their children's viewing. "After we sent the letter, we could see a change," recalls principal Eleanor Brussel. "The kids showed better concentration, better comprehension, an ability to think things through."

15. Clearly, there is no single antidote. For the children of today, and their progeny to come, TV watching will continue to be their most shared—and shaping—experience. Virtually all the experts agree, however, on one palliative. Instead of using TV as an electronic babysitter, parents must try to involve themselves directly in their youngsters' viewing. By watching along with the kids at

least occasionally, they can help them evaluate what they see—pointing out the inflated claims of a commercial, perhaps, or criticizing a gratuitously violent scene. "Parents don't have to regard TV as a person who can't be interrupted," says behavioral scientist Charles Corder-Bolz. "If they view one show a night with their kids, and make just one or two comments about it, they can have more impact than the whole program."

16. Reduced to the essentials, the question for parents no longer is: "Do you know where your children are tonight?" The question has become: "What are they watching—and with whom?"

Style and Structure

1. In the first paragraph, what device does the writer use to emphasize the power of T.V.?

2. (a) Reverse the order of the first two paragraphs. How would this effect the impact of the introduction on the reader?

   (b) Why does the author in his version place the thesis statement at the end of his introduction?

3. Why does the author include the ironic comment in the last sentence of paragraph 1?

4. Why does the writer employ statistical evidence in paragraph 2?

5. Examine the section of the essay from paragraph 4 to paragraph 12. What persuasive technique does the writer use? Is this an effective technique to employ given the topic and the projected reader?

6. Select two sections in which the writer employs direct quotation; rewrite them changing the direct quotation into an indirect quotation. Which has the greater impact on the reader?

7. If the writer is convinced of the harm that T.V. does, why does he include paragraph 3?

8. How does the subject of the last four paragraphs differ from the previous nine? Why is this an effective way to conclude this topic?

Thinking and Writing

a. As you may have noticed, the author of this article is concerned with the effect of television on *you*, i.e. upon the generation that has grown up with television as part of its everyday reality.

   Write an essay in which you examine the charges made in this article about the influence of television by relating them to your development and to the type of person that you have become. Be careful not to make the all too common reaction of saying, "There's nothing wrong with me," and then rationalizing that researchers are making mountains out of mole hills. Be as honest and careful as you can, especially when you find yourself disagreeing with the charges. We are not saying, of course, that you cannot disagree with the article, but simply warning you against falling into an obvious pitfall. Try to use reason rather than emotion to make your points.

Audience:

an "average" reader who has built up prejudices because of the sensationalized reports that he/she has encountered in the media. Thus your reader has come to hold opinions completely opposite to yours, but has never thought the problem out in terms of a real individual's development.

b. "If even half of the contentions of this article are true, then some controls should be placed upon what may be broadcast or else the people creating, sponsoring, and broadcasting should be made legally responsible for the results of their actions," was the comment of one person who read this article. Write an essay in which you support *or* refute this comment. If you support it, include in your essay concrete suggestions for legislation and/or controls. If you are going to refute the comment, include concrete evidence to support your argument. You might, for example, find supporting evidence in any television trade magazines.

Audience:

someone who is familiar with the television industry and is in a position to influence the type of programming being broadcast.

Send a copy of your essay to the company which sponsors a program which you find particularly obnoxious *and* to the CRTC.

Cool nerve required to play commodities

by Mike Grenby

1. It's a world of pork bellies, lumber, iced broilers, copper, corn and many other commodities. It's a world where a sharp, gutsy investor can make a real killing — and where any investor can just as easily lose his money.

2. You have probably heard about trading in commodities or commodity futures, and might have wondered if you should consider this investment field yourself.

3. "You need to have a net worth (excluding your house) of $50,000 to $75,000 before you should even consider commodities," said William Altow, manager of Conti-Commodity Services (Canada) Ltd.

4. "And you should be prepared to set no less than $7,500 aside to speculate in the commodities market."
   Merril Lynch's Murray Budd agreed.

5. "We have people sign a statement to the effect that they realize investing in commodities is highly speculative and there is a chance of substantial loss of money," he said.

6. Having warned people of the dangers, both Mr. Altow and Mr. Budd made it clear that "you can make a tremendous amount of money if you play the game right, but you have to have the temperament for it."

7. Here, very simply, is how you invest in commodity futures:

8. If you think the price of a particular commodity is likely to rise, you buy a contract in that commodity.

9. Example: You might buy a copper contract. This means you are ordering 25,000 pounds of copper for delivery at some future date—let's say December, 1979.

10. The price you pay is set by the market. As this is written, the price for 25,000 pounds of copper to be delivered in December, 1979 is 74 1/2 cents a pound.

11. That means the entire contract is worth $18,625.

12. However, you buy a contract like this "on margin." All you actually pay to the commodities broker is a deposit to show your good faith.

13. That deposit generally runs from 6 to 13 per cent of the total value of the contract.

14. So your copper contract might actually cost you only around $1,000.

15. You hope the price of December, 1979, copper will go up between now and that future delivery date.

16. Because you have made such a small deposit you are highly leveraged.

17. In other words, if December, 1979, copper goes up 20 per cent in price, your $18,625 contract will be worth $22,350—yielding you $3,725, a profit of 273 per cent on your original $1,000 investment (brokerage fees have not been considered in this example).

18. However, if the price is down 20 per cent when you sell, you will get only $14,900 for your $18,625 contract—a $3,725 loss, which means you will have to produce another $2,725 in addition to your original $1,000 deposit.

19. On the other hand, if you expect prices to fall, you can sell a contract—much like selling short on the stock market.

20. Again, you put up a good faith deposit of around 10 per cent of the price of the contract.
21. But this time, you make money if the price drops. Then, you can buy a contract at a lower price. Of course, if the price rises, you will have to pay more when you buy the contract, and so will lose money.
22. You as the speculator almost never actually take delivery of the commodity.
23. Commodity's Mr. Altow suggested that an investor should never actually put up more than about 20 per cent of his account.
24. That is, if you have $10,000 with which to speculate, spend only up to $2,000 on good faith deposits. Then, if the commodity's price goes against you, the $8,000 can be drawn upon.
25. The Association of Commodity Exchange Firms, Inc. suggests a commodity speculator should have or develop the following characteristics:
    • Cash funds which are genuinely "risk" capital.
    • The temperament and willingness to take losses (a survey of 8,782 speculators in grain futures showed only 25 per cent made a net profit).
    • An objective temperament. It must be brains over emotions every time.
    • The ability not to worry or lose sleep over speculating in this type of investment market. "Liquidate down to the sleeping point," as the saying goes.
    • The ability to develop a plan and stick to it.
    • The time to study the market and keep abreast of changing conditions.
    • The ability to keep an open mind, to be flexible and quickly see if an opinion of the market was wrong, admit it and act accordingly.
26. If you feel the commodities market might be for you, all commodities brokers have free pamphlets which explain how the market operates.

Style and Structure

1. Reverse paragraphs 1 and 2. Which order more effectively captures the reader's attention? How do the choice of words, content, and parallel structure contribute to arresting the reader's attention? What type of reader would this introduction appeal to?
2. Underline the topic statement of the article and draft a plan of the article's organization.
3. Why does the writer place the information contained in paragraphs 3 to 6 at the beginning of the body of the essay? Why

does he conclude this section with the information contained in paragraph 6?

4. Instead of describing how the commodities market works in general terms, Grenby chose to describe it through a couple of specific illustrations. Using the information contained in paragraphs 7 to 24, write a general description of how the commodities market works. What advantages does the "specific illustration approach" have over the "general description approach" in this situation?

5. Compile a list of the experts (or institutions) quoted either directly or indirectly in this article. How does quoting these sources affect the credibility of the article as a whole? How would this article have been impaired if the writer had not credited his sources of information and had tried to pass off his sources' ideas as his own (i.e. plagiarized)?

6. There are basically two ways to introduce lists:
   (a)The formal approach which uses a complete sentence followed by a colon to introduce the list (see paragraph 25).
   (b)The informal approach which integrates the list into the introductory sentence and never requires the colon (e.g. "Lola was asked to bring the blanket, the picnic lunch, and the suntan lotion.")
   In paragraph 25 why was the author forced by his material to use the formal approach?

7. How does the writer conclude his essay?

Thinking and Writing

a. 1. Consult one of the major newspapers or one of the weekly business newspapers for a list of the commodities or commodities futures (you might want to invite one of the business instructors at your college to come to class to explain how to read the commodities lists. You might also wish to discuss with this person how the commodities market works. Use a copy of the newspaper that is at least *6 months old*).

   2. Select a commodity that you think should be able to make you a profit by the delivery date indicated in the newspaper. Invest a theoretical $1,000 in your chosen commodity to cover a 10% deposit (e.g. $1,000 dollars would be worth a $10,000 contract). Now consult more recent copies of the newspaper and try to decide with each issue of the paper whether to sell or to keep your futures (don't cheat; looking at the price on delivery date causes the newspaper to self-destruct immediately!). Keep a running "history" of your future's price for each monthly period up to the point at

which you decide to sell or up to the delivery date. If you sell before the delivery date, consult the appropriate copy of the newspaper to find out whether your decision was the right one in light of the price on the delivery date.

Find out how much of a profit or a loss you would have made.

3. Write a report on the history, success or failure of your commodity speculation and the reasons for this success or failure. Write the report as if you were a broker reporting to your superior at an investment company trying to explain or justify your action.

b. Based on your experience with investing in commodities, write an essay aimed at the average person on the street in which you explain how the commodities market works and advise the reader on whether or not to become involved in this market.
Audience:
as indicated in the assignment.
Send a copy of your essay to a newspaper in your area (to be used as an article), or to a business instructor at your college.

Bio-engineering gone wrong

by Sheila Kulka and Barry Estabrook

1. In 1890 few Americans would have guessed that the seemingly innocuous lines from Shakespeare's *Henry IV*, "Nay, I'll have a starling shall be taught to speak nothing but 'Mortimer,'" would eventually lead to the deaths of 62 persons aboard a Lockheed Electra aircraft.
2. But for the misguided efforts of Eugene Scheifflin, a New York drug manufacturer and leading force in the American Acclimatization Society, the 10,000-bird-strong flock of starlings with which the ill-fated aircraft collided just after takeoff from Boston, would have never been found in North American skies.
3. Scheifflin had spent idle hours pursuing a perplexing avocation: it was his goal to bring all birds mentioned by Shakespeare to America's deprived shores.
4. But only 10 years after its 1890 introduction, the starling began showing clear signs that it was one species the New World would have been better off without.

5. Scheifflin's starlings spread rapidly from their first New World roost — ironically — beneath the eves of the American Museum of Natural History in New York's Central Park.

6. Within six years the black marauders were seen regularly in Brooklyn and Long Island. Spurred forward by a territorial nature that forces young starlings to seek new foraging areas, those first tentative New York flocks had spread to Halifax within 15 years, and by 1945 had become commonplace as far afield as British Columbia. Today starlings can claim title to being the most numerous of all bird species in North America.

7. Although some people thought the birds would benefit North America by eating insects, it fast became evident that Mr. Scheifflin's starlings preferred a varied menu of feedlot grain, corn, sorghum, rice, truck crops and fruit. Voracious, starlings consume up to twice their own body weight daily — an appetite that costs North American agriculture millions of dollars each year. And there is evidence that starlings are key villains in the spread of swine disease from feedlot to feedlot.

8. As pugnacious as they are voracious, starlings have no trouble out-competing less aggressive native birds. Flickers, wrens, bluebirds and martins — birds eating only insects — were forced from favourite haunts as starlings bullied their way to prominence.

9. But no one understands the nuisance of starlings as well as citizens of Waterbury, Connecticut, a town whose police force once staged a dawn shotgun war against the 250,000 starlings that called Waterbury townhall their home.

10. Citizens of Waterbury had to turn on windshield wipers when driving through town at dusk. Sidewalks were slippery from accumulated starling dung, and the downtown area was characterized by an irksome odour reminiscent of an ill-kept chicken coop.

Bestial ramifications

11. Since Noah filled his ark, man has been afflicted with an insatiable desire to shift animals far beyond their natural range. All of man's meddling has been backed by near total ignorance of the ramifications, and although some bestial transfers have met with (at best) marginal success, far too often they have resulted in irreversible natural disasters.

12. The most monumental meddling failure ocurred in 1859 when the merchant vessel *Lightning* pulled into an Australian port with a shipment of 24 European rabbits destined for the sheep ranch of Thomas Austin.

13. Mr. Austin's desire to bring this delectable, long-eared native of his homeland to Australia was perhaps understandable, but the gen-

tleman farmer would shudder to hear the contempt with which his name is held in that country today.

14. For a time, however, Austin was happy. Only six years after the first rabbits hopped from their cages onto his ranch, Austin was bagging as many as 20,000 per year. But within a decade rabbits had leapt the borders of Austin's estate and Australians were beginning to wonder whether they had a monstrous problem on their hands.

15. They did. On the dry Australian plains, it was found that five of Mr. Austin's fertile bunnies could consume the same amount of valuable grass as one sheep. One ranch, which supported 20,000 plump ewes before the first rabbit cast hungry eyes on its grassy hills, saw its capacity reduced to 2,000 sheep within four years.

16. In 1887 angry outbackers in New South Wales killed 20 million rabbits. By 1901 the problem had become so acute that Australians erected 2,000 miles of buried, rabbit-proof fence in a futile gesture aimed at stopping the spread of these pests.

17. Man fought a losing battle against these nimble foes until 1950, when germ warfare was called into the fray. Australian biologists innoculated several laboratory rabbits with a deadly South American rabbit disease. Released, these rabbits spread germs that killed 995 out of every 1000 Australian bunnies. With the rabbits decimated, deserts once again became productive pastures.

18. But Australians could soon face a second, escalated battle. It is now speculated that the rabbits may be developing an immunity to the South American disease.

Espeut's mongoose

19. A Jamaican planter named W. B. Espeut, in 1876, released nine mongooses (recently shipped from India) on his sugar plantation. Rats that had accompanied Europeans to this tropical island had become serious pests in sugar cane fields, consuming as much as one-fifth of the crop.

20. By importing the squirrel-sized mongoose to Jamaica, Espeut hoped to solve the rat problem. His plan worked. Those nine mongooses contentedly disappeared into his cane fields and, well-fed on rat meat, began to multiply.

21. Other planters, noting Espeut's fields were no longer plagued by rats, grew eager to get their hands on mongooses. Soon the little beasts were transported not only all over Jamaica, but to every sugar island in the West Indies.

22. By this time, however, the mongoose began to show his true colours. Noted for the speed and agility that permits them to kill cobras in their native India (although mongooses do lose the occasional battle), Espeut's introduction quickly devoured all Ja-

maica's rats and then turned its attention to other animals—
chickens, piglets, goat kids, lambs, kittens, puppies.

23. Before the mongooses' rampage was stemmed by natural forces,
    they had not only made it nearly impossible to raise small domestic
    animals in Jamaica, but had eliminated virtually all the island's
    native animals.

24. It is only by virtue of a miracle that these pests did not gain a
    foothold in North America. In the 1890's, western ranchers,
    plagued by gophers, had begun to introduce mongooses. By then
    aware of the dangers of these pests, scientists managed to stop the
    newcomers before populations became established.

25. When British farmers found that a new market had sprung up for
    live specimens of the thousands of house sparrows they had been
    killing each year to protect crops, they were understandably
    delighted—if not a little perplexed.

26. Once again, it was the Acclimatization Society movement of home-
    sick Europeans and this time they were attempting to introduce
    these chirping little birds to a new homeland in America.

27. Originally from southern Europe, house sparrows fast learned the
    ease of pilfering from man, and they have faithfully followed him
    everywhere he has gone.

28. By the spring of 1853, Mr. John Hooper of the Brooklyn Institute
    could proudly report to members of his organization that fifty
    sparrows released in a New York cemetery had done well and
    multiplied. "I have original notes taken from time to time of their
    increase and colonization over our great country," he wrote.

29. In Strathroy, Ontario, a Mr. L. H. Smith could claim that he had
    procured a good bargain on the 12 sparrows he had purchased for
    the princely sum of one dollar each. Not only were there now
    thousands of the little birds in his home town, but they had spread
    to become plentiful in "every town, city and village in this part of
    Ontario."

30. Once these fast-breeding birds became numerous in North
    America, they began to show some of the less desirable traits that
    made them so detested in their homeland. In orchards, they ate
    blossoms, buds and ripe fruit. They moved into ripening wheat
    fields in huge flocks, heavily damaging crops. In cities their drop-
    pings began to kill decorative plants.

31. Philadelphians, who had only recently cheered the release of 1,000
    house sparrows, were called upon in 1883 "to kill or otherwise
    destroy the small bird known as the English sparrow." Michigan
    offered a one-penny bounty for dead sparrows in lots of 25 or more.

32. Meanwhile, one enterprising New York landlady put the newfound
    pests to good use by serving sparrow pie to her lodgers, who
    reported favourably on the delicacy.

Carp-barrelling

33. Each year fish and wildlife authorities in Canada and the United States spend millions of dollars on programmes aimed at cutting back numbers of carp in our waters.

34. These hungry bottom feeders, with their unpleasant habit of devouring aquatic weeds and stirring mud on lake bottoms in search of food, can quickly render formerly clear waters unfit for habitation by any other fish species.

35. Shunned almost universally for both poor eating quality and inept fighting abilities, the carp now ranks as one of the worst plagues in North American waterways.

36. This, however, was not true in 1877 when Rudolph Hessel stood proudly before the United States Congress to receive applause for his successful planting of a breeding stock of carp in a pond near Boston.

37. Rumours spread that this supposedly fine-tasting European battler was now living on this continent, and it wasn't long before every constituent in the United States was clamouring for carp to be introduced in his area. Rising to the call, legislators made carp stocking a first-rate, pork-barrel issue. An election promise of carp for all was bound to garner votes.

38. But carp would have proliferated without extensive stocking programmes. All they really needed was a lift across the salty Atlantic. During spring floods they moved from watershed to watershed, gorging themselves on valuable aquatic plants and the spawn of gamefish as they traveled.

39. As fast as the carp fad had swept the land, it died. People, disappointed at the loss of native fish and no longer waxing eloquent about the carp's culinary and angling merits, began to demand elimination. But it was too late. By 1901 an American biologist studying carp for the federal government concluded that the best thing to do was to learn to live with the carp; it was here to stay. The biologist was correct.

Georgia-bound

40. The angler's world is rife with tall stories, but the eyes of Florida Game and Freshwater Fish authorities must really have rolled one autumn morning in 1968 when a bartender, holding three bizarre, pale-skinned catfish, started telling a story about how he was driving along this road north of Fort Lauderdale at 2 a.m. when he came across hundreds of these fish — all of them walking across the pavement.

41. The bartender must have exercised some of the fast talk for which his profession is noted. At any rate, he convinced the government

men to go out to the scene where they found several more of the mobile fish crushed on the pavement.

42. Today this scenario is no longer cause for raised eyebrows in the Sunshine State. The walking catfish has comfortably established itself as a Florida resident.

43. North America can thank Thailand for the walking catfish. These talented fish were originally introduced to Florida as two-inch long aquarium novelties, but no one thought to inform unsuspecting Americans of the strange little specimen's unfish-like manners.

44. Their perambulatory prowess went unrecognized until one day, during a heavy rainstorm, some catfish got out of their tank and crawled down to a nearby pond. They have never looked back.

45. The walking catfish is now at home throughout southern Florida, and has begun to turn its steps northward. Scientists speculate that walking catfish might (using stiff spines on their pectoral fins to draw themselves forward in a series of steps) someday move as far north as Georgia. Without natural enemies, they are overrunning Florida waters by out-competing native large-mouth bass and bluegills, vital to Florida's important freshwater sport fishery.

46. But not only do these Thai introductions walk, they fight. Walking catfish have been known to kill conventional catfish in fin-to-fin combat, and have forced piranhas to turn tail in observation aquariums.

47. Attempts to eradicate the walking catfish by poisoning have met with no success. Equipped with a lung-like organ, walking catfish can live out of water for 12 hours. Should the water of a particular pond drop to an uncomfortable level or become poisoned, walking catfish resident in that pond merely get up and move to another more to their liking.

48. Further south, another biological disaster is fast marching this way. In 1957, an uninformed beekeeper wandered into the experimental beeyard of Warwick Kerr, a Brazilian geneticist who had set out to improve the honey-producing capacity of Brazil's traditional European bees through crossbreeding with an African strain.

49. The unknowing beekeeper removed devices Kerr had installed on hives in his experimental beeyard to retain queens, and by the time the blunder was discovered, 26 swarms had escaped. The western world got its first taste of killer bees.

50. Leaving a trail of at least 150 dead humans and thousands of dead domestic animals, the released bees began to move away from Sao Paulo (the site of Kerr's experiment) at a rate of 200 miles per year. By 1990 they will have arrived at the southern borders of the

United States, and no one is sure what will result. One positive hope is that they will cross with gentler European strains during the course of their travels and arrive on this continent somewhat mollified.

51. But by no means has all man's meddling moved animals from the Old World to the New. Britons are still cursing the Duke of Bedford for releasing 10 American grey squirrels on his estate in 1890. The North American roughnecks made short work of displacing Britain's more mild-mannered red squirrels.

52. In the early 1900's, muskrats were sent from North America to Czechoslovakia in the hope of starting a new fur industry for Europe. The aquatic rodents took an immediate liking to their new home, and within 20 years escapees from fur farms had spread across the continent into areas where their affinity for constructing dens in dikes, embankments and roadbeds assured them a solid position on the exotic pest list.

Canada goose vs. sheep

53. Canadians, too, have had a hand in ecological meddling. Several Canada geese —those proud waterfowl whose seasonal migration stirs all of our hearts —were sent to gooseless New Zealand where they are now viewed with disdain. The unruly Canadians have become so numerous in some areas that they compete with sheep for food.

54. Man persists in his folly. Just over a decade ago, an Ohio Beagle club released thousands of those European rabbits of Australian renown, hoping to bolster hunts.

55. In the southern United States, fish and game men jealous of the North's ring necked pheasant (a Chinese introduction) are still attempting to convince a host of oriental gamebirds that Dixie isn't such a bad place after all.

56. New Mexican gunners are keenly eyeing a protected herd of wild Moroccan mountain sheep introduced to the state a dozen years ago. In Arizona there is worry about the new sheep competing with threatened native bighorns, and wildlife authorities have given the order to shoot the Moroccan immigrants on sight.

57. Meanwhile in Florida, pressure groups are springing up to encourage the introduction of 100-pound-plus Chinese weed-eating carp to help control the man-introduced water hyacinths that clog many inland waterways.

58. Hopefully Floridians will heed the words of naturalist George Laycock before introducing yet another exotic animal:
    "Release of wildlife into territory foreign to it involves, not a calculated risk, but a risk too great to calculate."

Style and Structure

1. How does the first paragraph encourage the reader to continue with the essay?
2. Instead of opening their article with the thesis statement, why did the writers choose to begin with a short narrative?
3. Underline the thesis statement and draft a plan of the article's organization.
4. From the reader's point of view, what are the advantages of presenting a series of illustrations of the thesis rather than just talking in general terms about the dangers of ecological tampering?
5. What level of knowledge about ecological tampering do the writers assume the reader has? How would this essay have to be different if it were aimed at a group of scientists specializing in the study of ecology?
6. Why doesn't paragraph 58 (including the quotation) function as an effective conclusion to the essay *as a whole*? Write a more effective conclusion.

Thinking and Writing

a. Write an essay employing non-technical language on *one* of the following topics:
   1. The successful introduction of one species into your local area (examine such things as crops, animals, biological insect control, birds, etc.).
   2. The destructive effects of the introduction of a species into your area (keep in mind that some species have been introduced accidentally).
   3. A future introduction of a species into Canada at present being considered (contact your local office of the Ministry of Agriculture for information).
   Audience:
   someone who has the same awareness of bio-engineering that you could expect from your friends who are not employed in agriculture, horticulture, botany or zoology.

b. Based on the data that you and the other students in your class discovered while researching section a., write an essay in which you make recommendations regarding future introductions of flora and fauna into the country.
   Audience:
   someone who has at least heard of the topic of bio-engineering, but who is perhaps not aware of all of its implications.
   Send a copy of your essay to the federal Minister of Agriculture or the provincial Minister of Natural Resources.

Good secretaries get harder to find as jobs call more for management skills

by Peggy McCallum

1. Bosses may not like it, and some of their secretaries may not either. But those who speak for secretaries seem to agree that the person who takes dictation, transcribes, types and files is fast becoming an anachronism.

2. Many secretaries, they observe, are half jumping and half being pushed into the role of executive assistant; the less ambitious are destined for typing pools and technical work. The evolution is seen as a result of radical new office technology, increased work demands on executives and women's liberation.

3. "Executives today need and expect much more than a technically competent secretary," Paul Douglas, an Edmonton-based management consultant, said. "They are saying they need a person skilled in public relations, leadership, organization and the management of their time. The manager wants a secretary as motivated as he is." His firm, P.A. Douglas and Associates Ltd., specializes in secretarial consulting.

4. Marvin Goodman, president of the Toronto-based unit of Manpower Temporary Services, an international temporary help firm, said his company recently had to develop more sophisticated applicant tests to keep up with such employer demands. "The ability of the employee to think, understand, initiate and adapt quickly — this was something (clients) found they were not getting."

5. Mr. Goodman thinks the biggest role changes will come at the middle-management level, where secretaries are most vulnerable to new technology. Word processors, machines that replace much typewriter work by producing edited, error-free texts at speeds of more than 2,400 words a minute, will likely have the greatest impact. (Two word processors can do the same work as five secretaries, estimated James Stevens, director of Documat Computer Documentation, a London, Ont., office systems consulting firm.) Dictation systems are expected to replace most shorthand work.

6. At this time, the profession is far from suffering with too many for too few jobs. "The demand is increasing. There's more demand than there is supply," Mr. Goodman said.

7. "In many instances good secretaries are hard to find because peo-

ple who have the capabilities for the job also have the capabilities to be good managers," said Vera Hall, Toronto chapter president of the National Secretaries Association (NSA International). Mrs. Hall was promoted from secretary to employee relations co-ordinator of Kimberly-Clark of Canada Ltd., Toronto, last June.

8. "The women's liberation movement has talked down the secre-tarial profession," she said. "And women have so many job options that just weren't there 10 years ago. I think many of the secretaries within my chapter welcome the opportunity for challenge as long as they are adequately compensated."

9. "In too many cases secretaries are taken for granted," said Elizabeth Murphy of E.R. Murphy and Associates of Toronto, training consultants. "I see a trend in secretaries wanting to move up (in responsibility), becoming more assertive. I see managers responding, but perhaps not as quickly as the women would like them to. It's a beautiful example of lack of communication: many managers say their secretaries don't want extra work. Managers still have stereotyped views. It's a habit."

10. Some executives are afraid that professional upgrading seminars for secretaries—for which registrations are on the increase—"will only make secretaries unhappy because their expectations become too high", Mr. Douglas said. But he admitted many execu-tives substitute the seminars, which cost a few hundred dollars, for raises. A rough average salary for a secretary is $15,000 a year.

11. A lot of secretaries who belong to professional associations say salary is not their biggest worry: "Once we prove we are profession-als, we'll be recognized," said Barbara Williams, Canadian district director of NSA. "But we must take the initiative. It won't happen the other way around."

12. The associations are fighting an uphill battle. The NSA has only 1,500 members in Canada, the Association of Administrative Assistants less than 500—together, an extremely small percent-age of the field, considering there are about 96,000 secretaries in Ontario alone.

Style and Structure

1. Underline the thesis statement.
2. Why does the writer include the last sentence in paragraph 2 in the introduction? Would a different ordering of the list have been more effective in the light of the rest of the essay?
3. What type of evidence does the writer use to prove her thesis? Do you find this type of evidence appropriate and sufficient?
4. The writer employs a fair amount of direct quotation in her essay. Change one or two of these passages into indirect quota-tion. Which approach is more effective?

118

5. Why does the writer enclose one of the sentences in paragraph 5 in brackets?
6. What relationship does the concluding paragraph have to the body of the essay? Write a conclusion that includes a recapitulation of the writer's main points.

Thinking and Writing

a. Recently, in Toronto, an executive instructed his secretary to go to the Motor Vehicle Licensing Bureau for the purpose of renewing his automobile license. When she refused on the grounds that it was not part of her job, she was fired.
Write an essay in which you defend *or* criticize the executive for firing his secretary.
Audience:
an average reader who would oppose your point of view on the question.

b. Write an essay in which you define your concept of the duties of a secretary and, based upon this job description, determine where your concept of a secretary's duties fits into the following quotation from the article:
"In too many cases secretaries are taken for granted. I see a trend in secretaries wanting to move up (in responsibility), becoming more assertive. I see managers responding, but perhaps not as quickly as the women would like them to. It's a beautiful example of lack of communication; many managers say their secretaries don't want extra work. Managers still have stereotyped views. It's a habit."
Audience:
someone who is familiar with the duties of a secretary, either from employing or being employed as a secretary.
Send a copy of your paper to a secretary that you know or to someone at your college who employs a secretary.

Riding with the Chosen Few

by Elliot M. Gold

The lawless image of the outlaw motorcycle gang has long since been distilled into movie legend, mostly based on the

exploits of the Hell's Angels. The reality of a motorcycle club, as seen by photographer Elliot Gold of Altadena, California, is somewhat different — and surprising.

1. We first heard the roar of the motorcycles when they were about half a mile away. I was covering a sparsely attended "Neighborhood Car Meeting" sponsored by a unit of the Los Angeles County Sheriff's Department in an Altadena schoolroom. The doors were open to let in the cool night air and, within a minute, the swelling cycle sound began to make it impossible to continue the discussion. We waited for the motorcycles to pass, but they seemed to be directly in front of the building. Suddenly, I realized the bikes were inside! Then, through the back doorway, a motorcycle appeared. Perched atop the bike was Jessie, The Power, a member of the "outlaw" motorcycle club called the Chosen Few. Followed by a dozen other members, he rode down the meeting's center aisle and parked at the front of the room.

2. When things calmed down, a sheriff's lieutenant explained that he had invited the club to dramatize the poor attendance of local citizens at these monthly meetings. I photographed the event and later sold prints to those who had attended. But my curiosity was aroused; so I sought out the local chapter of the Chosen Few and began to bring them prints. Each time I came, I would take more photographs and, finally, I suggested the possibility of doing a book on the club. The entire club voted to give me permission. Thus began an 18-month association with the Chosen Few during which I attended their meetings and parties and went on rides with them.

3. The Chosen Few was founded in 1961. First to join were Lionel, Little Frank, Bates and Champ, all blacks in their mid-20s from a south central Los Angeles neighborhood. "We just wanted to belong to something," Lionel says. Today, the club has 130 members in five chapters with names on the roster such as Blue, Slide, Hatch, Fast Eddie, Apache and Little Tony. They are a surprising mixture: more than half are married, over 90 percent are employed full time and the median age is about 29. The membership has included youth counselors, businessmen, an ex-policeman, an architect, a physicist, an importer-exporter and an ex-pro football player. There are alcoholics and those who are always loaded on drugs. There are also members who don't drink, smoke or take drugs at all. A love for motorcycles and a determined sense of brotherhood binds them together.

4. But most surprising to me was the racial mix: about 53 percent are black; 32 percent, white; and 15 percent, Chicano. It is, as far as anyone knows, the largest and perhaps only integrated outlaw motorcycle club anywhere.

5. The Chosen Few is an outlaw club by definition, since they do not

belong to the American Motorcycle Association (paradoxically, they cannot belong to the AMA because they *are* outlaws). "We run that line," Blue told me, "between the AMA and the one-percenters." The "one-percenters" are the fringe clubs, the "total outlaw" groups once represented by the Hell's Angels. The Few believe that such clubs account for 99 percent of the bad reputation that all riders have to live with.

6. Social activity includes parties and dances, but the main events are the "runs" held in the summer months often to points several hundreds of miles from Los Angeles. The Chosen Few make their runs in a double-file formation, sometimes followed by a support caravan of cars, trucks and campers carrying wives, girlfriends and children. Since small gas tanks are in vogue on the customized bike, fuel stops are frequent. A delay for a minor breakdown at a service station (the club will not leave one of its members behind) can turn into an occasion for an impromptu beer party on the spot.

7. The Chosen Few are keenly aware of their image. Their appearance on the road can seem menacing to some, and the riders are convinced they are the objects of envy, especially to women. Macho by nature, they are not prone to turn the other cheek, and they have had their share of violent incidents including bar-wrecking, assault and rape charges. It often starts, strange as it may seem, when outsiders, both men and women, come to them looking for trouble.

8. "Some of them are fools," Henry feels. "It seems to me that a lot of them want to see just how far they can push it." Henry is six-feet-five and weighs 300 pounds, and most of the members of his chapter are about six feet and over 200 pounds. Moreover, the brotherhood sticks together. Lionel, who first wore the cross of the Chosen Few, says, "The idea of seeing my colors on the ground, getting bodily harm done to them, that's what hurts me...like seeing the American flag dropped in the dirt."

9. My association with the Few introduced me to men who in the public's eye are deviants. I found men who would knock down an outsider for insulting a brother; yet these same men who lived by the wind would hurry home from work to be with their sick children and cry when they bury their club brother. In short, I found their subculture to be no different in many ways from the rest of society. But as one of them said to me about outsiders, "They'll never think of us as individual people like themselves."

Style and Structure

1. What is the reader led to expect after reading the first paragraph? Why is this a good way to attract the reader's interest to

the article? Why is it important to the writer's thesis for him to arouse an expectation which is really based on prejudice?

2. What purpose does paragraph 1 serve in the article?
3. What techniques does the writer employ to overcome our prejudices against bikers?
4. How does the final paragraph function in relation to the body of the article?
5. How does the final quotation relate back to the effect the writer tries to create in us in paragraph one?

Thinking and Writing

a. 1.One "theme" which underlies this article is that prejudices can be overcome by gaining knowledge about the person or group of people who are the subject of this prejudice.

Choose one group of people in your community who have traditionally been subjected to prejudice for religious, economic, racial or social reasons. One interesting way to approach this project would be to choose a group about whom you yourself have some negative feelings (e.g. Jehovah's Witnesses, East Indians, White Anglo-Saxon Protestants, the wealthy bourgeoisie, communists, welfare recipients, etc.) Investigate the history, customs, beliefs and social structures of the group that you have selected. Be careful not to be misled into believing the all too common popular myths about these groups; instead, try to see their point of view. Go to the sociological studies that have been done on the group, or to representatives or community leaders of the group (be prepared with good, objective questions; be careful not to make a fool of yourself with "when did you people stop beating your wives" types of questions).

2.Write an essay based upon your findings in which you present a sympathetic picture of your subject group, just as Gold did for the Chosen Few. Aim the essay at a reader who might normally be antagonistic to the group and try to persuade the reader that he/she has nothing to fear, hate or look down upon. Try to anticipate and defuse the most common myths about the group.

Audience:

someone who is prejudiced against the group that you have chosen.

b. Write a report which presents your opinion on whether or not obtaining more information about an individual, his/her needs, beliefs, customs and lifestyle actually reduces prejudice. Use concrete evidence from your experiences in section a. as a basis for your argument.

Audience:

someone who is aware of the prejudices in your community and is involved in trying to overcome them.

Send a copy of your essay to any organization in your community that represents a "minority group" or any organization in your community that has as its central purpose fighting the spread of prejudice.

The coming of an information society

---

by Edward Cornish

1. Many new technological systems will flood into our lives during the 1980s, but those in communications and computers may have the most revolutionary consequences. These new systems promise transformation in the ways we work, learn, play, shop, and manage our everyday lives.

2. No new technological breakthroughs are required for this transformation: the devices are already available and have begun to move into homes, offices, and factories. As this happens, the communications revolution long anticipated by scientists and engineers will actually occur.

3. To understand the information revolution, it is useful to look back at a few of the great historical landmarks in the collecting, synthesizing, and transmitting of information. If the computer is defined as any device for storing and processing information, it has an ancient history. Nature developed protoplasmic computers —brains—hundreds of millions of years ago. Animal brains evolved steadily through the eons, though far slower than electronic brains. The human brain, which appeared approximately two million years ago, represented a major advance over earlier models and gave enormous power to the species possessing it. This remarkable "wet computer" was almost certainly accompanied by a major breakthrough in communications—human languages. Thanks to these powerful computing and communicating abilities, man became the dominant animal on earth.

4. The next great breakthrough in information technology did not

occur until about 10,000 years ago with the invention of writing, which made it possible to encapsulate information and transmit it through time and space. With writing, information could be stored outside the brain and accessed years later for processing in another brain. The information could also be transported thousands of kilometers in its exact form—without being distorted by repeated passage through different human brains. To be sure, the method of transmitting the message was slow: a messenger proceeding on foot, horseback, or boat. Still, the communication system—primitive as it seems by modern standards—enabled the Roman emperors to govern territories ranging from Britain to Egypt.

5. Down through the ages, stupendous efforts were exerted to speed up communications. In the 1400s, the Incas had a system of messengers each of whom ran about one and a half kilometers at top speed to the next messenger; this relay system enabled a message to travel at the rate of about 240 kilometers per day across the Inca kingdom. No significant improvement on the Inca system occurred until the nineteenth century, but preelectronic communications systems enjoyed one last moment of glory—the Pony Express. Started by the U.S. government in 1860 to carry the mail from St. Joseph, Missouri, to the Pacific coast, the Pony Express lasted only 16 months but made a lasting impression on American consciousness. The "ponies" were actually horses, stationed 16 to 24 kilometers apart. Each rider rode three animals successively, covering at least 53 kilometers before passing the mail pouch to the next rider. The fastest trip ever made took 7 days and 17 hours, but the regular schedule was 10 days—hardly better than the Incas' system.

6. The telegraph, developed commercially in the 1840s, made communications virtually instantaneous over hundreds, even thousands of kilometers. But the telegraph stopped at the water's edge. Though the news of Abraham Lincoln's assassination could be transmitted by telegraph instantaneously to California 4,800 kilometers away, it could not cross the Atlantic. As a result, news of Lincoln's assassination took 12 days to reach London.

7. By the early twentieth century the telephone had largely replaced the telegraph, and cables linked Europe to America. Marconi patented his radio in England in 1896, but it was not until the 1920s that radio became a major medium of mass communications. Franklin D. Roosevelt, with his "fireside chats," turned radio into a major medium of politics in the 1930s. Motion pictures, which had evolved from the nickelodeon into the great silent pictures of the 1920s, began to talk in the early 1930s and had blossomed into color by the end of the decade. Television, demon-

strated experimentally as early as 1927, began to enter U.S. homes after World War II. During the 1950s, television swept into homes at a stupendous rate: in 1950, less than 10 percent of homes had television; by 1960, more than 90 percent of homes had succumbed to the one-eyed monster.

8. While radio and television were expanding furiously, developments were occurring elsewhere that seemed initially to have little bearing on mass communications. Large businesses and governments had vast amounts of information that needed to be handled economically and swiftly. One approach to information-handling was to use punched cards which could be manipulated mechanically, thereby making it possible to retrieve needed information more quickly. Rapid data-handling became particularly important to the U.S. military, which was trying to figure out ways to aim and launch missiles over very great distances. Human mathematicians operating with paper and pencil were simply too slow to perform the necessary calculations quickly enough. Nor could clerks get information from file drawers as fast as was required. So the military began putting funds into the development of electronic calculators—devices that later became known as "electronic computers" and then simply "computers." The experimental computers of the late 1940s and early 1950s were very large, often occupying a good-sized room, and were monstrously expensive. Furthermore, they were extremely stupid by today's standards. But during the 1950s, 1960s, and 1970s, the capabilities of the computers to manipulate data increased dramatically; equally dramatic was the decrease in their cost.

9. At first it seemed as if only large government agencies like the U.S. Census Bureau could use computers, and as if computers could be used for only a few purposes, such as solving certain types of mathematical equations. But as people gained more and more experience with computers, the electronic "brains" began to perform more and more tasks. And a funny thing began to happen: the computers began to "talk" to each other and to human beings by means of telephone lines, and telephone companies began to use computers to keep track of long-distance communications. So the barriers that once separated communications and computers into two fields began to break down. By early 1980, U.S. officials were in a serious quandary because the Communications Act of 1934 authorized the Federal Communications Commission to regulate electronic communications, but the Commission found it virtually impossible to find a legal formula that clearly distinguished between communications and data processing. In effect, technology had made obsolete the laws that were designed to regulate it!

10. The convergence of communications and computers is natural since both deal with information. Computers store and manipulate information; communications systems transmit the information from one point to another.

11. The importance of information is hard to overstate because we use information as the basis for all action. Without good information, we may blunder disastrously, but with it we can reach our goals quickly and easily. Thus better communications and information systems hold a tantalizing promise: they may be able to help us solve many of the problems besetting the modern world.

12. The speed of progress in computers has astounded almost everyone. Musing on microcomputers, Stanford University economist Edward Steinmuller has been quoted as saying, "If the airlines had progressed as rapidly as this technology, the Concorde would be carrying half a million passengers at 32 million kilometers an hour for less than a penny apiece!"

13. A writer for the *Washington Star* went even further:

    Had the automobile developed at a pace equivalent to that of the computer during the past 20 years, today a Rolls Royce would cost less than $3, get one million kilometers to the liter, deliver enough power to drive the Queen Elizabeth II, and six of them would fit on the head of a pin!

14. Such statements may seem to be mere hyperboles, but the microcomputer revolution has awed even its proponents. One expert, Adam Osborne, wrote a book called *Running Wild*, since that is what he said the microcomputers were doing. Osborne said neither government nor big business (nor anybody else) could halt the breath-taking advance of the silicon chip.

15. The rapid increase in the ability of computers to store and manipulate vast amounts of information led to speculation as early as the 1950s that computers might someday challenge the traditional paper-based information systems. Why couldn't the information in our daily newspapers be put into a computer and sent electronically into people's homes without the present cumbersome system, which involves the cutting down of vast forests for paper, the use of gas-guzzling fleets of trucks, and battalions of vendors and carriers? Why couldn't the contents of libraries be stored in computers so that the information could be accessed by users almost anywhere?

16. During the 1960s, studies were made by the Library of Congress and numerous other institutions to determine what role computers might play in storing and disseminating information. Many of the studies could be summarized as follows: yes, computers were technically capable of doing many of the things suggested by their enthusiasts, but the technology was insufficiently advanced to

make most such projects economically desirable. Still, there were exceptions to that rule. For example, the Library of Congress decided it would be desirable to computerize its card catalogs, and during the 1970s libraries in the United States and elsewhere adopted computers for many of their book-handling procedures. In effect, the libraries computerized "information about information"—titles and authors of books, reference numbers so books could be located, etc.—while leaving the bulk of the information in the form of books and other materials on paper.

17. Newspapers also began to adopt computers, and, by 1980, major newspapers all over the United States were thoroughly computerized. Instead of using a typewriter, a reporter types his or her article on a computer console, and the information is stored in the computer while various editors work on it. Instead of using pencils to edit copy typed on paper, the editors edit copy on a video display screen, a device looking much like a television screen but showing text instead of pictures. The system allows an editor to carry out all normal editorial tasks: words can be deleted, inserted, shifted about, etc. Once an article is ready to print, the computer generates the electronic signals needed to control the typesetting operation. But in its final form a modern newspaper is still a collection of large paper sheets on which articles and advertisements have been printed in ink.

18. The truly electronic newspaper—a contradiction in terms since it is *paperless*—appeared in Britain in the late 1970s. As happens so often in technological innovation, the breakthroughs did not come from the traditional provider of the service. Instead of British newspapers pioneering the electronic newspaper, the British post office and the British Broadcasting Corporation (BBC) established information services that could be described as electronic newspapers: news can be called up on a video screen and read whenever one wishes. For instance, a subscriber may select "headlines" and then press the appropriate buttons on the mechanism (which is about the size of a pocket calculator). The headlines then appear on the screen. After reading them, the viewer can call up other subjects such as "foreign news," "consumer news," "people," "weather," etc. An electronic "newspaper" may have hundreds of pages of information in its memory.

19. The broadcast versions of the electronic newspaper, such as the BBC's, allow the viewer to call up a wide variety of information that is being broadcast simultaneously. The viewer has the feeling of being able to interact with the system, but the interaction is really limited to the electronic equivalent of looking at different pages in a printed newspaper. By contrast, the electronic newspaper provided by the British post office has the technical feasi-

bility of allowing the reader to contact the editors of the newspaper. The reason is that the post office's electronic newspaper is transmitted by telephone lines; being two-way, the system allows a viewer to ask for any information in the post office memory bank. Many thousands of pages of information can be made available, since the system is not limited by the constraints of the airwaves. The post office system, because of its enormous information capacity, provides a bridge from the electronic newspaper to the electronic library. The contents of hundreds of thousands of books can now be put onto computer tape, and people can have the material displayed on their home viewing screens.

20. The terminology of the new electronic information systems is unsettled, but the word "teletext" is often used to suggest a system employing a television signal for transmission while "viewdata" (or "videotext") is often used in cases where the information is transmitted by cable or telephone lines. However, these terms are still used rather interchangeably.

21. No one knows how rapidly the new electronic information systems will catch on. So far, the British systems have not proved outstandingly popular, in part because of the substantial costs involved. If more people acquire home computing equipment (for whatever reason), the way will be open for the electronic information systems to move in more strongly.

22. A French system known as Antiope is currently being introduced into the United States. The terminal required to receive the Antiope information is small enough to be built into an ordinary television set and will raise the price to only about 10 or 20 percent above the price of a normal color TV. With Antiope, you can use a simple, hand-held key pad, about the size of a pocket calculator, to call up the latest news, sports, stock market prices, weather, traffic reports, information on television programs, etc. Moreover, the Antiope organization is already planning to add airline and rail schedules, theatre and movie listings, listings of educational courses, and a wide variety of other information.

23. In France, where Antiope was developed, the telephone company is already planning to abolish the traditional telephone directory and, in its place, give every phone subscriber an Antiope terminal. Providing millions of terminals free of charge is believed to be cheaper in the long run than providing paper directories.

24. AT&T has already run a "concept trial" in Albany, New York, to test reactions from residential and business participants to the idea of electronic "yellow pages." Today's yellow pages have serious limitations. They are difficult to update and so costly the average person who has a house to rent or an automobile to sell finds advertising in them impractical. But if telephone companies make

their yellow pages electronic, it will be possible for them to invade the classified ad market, which is one of the richest sources of newspaper revenue. Unfortunately for the newspapers, the electronic systems appear to be inherently cheaper and faster. It is at least theoretically possible for someone who wants to sell a sofa to advertise it on an electronic system and have it actually sold within a few minutes of deciding to put it on the market!

25. Conceding probable defeat, newspapers are now actively trying to get into the electronic act themselves. Eleven major newspapers, including the *New York Times, Los Angeles Times,* and the *Washington Post*, have been selected to join a national computer data network and will supply their entire editorial material every evening to a service based in Columbus, Ohio. The service, CompuServe Information Service, is available to anyone with a home or office computer at a time-sharing fee.

26. The electronic newspaper system began when the *Columbus Dispatch* joined the program. Subscribers can call up any of the articles in the newspapers and the newspapers will receive 20 percent of the time-sharing charge levied on the subscriber. Initially, only editorial copy will be supplied, but the newspapers are expected to sell national ads on the computer media soon.

27. Another experiment is under way in Coral Gables, Florida, where Knight-Ridder Newspapers is supplying news, advertising, and other consumer services via 200 personal computers installed at no cost in selected homes. If viewers want to order goods they see advertised, they can type messages in their terminals to say where they want the goods delivered, along with the necessary credit card information.

28. The growing use of computer terminals may greatly speed up the arrival of the electronic newspaper. The Source Telecomputing Corporation of America, based in McLean, Virginia, allows its subscribers to access all kinds of information, including the United Press International dispatches from around the world and the *New York Times* Information Bank. In addition, Source subscribers can post messages on an electronic bulletin board, send messages to each other, and play electronic games. The availability of these other services means that people have a variety of reasons for acquiring a computer terminal that, once acquired, can be used for accessing newspaper-type information.

29. The advent of electronic information systems means that people will be able to get more up-to-date information in their areas of interest than is possible with the present publishing methods. Already, book publishers are recognizing the challenge of electronic publishing and are moving into the field themselves. According to one industry estimate, U.S. elementary and high schools

spend about two billion dollars a year on instructional materials. About 3.5 percent of the total goes for computer-based equipment. By 1985, according to one forecast, computer spending may jump to 14 percent—four times greater. Textbook publishers are putting material into computer form so that more people can get computerized instruction.

30. Meanwhile, in the scholarly world, computers and telecommunications are having a wide variety of impacts. For instance, two authors thousands of miles apart may use a computer as a communications link while they are collaborating on a "paper." Each author suggests ideas, paragraphs, clarifications, etc., and watches for misspellings by the other. Eventually the "paper" is completed, and the question then becomes what to do with it. One approach would be to put it into a traditional journal printed on paper. Another approach, however, would be to keep the article in the computer and let other scholars access it by means of their computer terminals. In this way the paper would go only to those really interested in it, and a large amount of paper and mailing costs would be saved.

31. The concept of "networking" has emerged as one of the most exciting ideas in the information area. In a sense, the concept is so natural that one might wonder what the excitement is all about. Networking really implies little more than a shift in the way we view the storage of information. Information can be stored in a large central location, such as a huge computer. However, the same information might be stored in smaller computers at a wide variety of locations. The arrival of microcomputers, which can be bought by ordinary people, has meant that it is possible for a person working in his or her basement to develop a computer program and/or data base that many other people can use. When a system is connected into a network linking up other people's systems at other locations, the individual computer user suddenly has access to enormous resources and also becomes a resource for other people on the network. An individual in the network can be both a user and a supplier of information transmitted by the network.

32. Hundreds of computer networks now are springing up all over the United States. In some instances these networks may consist of nothing more than a few individuals who share an interest in something. In other cases the networks have thousands of individual and organizational members and have easy access to vast stores of information. The networks make it possible for ordinary people to access huge data banks, such as the Index Medicus (medical index), maintained by the National Library of Medicine in Bethesda, Maryland. As these networks grow, each individual will

have increasingly easy access to more and more information. To an increasing degree, we will all be able to find out almost everything we want to know about anything whenever we want it.

33. The impacts of the communications revolution will continue to be pervasive, unsettling, subtle, and mysterious. The new technologies in communications and computers—sometimes abbreviated to "compunications"—will help us to save energy, prevent crime, drive more safely, do more of our work at home, and remove much of the agony of such chores as preparing our income tax returns. On the other hand, the compunications revolution may be expected to destroy many people's jobs and provide new opportunities for crime.

34. The information revolution may also change our views of ourselves. Down through the centuries, human beings have taken pride in their knowledge, even giving themselves the name *Homo sapiens* or "knowing man." But already some computers are smarter than human beings—at least in some respects. In 1980, human and computer chess players squared off at the National Conference on Artificial Intelligence, held at Stanford University in Palo Alto, California. Paul Benjamin, an expert-ranked human from New York City, won one game from a computer but lost a second. An exhausted Benjamin congratulated his opponent for its "brilliant tactical" play. "I was definitely inferior," he admitted ruefully.

Style and Structure

1. A good introduction contains a thesis statement and an indication of the approach to be taken in the body of the essay. Underline the thesis of this article.
2. In paragraph 2 the writer hints at his approach to the topic when he says, "The devices [1] are already available and [2] have begun to move into homes, offices, and factories." Does Cornish maintain this approach consistently in the following sections:
   (a) British systems: paragraphs 18–21;
   (b) French systems: paragraphs 22–23;
   (c) American systems: paragraphs 24–32
       (i) Does the author describe the systems?
       (ii) Does he show how they are moving into homes, offices and factories?
3. (a) What aspect of the subject does Cornish develop in paragraphs 3 to 14?
   (b) In paragraphs 12 and 13, what do the quoted comparisons accomplish?

(c) From your answers to 3(a) and 3(b), draw up a profile of the intended reader.
4. Paragraphs 33 and 34 form the conclusion of the essay.
   (a) What function does each of these paragraphs serve?
   (b) Are both of these functions legitimate for a conclusion? Why?

Thinking and Writing

a. The article presents a variety of uses of "compunications". Choose the one most attractive to you, and write an essay explaining its advantages so that your reader will want to have a terminal in his/her home.
   Audience:
   someone who knows nothing of the new compunications systems.

b. Cornish says, "These new systems promise transformation in the ways we work . . . ." Write an essay on the positive and negative effects such systems may have on the profession for which you are preparing.
   Audience:
   someone presently working in the profession you have chosen. Send a copy of your essay to the person in charge of training you for this profession.

How Telidon may change your life

by Robert Fulford

1. As a household appliance, Telidon may be the most significant event since the telephone. As a way of selling products and shaping the marketplace, it may be the most significant event since television. These are both at the moment extremely chancy propositions, but there is no doubt that a highly sophisticated new form of communication is being created and that Canada is now a leader in its development.
2. Telidon is the system of videotext, or two-way TV, developed at the Department of Communications in Ottawa. The people who created Telidon believe it is the best such system available, and

there is some evidence to support their belief. Several federal agencies in Washington chose Telidon for a field test over Britain's Prestel and France's Antiope, both of which have been more extensively used in tests in recent years. The government of Venezuela has also chosen Telidon for an experiment in communications.

3. Telidon's early success has enormous implications. It may mean that Canada will have a major role as a creator and producer rather than an importer of equipment in the next telecommunications revolution. It may mean that our government engineers have placed us at the centre of a new communications industry rather than on the periphery, where we have so often lived in the past.

4. But as the field tests of Telidon get seriously under way—mostly in Canada—some questions arise. Is there, in fact, a genuine revolution coming? Is Telidon (or some system like it) so valuable that people by the millions will want it or will be persuaded they want it? If the answer is yes, if some large number of homes are equipped with Telidon in the next ten years or so, how will this affect existing institutions?

5. Telidon is an impressive piece of equipment. It consists of a microcomputer, a keyboard, and a television screen—probably the screen that is already used for watching programmes. The screen shows words, numbers, and drawings. You sit at the keyboard, or hold it on your lap, and use it to call up information on the screen. And you can call up, theoretically, *any* information. At the most primitive level you call up the cost of a can of corn at the supermarket. At the most sophisticated level you call up all the information in the British Museum. The determining factor is demand. If the owners of Telidon sets want corn prices, they can have them. If enough of them want the contents of the British Museum, they can have that too. At this stage no one knows what they will want, so no one knows how Telidon will develop. (In 1940, when television was about where Telidon is now, no one understood either the kind of medium it would become or the extent of its growth.)

6. The accelerating development of computers makes Telidon's possibilities almost limitless. Storing vast quantities of text and pictures is of course expensive, but it grows steadily less expensive. Efrem Sigel pointed out in *Videotext: The Coming Revolution in Home/Office Information Retrieval* that "the cost of computer storage is dropping by thirty-five per cent a year, while the cost of performing a given computer operation in a microprocessor is falling nearly as fast. Storing millions of pages of text information in computers was once wildly impractical because of the cost. Today

it is already practical for certain kinds of information. . . ."

7. Some obvious applications can be imagined. A theatre-goer wants information about the plays in town. She consults a little booklet of standard codes and punches the code for theatre. A list of plays appears. She chooses one. The screen announces the cast, author, and director and shows a drawing of the star. She punches more keys and she sees a selection of the reviews. She punches more and sees a plan of the theatre showing which seats are still available. She chooses her seats and punches another code. She has reserved her seats and charged them to her credit card number.

8. Someone else is considering buying a house. He calls up real estate listings and indicates the district he wants and the price he wants to pay. The screen shows a list of addresses. He chooses one. A drawing of the house appears on the screen. He punches more keys and a floor plan appears, followed by credit terms, taxes, and the rest of the information real estate agents normally provide. Without leaving his living room he has learned as much about the house as he could learn without actually visiting it.

9. It's a long way, of course, from the communications systems of the present to Telidon. Between here and there are hundreds of millions of buying decisions and billions of dollars. The supporters of Telidon are still not sure how these decisions will be made—or even *if* they will be made. At the moment the equipment is almost ready for mass production, but will there ever be a mass that justifies the production? Or will Telidon go the way of Facsimile, the system that was supposed to eliminate newspaper delivery by electronically transmitting your newspaper directly into your house? (In the 1940s Facsimile also was technically feasible, but no one ever figured out how to pay for it. Certainly newspaper readers weren't going to pay out a few hundred dollars each just to eliminate the paper carrier. So it never happened.) Television became popular because people could see that it was entertaining: the user-benefit was obvious to anyone. Telidon's user-benefit isn't so clearly evident.

10. There are those who believe Telidon will make its way into our households as a toy—that Telidon entrepreneurs will create so many games that playing with Telidon will become a gigantic international fad and people will buy it for that reason. Douglas Parkhill, the assistant deputy minister who supervised the creation of Telidon in the Department of Communications, does not see it that way. He thinks games involving computers and TV screens will become even more popular but that you won't need Telidon to play them. You can buy them in a cheaper form.

11. Parkhill imagines a more gradual market entry. He sees Telidon making its way slowly into society through business and public

institutions. Businesses will use it as a way of communicating instructions and information among employees. Public institutions will use it as an information or propaganda system: the Venezuelan government is about to place it in booths around Caracas to inform semi-literate migrants to the city about government services. Parkhill envisions companies feeding Telidon advertising into hotels. In one way and another, a large part of society will thus become accustomed to Telidon. After that it will require only a few energetic and well-financed entrepreneurs to begin supplying it (probably over existing TV cable systems) to homes. And after that. . . .

12. A great many things may happen, not all of them pleasant. If Telidon indeed becomes popular, in the way that telephones and TV sets are now popular, then certain institutions will be profoundly shaken. My guess is that, first of all, Telidon will mean the end of daily newspapers in their present form.

13. Newspapers draw roughly a third of their revenues from classified advertising. Telidon, once widely installed and accepted, will quickly take away all of that. It will provide better service, more cheaply, by eliminating waste. When I buy a $50 classified ad in a newspaper, the newspaper has to print it 100,000 times just to reach the thirty people in town who want to buy my stereo. Telidon will simply insert my ad in the computer and *only* those people in the market for my stereo will call it up. Along the way we'll save those 99,970 bits of newsprint on which my ad would have been printed. Keyboarding my ad, inserting it in the computer, may not cost any more than typesetting it at the newspaper.

14. Classified advertising is Telidon at its most primitive. One can imagine the Telidon entrepreneurs, as they grow more imaginative and their equipment grows more sophisticated, drawing away many forms of display advertising, such as the pages devoted to supermarkets. The only kind of advertising they won't be able to take (so far as anyone can guess) is the kind that consumers won't be prompted to call up—the kind that attempts to enhance the value of a product by glamorous settings and the kind that sells products no one would think of until they are advertised, such as vaginal deodorants.

15. Douglas Parkhill imagines Telidon, as it moves through its first few phases, developing in a dozen other ways. It may bring electronic mail, changing the postal service entirely: you compose a letter on your screen, then transmit it electronically to the recipient, whose computer holds it until he or she is ready to read it. Parkhill thinks newspapers and magazines may be transmitted by Telidon—though the screen will have to become easier to read before that happens. Writers may offer their work

at a fee on Telidon, bypassing publishers. University courses by Telidon may be offered, for those who enjoy loneliness.

16. In the book *Gutenberg 2: The New Electronics and Social Change,* the novelist and publisher David Godfrey writes that Telidon and related developments are about to produce not just a slight alteration in the way we receive information, "but a quite magical change, a change almost as exciting as the first telephone must have been in rural areas, but with an impact far more fundamental." Certainly television did that. Telidon may well do the same: change our lives in ways that no one, not even its creators, can now imagine.

Style and Structure

1. A good introduction contains a thesis statement and a brief indication of how the body of the essay is organized.
   (a) Underline the thesis statement in Fulford's introduction (paragraphs 1 to 4).
   (b) Locate the part of the introduction that points out how the body of the essay is organized. How does this device help the reader?
2. What devices does the writer use in paragraph 1 to get the reader's interest and attention?
3. Paragraphs 2 and 3 tell us a great deal about the intended reader of this article. Describe this reader and discuss why Fulford found it necessary to include these paragraphs.
4. Using the information located for question 1(b), draw up a plan of the organization of the body of the essay.
5. The body of the essay has three main divisions. What is the relationship of the first sentence of each to the remainder of that section? Why is this an effective structural device?
6. What is the relationship of paragraphs 7 and 8 to paragraphs 5 and 6? Why, then, does the author include paragraphs 7 and 8?
7. What devices does the writer use in the concluding paragraph to tie it to paragraph 1? Why?

Thinking and Writing

a. Fulford states, "If the owners of Telidon sets want corn prices, they can have them. If enough of them want the contents of the British Museum, they can have that too. At this stage no one knows what they will want, so no one knows how Telidon will develop."
   Write an essay in which you outline a use for Telidon that you would personally find valuable. Be sure to use one or more specific illustrations.

Audience:
someone who knows nothing about Telidon.

b. From the essays written by class members for section a, select the three uses of Telidon that you believe will prove most practical and most popular. Write a report outlining these uses.
Audience:
someone who works with Telidon and will be responsible for developing its programs.
Send a copy of your essay to the public relations department of Telidon.

Earth's biggest blast

by Walter Sullivan

1. A Czechoslovakian scientist has come up with a new explanation for what was by far the largest — and most mysterious — explosion ever recorded on earth.
2. The blast, high in the air over the remote region of Podkamennaya in Siberia on June 30, 1908, blew down trees for 20 to 30 miles in all directions. Horses 400 miles away were blown off their feet, and residents of a trading station 40 miles away were knocked unconscious and suffered flash burns.
3. The explosion was equivalent to a 10- to 15-megaton nuclear device and devastated an area of about 1,500 square miles.
4. Investigation of the event was hampered because its location was so remote that no scientist reached the area until 19 years later, although probably no phenomenon in history has evoked so much scientific speculation. These have ranged from suggestions of spontaneous nuclear explosions, alien spaceships crashing to earth and falling comet heads.
5. The comet-head theory has now received support through a little-noticed proposal from L. Kresak of the Slovak Academy of Sciences in Bratislava, Czechoslovakia. He suggests that the blast occurred when a huge "boulder" shed by Comet Encke exploded in the atmosphere. Mr. Kresak noticed that the June 30 explosion coincided with the peak of an annual meteor shower. Such showers of "shooting stars" occur when the earth passes through debris left by a comet that has been partially torn apart during repeated close passes by the sun.

6. The shower that peaks on June 30 each year originates in the constellation Taurus and is attributed to debris from Encke, a comet that orbits the sun every 3.3 years.

7. Mr. Kresak believes that the components of comet fragments that make comets and their tails glow are gradually boiled away by solar heat, leaving only "cometary boulders." These, he reported recently in the Bulletin of the Astronomical Institute of Czechoslovakia, probably constitute "an overwhelming majority" of interplanetary objects one to a hundred yards in diameter.

8. According to his hypothesis, such an object would become so hot during its plunge through the atmosphere that it would explode in a catastrophic manner. When large meteorites hit the earth, they generate explosions sufficient to gouge out craters, but no crater was formed by the Siberian blast, possibly because the "boulder" was not large enough to do so.

9. In recent years, scientists have noted many features of the 1908 blast resembling those of a powerful nuclear explosion. According to a recent account in the British journal *Nature*, a small amount of excess radioactivity has been found in the area.

10. Furthermore, the trees at ground zero—the point directly below the explosion—were not blown down but were stripped of bark and branches like telephones poles, an effect also seen at Hiroshima after the atomic bomb.

11. In 1967, the prestigious scientific journal, Soviet Physics-Doklady, published an analysis by Alexei V. Zolotov of the Ioffe Physio-Technical Institute of the Soviet Academy of Sciences, who had accompanied an expedition to the site. He concluded that the effects were those of a thermo-nuclear explosion, such as that of a hydrogen bomb. The nuclear explosion idea was again argued in 1975 by Professor Ari Ben-Menahem of the Weizmann Institute in Israel. He analyzed records of shock waves recorded around the world both in the atmosphere and within the earth—the entire planet trembled from the blast—and concluded that the explosion was probably "an extra-terrestrial nuclear missile" of 10 to 15 megatons.

12. Last summer, the theory that the blast was the explosion of a nuclear-powered space ship was revived in reports widely circulated by Tass, the Soviet press agency. Despite all these arguments, most scientists have found the nuclear explosion idea far-fetched and prefer such explanations as the fall of a comet head.

13. But in 1965, the Nobel laureate Willard Libby and two colleagues questioned the comet theory because no comet had been seen approaching the earth. They suggested, instead, the fall of an "antirock"—a meteorite formed of antimatter.

14. Each atomic particle has a twin that is identical but opposite in

138

such characteristics as electrical charge. These are the particles of antimatter and when such a particle meets one of matter, they annihilate one another in a violent burst of gamma rays.

15. This reaction would account for the explosion and also create a large amount of radioactive carbon which should later have become incorporated into the trees at the blast area. Dr. Libby and his colleagues found a small excess of the carbon in rings formed in two trees during 1909, but they concluded that it was not sufficient to support the antimatter idea.

16. In 1973, two scientists at the Centre for Relativity Theory of the University of Texas proposed that the event was caused by a tiny black hole, a hypothetical object compressed to such density that its gravity would not permit the escape of light. Such an object, they reasoned, would go through the earth.

17. Their much-publicized proposal helped bring the concept of black holes wide public attention, but did not gain any scientific adherents.

18. The most widely accepted view of comet heads is the "dirty snowball" hypothesis of Fred L. Whipple at the Smithsonian Astrophysical Observatory in Cambridge, Mass. He sees them as a mixture of dust and frozen gases but adds that he is not convinced of Mr. Kresak's boulder theory, but "has an open mind."

19. While the comet-fragment proposal is the front-runner at the moment, the mystery may never be settled to the satisfaction of everyone. At least not, as Professor Ben-Menahem has pointed out, until there is a recurrence. In that case, though the mystery may be cleared up, the other consequences may be disastrous, especially if the explosion occurs over an inhabited area and is mistaken for a nuclear attack.

Style and Structure

1. Another possible opening statement for this article is:
   "A Czechoslovakian scientist has introduced a new theory about the 1908 explosion in Podkamennaya, Siberia."
   From the point of view of the reader, would this introduction be as effective as the one in the article? Give reasons for your answer.

2. What purposes do paragraphs 2 and 3 serve in the introduction? How does the writer's choice of words and illustrations heighten the dramatic effect?

3. List in order the different explanations for the explosion presented in the article.
   (a) Can you detect a logical reason why the writer has presented the theories in the order he does?
   (b) Underline the first sentence in each explanation. How

does this sentence function in relation to the rest of the explanation?

(c) Where does the topic statement appear in the section dealing with antimatter?

4. How does paragraph 18 help to unify the article?

5. In the concluding paragraph the writer summarizes the article in the first sentence. For what purposes does he use the remainder of his conclusion?

Thinking and Writing

a. Write an essay in which you either support or refute the proposition that "the Podkamennaya blast was the result of extraterrestrial visitation." Although you may never have heard of this explosion before, there is quite a large amount of material written on it. The newspapers, magazines and books in your library should provide extensive information. (Be sure to use such aids as *The Reader's Guide to Periodical Literature*, *The Canadian Index*, or the index to a major newspaper to save yourself time and effort.)

Audience:

someone who is only aware of the sensationalized aspects of the blast and yet would take a position on the proposition that would be opposed to yours; an average "non-scientific" reader.

b. Write an essay in which you argue for *or* against the theory that the earth has been visited by extraterrestrial beings. You will find such books as *Chariots of the Gods* and *Crash Go the Chariots of the Gods* useful when researching the topic, but be careful to document your sources of information.

Audience:

the "average" reader of a science magazine who could be expected to have some knowledge about the topic, would prize logical thinking, and would oppose your position on the theory. Send a copy of your essay to the editor of a science magazine.

Winter camping can be fun

by Berndt Berglund with Jack Batten

1. Not very long after I came to Canada, I was snowshoeing in the Yukon when a blizzard blew up. I was with an Indian guide that

day, moving behind him, and the snow made it difficult for me to see ahead. So I pushed my parka top back. In a few minutes, my hands and feet became painfully cold and I found it harder to walk.

2. The guide turned and looked at me. Immediately he grabbed my parka top and pulled it tight on my forehead. Within five minutes, the warmth started to return to my hands and feet. I had learned a valuable lesson about coping with cold: To keep your hands and feet warm, cover your head.

3. The body is a complex radiator, and one of its quirks is that the degree of heat in the head has a direct correlation to the heat in the extremities. If your hands and feet are cold, put a hat on. If you feel overheated, don't uncover your head; unzip the front of your parka. My guide understood the hat-on-the-head lesson from his people's long experience in the wilderness. And it is the sort of practical knowledge that you must grasp if you want to get in on the fun of winter camping.

4. Many Canadians, I've discovered, are keen to do so. Winter camping opens the door to all kinds of family activities, such as cross-country skiing, ice fishing, hunting, and cold-weather tramping. And it is a perfectly safe and invigorating experience as long as you approach it with care and preparation. The key step is to buy the correct equipment and make proper use of it in the wilderness. Tempted? If you are, here is some guidance that will enhance your pleasure.

5. *Clothing.* From the skin out, here's what you should wear: Norwegian string-net underwear, long-sleeved woolen shirt, woolen pants, silk socks under woolen socks, silk gloves under woolen mittens, and a parka jacket with a sturdy hood.

6. There's a reason for each item. Take the underwear. The best insulation the body has is supplied by the layer of air that clings to it; and string-net underwear doesn't interfere with this clinging air. Be certain, too, that the underwear is made of cotton, because cotton admits the wetness from the body's sweat and passes it on to the wool of the shirt without getting wet itself. Silk has the same property; hence the silk gloves and socks. You don't want anything wet next to your skin in frigid temperatures.

7. *Boots.* For dry snow, wear traditional Eskimo mukluks. When you're not wearing them, leave them outside your tent or trailer so they won't develop moisture. For all other conditions, wear waterproof, insulated sports or snowmobile boots. Make sure you put waffle-woven insoles into them, because they preserve that all-important clinging air.

8. *Food.* To generate the heat that'll keep you functioning in sub-zero temperatures, you must plan on digesting 2000 extra calories per day. Work out menus that are high in fat content. Stay away from

dehydrated solid foods, and use canned foods instead. Corned beef and pork and beans may not sound like gourmet's delights, but you'd be surprised how delicious they are beside a campfire at 30 degrees below zero.

9. *Drink*. Never neglect the minimum two quarts of fluid everybody needs every day. The best kinds are tea and soup. When you're out on the ski trail or strolling through the woods, call a halt every now and then to heat up a brew of tea. Another liquid I take regularly is orange drink: two glasses a day of melted snow and orange-flavor crystals. A point to remember is that exposure to extreme cold and alcoholic spirits don't mix. (Alcohol slows down mental and muscular functions, and lowers body temperature by causing the capillaries to dilate.)

10. Liquids are also a reliable alarm clock. Drink three glasses of water or tea, and you'll be awake early and anxious to go to the bathroom. This introduces another problem.

11. *Toilet*. If you don't urinate properly — a tough trick in the wilderness at sub-zero temperatures — then you're going to end up with dangerous wetness in your sleeping bag or run the risk of frostbite outside. And what compounds the difficulty is that in cold weather you have to urinate much more often than in warm weather.

12. Here's my advice. Take along a supply of small, plastic garbage bags. Put three or four inside your sleeping bag, for use one at a time as required. Then, twist the top of the bag until it's tight, apply the wire tie, and empty the bag later. On a cold, windy day, to avoid frostbite or wetness on the clothing, simply use the bag and empty it.

13. Now that's fine for men, but how about women? Well, there is a new and ingenious invention available called a feminine hygiene device (FHD). I know that it works because in 1975 I took 40 female nurses on a 12-day program of winter training at Sioux Lookout in northern Ontario. The temperature, adding the wind-chill factor, was 70 below zero. They said the FHD was 100-percent effective.

14. *Sleep*. Can you stand a mummy bag? It is a sleeping bag that encloses every part of your body except the face. It's tricky to master; you have to learn to take it with you when you turn. If you turn inside it, you'll end up in a corkscrew position. But if you can handle it, the mummy bag solves all your winter sleeping problems. Otherwise, buy an ordinary rectangular sleeping bag. Forget about air mattresses and cots because they leave cold air in the space between you and the ground. Take three or four inner linings along and, when it's colder than usual, use them to build up protection inside the bag.

15. Ideally, your sleeping bag should sit on three or four inches of snow; temperatures there will be several degrees higher than ground

142

level. Throw down a mat of polyurethane foam three quarters of an inch thick as insulation. Then lay your sleeping bag on top of the mat and you're set for the night.

16. *Other equipment*. Any good sturdy tent will do, and you'll find it's just about as easy to set up in cold weather as in warm. If you find it difficult to drive stakes into the ground, secure the tent to trees, logs or rocks — or place heavy gear in the tent corners to hold them out. Whatever heater you choose, be certain you buy the proper fuel. Carry two containers of waterproof matches, one in your pants pocket, the other in your packsack. When you are packing, place your sleeping bag at the top of the sack; this will distribute the weight better and make lifting and walking easier.

17. Finally, go to a familiar site. National and provincial parks are an excellent bet because there'll be rangers and other people in the neighborhood who can help you in a crisis. Before you set out, make sure you tell someone exactly where you're going and when you'll be back. If you're not home by the designated hour, a search-and-rescue operation can be organized quickly. Don't be unreliable about the duration and locale of your camping — like the man who went hunting near Kapuskasing, Ont., in 1971. He wasn't home by his stated time, and a relative gave the alarm. The air force, the police and local people started to search an area of 256,000 square miles. On the tenth day of the search, the hunter walked cheerfully out of the bush wondering what all the fuss was about. He'd met a couple of buddies and simply extended his hunting trip. His thoughtlessness cost taxpayers $300,000.

18. Once you've taken all precautions, you're free for winter fun. Maybe you'll even try my sport from the Yukon, snowshoeing. It's tough to master; or so I thought until my daughter took it up a few winters ago. I always considered myself an expert, but now she's out in front of me. And she's all of 12 years old.

Style and Structure

1. Why does the writer open his article with an anecdote instead of a thesis statement? Why does he select this particular anecdote?
2. Underline the thesis statement and draft a plan of the essay's organization.
3. The writer seldom recommends or condemns a piece of equipment without an explanation. Why is this approach superior to simply offering a list?
4. What purpose does the last sentence in paragraphs 4 and 10 serve?
5. Do the headings (food, clothing, etc.) help or hinder the reader's comprehension of the material? Are the sections they

introduce organized in any particular order? For what types of essay development would the "headings" approach be inappropriate?

6. Why is the conclusion weak? Write a more appropriate conclusion. Why is yours more appropriate? (You might want to compare your conclusion with those of others in your class.)

Thinking and Writing

a. 1. One of the most difficult writing situations is one in which you have to explain ideas or processes that you know very well to someone who has no knowledge whatsoever about the topic. The mind subconsciously uses the "jargon" that comes from familiarity with the topic, or assumes that another person's thinking patterns operate in exactly the same way as yours do, or makes leaps of logic that are clear to you but baffling to the reader.

   In order to get some idea of the difficulty of this task, write a short essay in which you explain to a reader who knows absolutely nothing about the topic how to carry out some relatively simple task (e.g., how to sharpen a pencil, how to light a cigarette, how to open and close a door).

   2. The class will divide itself into pairs and exchange papers. One at a time, each partner will act out the task exactly according to the written instructions. Remember that you are playing the role of someone who knows nothing about the task. If, for example, you are given instructions on how to light a cigarette, that say "put the cigarette in your mouth", do just as you are told and put the whole cigarette in your mouth. You may add further oral instructions as you see your reader beginning to do something incorrectly, but only after you observe the procedure going wrong. Do not give a running commentary on your intentions.

   3. Rewrite the essay. Incorporate all of the changes that you found necessary to communicate your message accurately. Submit all drafts of this essay to your instructor.

b. Articles such as this one can sometimes be dangerous. They may make a hazardous endeavour sound glamorous and attractive to very inexperienced readers. Write an essay that would serve as a publication put out by the Ministry of Natural Resources warning people of the dangers of winter camping and advising them of the correct way to go about it.

Audience:

a reader who is completely unfamiliar with the subject and who may have only very limited experience with outdoor winter activities.

Send a copy of your paper to one of the following agencies and enquire whether the group would be interested in using the paper as an educational publication:
a local Conservation Authority;
the local Parks and Recreation Department;
the superintendent of a provincial or national park; or
a local chapter of the Boy Scouts.

Fiber optics: a growing technology

1. As a new technology for data transmission, fiber optics is expected to spawn a market of at least $1 billion within a decade, according to one U.S.-based market research firm. Another has forecast a worldwide market totalling more than $1.58 billion through the 1980/1990 decade.
2. Although the largest part of this market is expected to come from the telephone industry, other significant applications of fiber optics are already being found in electronic data processing, cable TV, military and industrial equipment.
3. Fiber optics technology involves the transmission of light along a solid fiber of glass or plastic. The fiber is typically only a few thousandths of an inch in diameter—not much larger than a human hair. The material is treated so that light remains inside the fiber as it travels from the light source at one end to a light detector at the other. Very little light escapes through the wall of the fiber.
4. Information or data can be transmitted along with the light so that fiber optic cable can be used in place of copper cable in telecommunications and information systems. Fiber optics has the advantage that the cable is much smaller in size than the copper cable necessary to transmit equivalent data. Fiber optics systems are also immune to electrical interference and remote eavesdropping.
5. Unlike copper cable, the principal raw material for which is subject to shortages and pricing fluctuations, optical fiber is made basically from sand which, as one market research report points out, is in plentiful supply in all of the continents of the world and "the price is right". However, considerable skill is needed to avoid tiny bubbles or impurities which interfere with the fibers' light-carrying capability.

Meeting the market

6. Companies both large and small are developing new products to meet the requirements of the burgeoning market.

7. A complete fiber optic link for data communications applications that requires no expertise in optical design, calibration or adjustment has been introduced by Hewlett-Packard. Their HFBR-0010 low error rate fiber optic link system comes ready to hook up. It consists of a digital transmitter, a digital receiver, a single fiber 10 metre connector/cable assembly and complete technical literature. Each of the components is available separately and the connector/cable assemblies come in five standard lengths, with a maximum distance of 100 metres.

8. Typical applications of the new link include large computer installations; distributed processing systems; hospital computer systems; power plant communications and control; process control; secure communications; aircraft or shipboard data links; high voltage or electromagnetic field research; remote instrumentation systems; and factory data collection. The HP fiber optic system can replace traditional wires to provide a communications link between computers, computers and their peripherals, and computers and other digital instruments.

9. Canstar Communications of Scarborough, Ontario, is a company working on a variety of projects in different fiber optics market application areas. Its Advanced Systems Division was awarded a $2 million subcontract by the Harris Corporation of Florida to supply and install a 50 km optical cable subsystem for Alberta Government Telephones. The cable is designed to carry a total of 20,160 simultaneous telephone conversations along twelve optical fibers designed for low loss light transmission.

10. Canstar has recently announced the availability of fiber optic directional couplers designed for use as both taps and feeds in fiber optic systems. Used as taps, the couplers serve to divide the optical power in a single channel and distribute it among one or more secondary channels. For instance, they permit the attachment of several computer terminals to a single data bus for multi-drop systems. As feeds, the couplers can be used to feed signals from one channel into another to merge channels to or from an optical source. The couplers are packaged for industrial and telecommunication applications.

11. According to Dr. Mike Dudley, Director of Canstar's Optical Fiber Products Division, these couplers have the capability of being adaptable to future high volume, low cost commercial applications such as, for example, CATV. Since the design permits the introduction of high quantity manufacturing economies, "Fiber optic couplers are no longer complex multicomponent laboratory

curiosities," said Dr. Dudley. "They can now be confidently engineered into communications and data networks with the realistic expectation of consistent performance and future cost savings."

12. The 3M Company's Electronic Products Division has introduced a TTL-compatible fiber optic data link which combines two transceiver (transmitter/receiver) modules and a preterminated duplex cable 30 metres long. Interconnection of the link to a PC board is accomplished by bringing the necessary signals to a standard 3M PC board header. The transceiver module measures $3/8$ x $1 1/4$ x $2 1/2$ inches and is thin enough to be used in a card cage without modification. The data link uses a duplex cable with two discrete low-loss plastic-clad silica fibers in a PVC-jacketed flat cable configuration that permits simultaneous transmission and reception of data. A reinforced cable is available for additional protection of optical fibers in longer or rugged wiring applications. Cable attenuation typically is 30 dB per kilometre, and connector attenuation is 1 dB per mated pair.

13. Fiber optics technology is being used in an office printer to produce high-quality printed documents 50 times faster than conventional typewriters. The intelligent "Image Printer" was recently unveiled by Wang Laboratories Inc. It converts characters from a CRT screen into light images that are "painted" by fiber optics onto plain paper coated with a dry toner such as that used in copiers. This combination of technologies produces an original document of typewriter-like quality at a rate of 18 pages per minute. By comparison, a conventional typewriter output device produces only one page every three minutes while standard printers usually put out about one-half page per minute.

14. A pioneer in fiber optics, the Du Pont Company first made its "Crofon" flexible plastic fibers line commercially available in 1969. Best known for their function in dashboard illumination and headlight and taillight monitoring in automobiles, "Crofon" fiber optics are now finding use for signal transmission in electronic equipment, electrical controls, business machines and communications equipment, as well as in advertising displays, signs, medical equipment, aircraft, detection devices and photographic systems.

15. The firm has designated "Pifax" as the trademark for its fiber optic cable line used for data communications. It was formerly known as PFX fiber optic cable. "Pifax" fiber optic cables, designed for short and medium-run lengths of under one kilometre, are reinforced with "Kevlar" 49 aramid fibers in a protective jacket of "Hytrel" polyester elastomer. They offer large diameter cores, large numerical apertures, hard cladding and easy connection.

An experimental kit

16. To help control and circuit designers to evaluate fiber optics and demonstrate how readily available, low-cost semiconductor components may be used to construct dc control and digital communications systems, AMP Inc. has produced the "Optimate" fiber optic experimental kit.

17. The kit provides the semiconductor devices for transmitter and receiver circuits, circuit boards, waveguides, connectors, tools, and instructions to build several different fiber optic systems. Experimenters can construct systems which are TTL and CMOS compatible, which are operational for most low frequency data links and short length experiments. Links up to 20 metres (for one megabit systems) and as long as 45 metres (one kilobit systems) can be produced.

18. The kit will not produce "saleable" systems, but it can bring an experimental fiber optic link to about 85 percent of the way toward a final commercial design.

19. Fiber optics offer many advantages for data transmission, such as immunity from interference, dielectric isolation, reduced size and weight, increased bandwidth, increased safety, installation ease, and less vulnerability to "bugging". The next decade should provide a wealth of applications which, at this time, we can only imagine.

Style and Structure

1. This article was written for professional engineers. Why would paragraph 1 attract the attention of such a readership?
2. Underline the thesis statement and draft a plan of the essay's organization.
3. What does the writer do in paragraphs 3 to 5? What assumption is he making about his readers by including this information? What assumption would he be making if he excluded it?
4. What function does paragraph 7 serve?
5. How is the information in paragraphs 6 to 18 organized? How does this organization meet the requirements of engineers interested in how the latest developments in fiber optics apply to their companies?
6. How does the final paragraph serve as a good conclusion?

Thinking and Writing

a. Write an essay on "Fiber Optics" that is intended to be an article in one of the general circulation newspapers in your area. You may want to use basic information from the article or from other authoritative sources, but be careful to adapt your

148

vocabulary, total length, structure and organization and so on, to fit your particular audience.

Audience:

a reader who has so little involvement with technology that he/she has never even heard of fiber optics.

b. Select a basic concept, process, or other technical description from your area of specialization and explain it in language which the non-specialist can understand. An electrical technology student could describe parallel and series circuits; an early childhood student could define the psychological term "projection". Do not forget to use illustrations and examples where their inclusion will help clarify your description.

Audience:

a reader who has no knowledge whatsoever about your subject and only the vaguest notion about the field from which it is drawn.

Send a copy of your paper to a local newspaper; ask them to use it as an article.

What do we really know about psychic phenomena?

by Laile E. Bartlett

1. A mother dreamed that in two hours a violent storm would loosen a heavy chandelier which would fall on her baby's crib. She awoke her husband. "A silly dream," he said. "The weather is clear. Go to sleep!" But she brought the baby to her bed. In two hours a storm came up, and the light fixture fell on the crib.
2. Eating lunch at school, a 13-year-old girl "heard" her little sister screaming. She ran home to find the child had cut her hand almost in half. She summoned the doctor, who arrived in time to save her sister from bleeding to death.
3. This is the world of Psi (psychic phenomena) — or ESP (extrasensory perception), as it is often popularly known. It has been blocked off from us by our conditioning. For decades we've been taught that what is "real" is only what our five senses perceive. Today some scientists tell us that Psi is our new frontier. They see a future world where we can be in instant touch with others around the globe, hurdle time and space with a leap of the mind, know the

future, the past and the present, and cure our ills through the power of the mind.

4. Yet Psi is controversial. It is an open invitation to charlatans who prey on confused and eager seekers. For many, it opens a closet they'd rather keep shut: "My dreams keep coming true. Am I going crazy?"

5. There has been small place for the psychic in the standard scientific world. Paul Kurtz, professor of philosophy at the State University of New York at Buffalo, speaks for many skeptical scientists when he says: "We are disturbed that only so-called positive results are published. The public rarely hears about negative findings, which are considerable." But Stanley Krippner, chairman of a Psi advisory committee at the Smithsonian, takes issue with Kurtz, saying, "In the ten years of our work in ESP and dreams at Maimonides Medical Center in Brooklyn, N.Y., we published all our results, negative or positive. For many years parapsychologists have been the outcasts of science. Fortunately, this is changing because of recent improvements in experimentation."

6. Pinning down psychic phenomena is a slow, exacting process. Because the whole field is on trial, serious Psi researchers are super strict in their methods and conservative in their professional reporting. Nonetheless, from their experiments here's what we know:
   People can and do communicate by means other than five senses: telepathy.

7. Telepathy comes through in everyday incidents and serious warnings. A waitress "gets the message" and hands a man his order before he gives it. A Texas teacher breaks a rule and leaves her students to be near the telephone. It rings: "Come at once; your sister is dying."
   People can and do pick up information on remote or hidden objects, persons or events: clairvoyance.

8. Under laboratory controls at Stanford Research Institute, scientists Harold Puthoff and Russell Targ studied the clairvoyant abilities of controversial Israeli Uri Geller. Seven times in a row, Geller accurately drew a picture hidden in two sealed opaque envelopes. Ten times without error, he identified which of ten identical sealed cans contained an object. The odds are one in a billion!

9. The Stanford Research Institute also verified clairvoyant abilities in six subjects with no previous psychic experience. All were able to describe in detail distant "target areas" picked by the scientists.
   People can and do sense what is going to happen before it takes place: precognition.

10. In one of 15,000 validated cases compiled by Louisa Rhine of the

Institute of Parapsychology in Durham, N.C., a 19-year-old California girl canceled plans to go to a funeral. She "had" to get to her mother. When she got home, her parents were calmly sitting in the living room. She "had" to get them out of their chairs. She claimed to be hungry and talked them into a snack in the kitchen. No sooner had they left the living room than a car crashed into the house, destroying the chairs in which the parents had been sitting.

11. So accurate have "hunches" of major events proved to be that premonitions registries have been set up in New York and California. A few of the "hits" in registry files are the tragedy at Chappaquiddick, space-program failures and Martin Luther King's assassination.

People can and do move or affect objects without touching them: psychokinesis.

12. After watching a film of the great Russian sensitive Nina Kulagina moving objects by gestures only or with her eyes, Felicia Parise of the Maimonides Dream Laboratory performed some of the same feats under controlled conditions.

13. Bernard Grad, a biochemist at McGill University in Montreal, moistened seeds with water "treated" by a healer. Compared with a control group using ordinary water, "treated" seedlings grew faster and weighed more at the end of the strictly monitored experiment. Impressed with Grad's work, biophysicist M. Justa Smith of the Human Dimensions Institute, Canandaigua, N.Y., demonstrated that an enzyme "treated" by the same healer showed significantly more activity than the "untreated."

14. With so much evidence now established concerning these four Psi or ESP phenomena, what about the scientific search for conditions under which they operate? Some discoveries so far are the following:

   (i)   Distance doesn't seem to matter. ESP has been recorded in the same room, and from outer space.

  (ii) People who believe in ESP, or want it to work, usually do better at it.

 (iii) People who feel close to each other appear to communicate better.

 (iv) Shock events, such as accidents and disasters, come through — or are reported — much more often than neutral or happy ones.

  (v) ESP is more effective in altered states of consciousness such as deep relaxation, hypnosis and sleep. Most of the reported cases of precognition occur in dreams.

15. In some areas, there is less scientific consensus: Do psychic healers really heal? What about reincarnation? Is there such a thing as an "out-of-body" experience?

16. Psychologist Charles Tart, of the University of California at Davis,

discovered a "Miss Z" for whom out-of-body experiences were so normal that when she was a child she thought everybody had them. In an elaborately prepared experiment, he arranged for her to sleep in a lab, with electrodes recording her brain waves, and "read" a randomly chosen five-digit number put on a shelf high over her head. While confined to her bed by the medical paraphernalia, she "floated up" and correctly identified the number.

17. The major dilemma in all such experiments is *how* do you get scientific validation for Psi? The very tools and technology which would document psychic phenomena are based on the old premise that scientific fact is only what you can measure and observe. However, such metaphysical material by its nature resists capture, often going dead or turning off in a laboratory situation. Many people are instantly constrained when hitched up to a machine in a cubicle.

18. A noted psychic healer, Olga Worrall, recalls: "The first time I concentrated on a damaged leaf for a healing experiment, I 'burned it up.' I had to 'tone down' for the laboratory." Most of those who can work at all under laboratory conditions tend to taper off after a time — what scientists call the "decline effect."

19. Psychic Ingo Swann is a striking example of this scientific dilemma. Though he has been dramatically successful as a subject in rigidly controlled lab experiments — for instance, making temperature readings on instruments in insulated containers hotter or colder by force of will — indications are that such feats reveal only a portion of his psychic potential.

20. In out-of-body experiments — or remote viewing, as some researchers prefer to call it — Swann can "go" to any spot on the globe, given its latitude and longitude, and sketch correctly the mountains, rivers, roads and buildings just as they are at that point.

21. When asked in an experiment at the American Society for Psychical Research in New York to "go" to a hidden box and describe its contents, Swann rejoined, "You forgot to turn on the light in the box. It's dark." He was correct!

22. But these are minor accomplishments compared to what Swann and his colleagues seem able to do on their own. Once, filled with ennui by months of lab work in California, Swann phoned his friend, psychic Harold Sherman, 1500 miles away in Arkansas, and proposed they take a 600-million-mile trip together and "go" simultaneously to Jupiter, which neither of them knew anything about, but which Pioneer 10 was scheduled to pass. Sherman agreed. Their respective observations of colors, landscapes, atmosphere and other conditions were filed the next day with astrophysicists and showed remarkable convergence. Nor were they far off from the Pioneer 10 data.

23. Challenged by a science editor, they turned their attention to Mercury, by which Mariner 10 was soon to pass and radio back data. Prevailing opinion was that Mercury had neither atmosphere nor magnetic field. Yet each psychic reported a thin atmosphere and a magnetic field — confirmed by Mariner 10 within the month.

24. On one thing numerous authorities agree: everyone has some degree of Psi. In not too many people, however, has the power begun to surface, and experts caution against trying to force it. California clinical psychologist Allan Y. Cohen points out, "There are at least 2000 documented cases of individuals needing psychological help, because of symptoms caused by prematurely and forcibly trying to develop psychic powers." Ernest Pecci, whose psychiatric specialty is "salvaging psychic casualties," warns against pushing into the unknown Psi jungle without guides and help. We must avoid phony gurus, drug-induced "trips," and take our cues from serious scientists.

25. We may not know exactly *what* Psi is, or exactly *how* it works, but we do know *that* it works. And as pragmatists we are already employing it:

26. ▶ *In detective work.* A major retail chain in Toronto engaged a man with precognitive abilities to spot people about to shoplift. He's correctly tabbed thousands — even predicting *what* they will take minutes before they do take it.

27. Psychic Gerard Croiset of Utrecht, the Netherlands, is noted for unraveling many crimes. He can pick up cues on the telephone. Once, called from a town some miles away to help locate a missing man, Croiset was able to say that the man had committed suicide by jumping off a bridge. His description of the locale was so accurate that police found the body by that afternoon.

28. ▶ *In locating resources.* Clairvoyance is now being used to find water, minerals and archeological treasures. On play-by-play instructions from psychic Aron Abrahamsen, for instance, geologist-archeologist Jeffrey Goodman dug up deeply buried artifacts in Flagstaff, Arizona, which were over 100,000 years old — what could be the oldest clear-cut evidence of man in the Americas. Of Abrahamsen's 58 specific predictions tested so far in this case, 51 have proved correct. "ESP is replacing the spade as archeology's primary tool," says Goodman.

29. ▶ *In health work.* Psychic healings may become commonplace someday. It is estimated that 70 percent of illnesses are brought on by stress and thinking oneself sick. "If you can think yourself sick, why not think yourself well?" asks osteopathic physician Irving Oyle. He is part of a growing network which practices "holistic" medicine, based on the power of consciousness to influence the

body. "Treating disease through the mind is the coming thing in medicine," he declares. "But don't put me in the spook section. I'm just a family doctor turned medical researcher, trying to find out what it is that gets people well."

30. "One can become aware of the flow of energy within oneself and use it," says Jack Schwarz. He can control his bodily functions much as do the yogis in India. He can thrust an unsterilized knitting needle through his biceps, with no pain, bleeding or subsequent infection, the wound closing when the needle is withdrawn and healing completely within a day or two. Schwarz's ability has been observed in the research department of the Menninger Foundation and elsewhere. A number of researchers believe that his self-healing ability can be learned. Schwarz devotes himself now to his own Aletheia Psychophysical Foundation in Oregon and teaches doctors and others "energy flow" techniques for preventing and healing disease.

31. Beyond all this, Psi presents us with hints of a universal unity. Individual consciousness, it would appear, is part of a consciousness we all share. Each of us is part of everyone and everything in the universe. "Thou canst not stir a flower without troubling of a star," as visionary-poet Francis Thompson put it.

32. The deeper the psychic scientist probes, the closer he comes to the mystical religious vision. The Unity, the One, is the central concept and experience of all mysticism.

33. And the more the physicist, traditional defender of materialist science, dissects physical reality, the closer he edges toward that same view. Quantum physicist Max Planck noted that it is impossible to obtain an adequate version of the laws we are seeking unless the physical system is regarded as a whole.

34. It was this Oneness that struck astronaut Edgar Mitchell on his trip to the moon, "merging the boundaries of the self with the cosmos." Then and there, Mitchell pledged his life and career to the understanding of consciousness, and its effect on the human condition. "We can't all go to the moon," he admits, "but perhaps the deeper awareness of Psi processes can provide the same perspective."

35. People were aghast when Copernicus proclaimed that the earth circles the sun. But the new view won out.

36. We may be at another such turning point today. In the words of Willis Harman of Stanford Research Institute, "Psychic research in the next few decades may be destined to have an impact comparable to the impact a few centuries ago of Galileo and Copernicus."

Style and Structure

1.   Why does Bartlett begin the article with two illustrations?

2. Although Bartlett goes to great lengths to appear objective in the introduction (paragraphs 1 to 5), she is, in fact, carefully manipulating the reader to believe in the validity of Psi phenomena. What techniques does Bartlett use to manipulate the reader?

3. Underline the thesis statement and draft a plan of the article's organization.

4. (a) In paragraph 6 Bartlett claims, "... serious Psi researchers are super strict in their methods and conservative in their professional reporting." Examine the evidence she presents in paragraphs 7 to 13; which "proofs" actually conform to her claim about the methods of serious Psi researchers? In the cases where scientific evidence is cited, does Bartlett (i) give us enough information to form an independent judgment, and (ii) furnish adequate proof that the experimental controls were "super strict" and conservatively reported?

   (b) To whom does the "we" in the last sentence of paragraph 6 refer?

   (c) Where else in the rest of the article does the author use similar manipulative techniques?

5. (a) In the conclusion (paragraphs 31 to 36) the writer attempts to enhance the prestige of Psi by associating it with things which our society has traditionally taught us to respect. What does the writer associate Psi with? On the basis of what you are told in the article, are the comparisons valid?

   (b) In spite of the writer's lack of objectivity, why is this a good conclusion for the article?

6. (a) Underline any words you do not understand.

   (b) Try to figure out the meaning of the word from its position in the text.

   (c) Look the word up in a dictionary to see how close you came.

Thinking and Writing

a. Many people claim to have had psychic experiences of one kind or another, and most of us know a person who has had such an experience.

Write an essay in which you describe the experience as objectively as possible and analyze the experience to determine whether it is a genuine example of Psi. As you present your evidence, try to anticipate and refute the objections of someone who opposes your interpretation of the experience.

Audience:
an intelligent reader whose beliefs about the existence of psychic experiences are the opposite of yours.

b. Write an essay in which you support *or* oppose the proposition "all claims of Psi phenomena are fraudulent, manifestations of mental illness, misinterpretations of chance occurrences or the daydreams of ambitious pseudo-scientists".
Audience:
an intelligent reader who has had some experience or is widely read in the field of psychic phenomena.
Send a copy of your essay to someone who advertises in your local newspaper that he/she is working in the field of psychic phenomena, or a member of the clergy whom you know.

Reign of terror

by Jorge Nef

1. In March 1978, Aldo Moro, a leading figure in Italy's ruling Christian Democratic Party, was kidnaped in a street ambush in Rome. His five bodyguards were shot to death. The radical Red Brigade, notorious in recent years for its daring kidnapings and "knee-cappings" of officials, politicians and businessmen, claimed responsibility. The terrorists demanded the release of 14 of their comrades being tried or serving sentences for previous offences. The government refused to bargain. For nearly two months a virtual state of emergency obtained throughout the country, but all attempts to find the former premier proved futile. Eight weeks after the abduction, on May 9, 1978, Moro's bullet-ridden body was found in the trunk of an abandoned car near the Christian Democratic Party headquarters.

2. Moro's kidnaping has been widely publicized around the world. Less attention, however, has been paid to the equally alarming growth of Italian rightwing terrorism. Before the *Brigate Rosse* went into action, well financed and organized neo-fascist groups had resorted to what they called "armed propaganda." For instance, on May 28, 1974, a group known as *Ordine Nero* (Black Order) exploded a bomb at an antifascist gathering in Brescia, killing seven persons and injuring nearly 100. On August 4 of the same year, this group claimed responsiblity for a bomb attack on the Rome-Munich express near Bologna which killed 12 and maimed or severely wounded nearly 50. In a communiqué *Ordine Nero* stated that the attacks were a warning to the Christian Democratic government to stop its "leftist-leaning" Marxist stand. "The Nazi flag did not die in Berlin in 1945," the communiqué said.

"It still lives for a powerful fascist and Nazi Italy. Nazism will return for the salvation of a renaissance Italy." At least eight such fascist action groups are operating in Italy. They maintain an arm's-length relationship with the country's legal neo-fascist party, the MSI. They fear a Communist victory at the polls, and in certain ironic ways their immediate objective is not different from that of the extreme Marxist left (which is also bitterly opposed to the legal, highly bureaucraticized and labor-controlled Communist Party). Curiously enough, despite their abysmal ideological differences, the terrorists of both Left and Right want an end to the present Italian state.

3. These examples illustrate the complexities of the terrorism that in our generation has permeated the fabric of national and international politics. It is present in many societies — new and old, democratic and non-democratic, developed and backward. It is practised by both the Right and Left, by rabid nationalists and by antinationalists. In our shrinking global village, terrorism of all kinds comes to us daily over the teletypes and through the tube. We are informed of the ongoing, apparently senseless cycle of killings and bombings in Northern Ireland. We are shocked by the murder of Israeli athletes at the 1972 Munich Olympics. We are stunned by the seizure of a train in the Netherlands by South Moluccan exiles. We hear of airplane hijackings, airport hand-grenade attacks, group kidnapings and assassinations by assorted terrorist organizations whose names and objectives are difficult to remember. It would not be too much to say that we are stalked by the phantom of terrorism.

4. Insurgent terrorism receives most of the publicity, but it is only one side of the coin. What about the state as terrorist? Those governments that Amnesty International has classified as the worst violators of human rights, regularly and as a matter of policy practise torture, assassination, bombing, hostage-taking and other forms of intimidation. Both the black supremacist regime of Idi Amin in Uganda and the more businesslike white supremacist regime in South Africa practise terror on a large scale. So do Chile and the Philippines. Even allegedly democratic, "civilized" regimes find themselves engaged in dirty business, either on their own or through support for another regime; witness the recent U.S. Senate exposés of CIA involvement in assassination plots and coups d'état, in dealings with the underworld and in the financing of overseas terrorist groups. State terrorism sometimes allies itself with private entrepreneurs of terror, either groups like the IRA or individuals like Carlos. A number of states — Libya, Iraq, the USA, the USSR and Egypt — have contributed to international terrorism. To be sure, repressive governments use soft words like

"law enforcement," "national security" and "counter-insurgency," euphemisms designed to persuade people that state-sponsored violence has a higher purpose and thus is justifiable. But as always, terrorism is being used to attain political objectives. It is the politics of fear.

5. To explain contemporary terrorism is risky because there are those who feel that attempting to understand terrorists is tantamount to sympathizing with them. But condemnation without comprehension is of little practical or even moral value. How can we devise a strategy of containment without trying to understand the nature of the beast? Terrorism has to be seen in relation to other manifestations of violence which plague modern civilization, such as war.

6. A depressing feature of terrorism is that like war it is a rational political strategy. Despite the myth that terrorists are criminal psychopaths, most available evidence suggests that even the bloodiest of them are not particularly psychotic. We may think of them as fanatics or true-believers, possessed by self-righteousness and able to rationalize the most ruthless actions. Like soldiers and policemen they operate under extreme stress, and the anxiety and abnormal behavior they exhibit can be seen as normal. This is not to say that the objectives of terrorists are reasonable or realistic or have a good chance of success. Risk and the possibility of failure are present in any human endeavor — in war, business and politics — and success more often than not can be seen only in retrospect.

7. The general and often deliberate confusion of terrorism with criminal or psychotic behavior precludes the understanding of its essentially political nature. We cannot put the actions of the IRA in the same category as Al Capone's St. Valentine's Day Massacre, the Manson murders, or, more recently, the horror of Jonestown. The orgy of mass murder and torture unleashed by the Guatemalan Special Forces against peasants and villagers in the Zacapa region in the early 1970s may have appeared insane, but Colonel Arana Osorio (nicknamed "the Butcher of Zacapa") was carrying out a carefully organized contingency plan to destroy local support for the guerrillas who threatened the Guatemalan establishment. The FLQ terrorists who kidnaped James Cross and murdered Pierre Laporte were guilty of crimes under the Criminal Code of Canada, but they were uncommon criminals; the FLQ's lawbreaking was directed against a legal system whose legitimacy they challenged.

8. One of the political objectives of terrorists is propaganda, the "propaganda of the deed." It provides a rallying cry for a cause (e.g., "a free Palestine"). Bloody stunts such as the killing of hostages by the Red Army Faction at the West German embassy in Stockholm

in 1974 and the bombing of the Le Mon House Restaurant by the IRA in 1978 were intended to produce a high publicity return. When the Popular Front for the Liberation of Palestine blew up three airliners in Jordan in September 1970 it achieved unprecedented media success; after releasing more than 300 hostages in front of television cameras, the PFLP put on a pyrotechnical show that reached the most remote corners of the world — instant terror in our living rooms. The plight of the Palestinian refugees was in front of us in living color, several times a day.

9. Contemporary terrorism has shifted its focus from the assassination of political leaders to random terror against innocent civilians. It has erased the distinction between combatants and noncombatants, a trait of all forms of modern warfare. Terrorists go for the soft underbelly: unsuspecting civilian targets. The victim and the ultimate political target are generally not the same. For instance, when the Japanese *Rengo Sekigun* (Red Army) struck at Israel with an assault on Lod Airport in Tel Aviv on May 30, 1972, most of the 28 victims were not Israelis but foreign tourists, including a group of Puerto Rican Christians. Random terror increases the emotional impact of the action, delivering "more bang for the buck." It is a question of cost-benefit, feasibility and expediency. The levels of force employed by terrorists, it should be noted, are modest in comparison to conventional or guerrilla warfare. The Arab-Israeli war of 1967 produced many more casualties to the Israelis than all the sensational terrorist attacks since then, and the political impact of *fedayeen* terrorism has been far greater than that of all the Arab armies combined.

10. Terrorism is the preferred option for a weak party fighting a strong one. Instead of fighting on the battlefield, terrorists try to turn the adversary's might into a political liability. They provoke a spiraling escalation of terror and counter-terror up to the point at which repression becomes uneconomical or unbearable for its perpetrator. This sort of political *jiu-jitsu,* making a heavy adversary trip by his own impulse, has been successfully applied on numerous occasions. One such instance was the campaign of massive murders launched by the Irish Sinn Fein (the IRA) in November 1920. British military overreaction, especially by the auxiliary Black and Tans, resulted in the Croke Park massacre of November 21, 1920, in which scores of spectators at a stadium were randomly shot by soldiers. London was put in an untenable position and finally had to sign the Irish-Anglo Treaty of 1921, the first step toward full independence.

11. A disturbing aspect of terrorism is that it becomes legitimized. The fact is that one man's terrorist could be someone else's liberator. Acts of violence committed by the other side are terrorist, while

those committed by our side are self-defence or necessity. When the Zimbabwe African National Union launches guerrilla raids in Rhodesia, the regime in Salisbury, which is not recognized internationally, refers to such raids as terrorism. Rhodesia's own attacks on refugee camps in neighboring Zambia and elsewhere are "punitive actions." For most Africans, however, ZAPU's actions, no matter how callous, are a legitimate "war of national liberation."

12. In the end, historical vindication for violence, like that for war or revolution, depends on its effectiveness. Many states have been founded on terrorism: General Grivas in Cyprus, Houari Boumedienne in Algeria and Jomo Kenyatta in Kenya all were cleansed of guilt when their causes were won. In British-occupied Palestine in the 1940s two militant Zionist groups, *Lehi* (the Stern gang) and *Irgun Zvai Leumi* (National Army Organization) engaged in assassination of British officals and soldiers and in the systematic harassment of Arab civilians; *Irgun,* under the leadership of Menachem Begin, was responsible for the spectacular attack on the King David Hotel in Jerusalem in 1946, which resulted in more than 200 casualties. There is little doubt that many of *Irgun's* deeds accelerated the British decision to allow the partition and subsequent creation of the state of Israel in 1948. *Irgun* and its leaders have been "absolved by history."

13. The roots of contemporary terrorism go deep. We find examples of terrorism in the Zealots of Roman-occupied Jerusalem in the first century, and in the Persian sect of the Assassins (or hashish-eaters) in the 11th and 12th centuries. The word *terrorisme,* however, is of more recent origin. It meant first the state-sponsored carnage of counter-revolutionaries during the period of the French Revolution known as the Terror (1793-94). The term was later used to refer to the method of those who committed acts of violence *against* the state. In the 19th century, through the anarchist writings of Blanqui, Kropotkin, Bakhunin, Most and Nechaev, terrorism became an elaborate political doctrine with a creed and its own methods and techniques.

14. One of the basic strains of 19th-century terrorism was nationalism. Self-determination was the rallying banner of the Italian *Carbonari* in the 1830s, the Irish Fenians in the 1850s and the numerous pan-Slavic organizations that emerged at the end of the century. On June 28, 1914, in the town of Sarajevo in Bosnia, terrorism accomplished its greatest feat: a Serbian high school student, Gavrilo Princip, shot and killed Archduke Francis Ferdinand of Austria-Hungary and his wife Countess Sophie Choteck, Duchess of Hohenberg. These pistol shots ignited the fuse of the First World War. For all their drama, however, *Carbonari,* Fenian and Balkan terrorists were not directly responsible for national

independence. What they did was stiffen the resolve of the population to attain independence at any cost. They helped create martyrs, myths and a romanticized folklore which was capitalized on by later nationalists. In the Irish case, for instance, the successful terrorism of the '20s was built on a long history of repression and defeat.

15. The anarchist and nihilist terrorism that mushroomed in the 1880s and 1890s in Czarist Russia—and to a lesser extent in France, Spain and the United States—sought social revolution. In the United States, anarchist terrorism played a leading role in the early stages of the labor movement, and it was an anarchist who assassinated President McKinley in 1901; by the 1920s, however, with the bureaucratization of labor unions, these early strains were all but gone. The most famous group was the Russian *Narodnaya Volya* (People's Will), which was responsible for the killing of Czar Alexander II in 1881. The *narodikniki* and their successors, the Battle Organizations, had been effectively destroyed by the *Okrhana* secret police by 1905, the time of the first abortive Russian revolution. The brutality of the repression unleashed by the regime, however, had wiped out any vestige of middle-class support for the monarchy. In 1917 the mass organizations—the Revolutionary Socialists and subsequently the Bolsheviks—harvested the fruits of rebellion whose seeds had been sown by the early terrorists. After the October Revolution, anarcho-nihilists and other terrorist groups were wiped out by the new Soviet regime. Both Lenin and Trotsky contemptuously referred to the revolutionary terrorists as bourgeois romanticists.

16. A new strain of terrorism emerged after the First World War as a result of middle-class reaction to the spread of revolutionary ideologies. This was vigilantism; it became, in some instances, fascism. In Macedonia, Bulgaria, Romania and Japan, ultra-nationalist organizations such as Antonescu's Iron Guards, Japan's Black Dragon and the Croatian *Ustashi* imposed a reign of fear. In Germany these took the form of the *Frei Korps,* created to fight leftist unrest in 1919, and the "patriotic" *Geheimbündler* of the early '20s. These vigilante groups used terror not only to silence their opponents but to justify their ascension to power. They alone, it was stated, could control the violence. This two-sided strategy, mixing private with state terror, paid enormous dividends. Hitler's *Sturmabteilungen* and Mussolini's *squadristi* paved the road to power. With fascism and Nazism in control of the state these groups became part of the legalized terror of the New Order. Generous German and Italian financing facilitated the spead of white terrorism throughout Europe; among the victims were King Alexander of Yugoslavia and the French foreign minis-

ter, Jean-Louis Barthou, both assassinated by the Croatian *Ustashe,* and the Austrian chancellor, Englebert Dolfuss, murdered by a gang of Austrian Nazis. These events prompted the League of Nations to propose a Convention for the Prevention and Punishment of Acts of Terrorism in 1937. Needless to say, the convention was never ratified.

17. While fascist terror spread throughout Western Europe, state-sponsored terror had swept the Soviet Union during the '30s. Stalin's purges made Red Terror virtually a form of government. Then a frightened Europe experienced the ultimate terror: the Second World War. A major lesson of the war was that terrorism needed a solid political and military foundation; this had been suggested by the rise of fascism in the '30s, and it was confirmed by the experience of the *maquis,* the *chetnicks* and the *partisani* in the antifascist resistance. Technologically, the war expanded the destructive capabilities of terrorists in the areas of communications, electronics, small arms and explosives. Organizational technology became equally perfected. Psychologically, the war made extremely brutal acts — Hiroshima, Dresden, the firestorm over Cologne — quite acceptable.

18. With the collapse of the European empires following the war, "national liberation movements," combining mass organizations, rural guerrillas and urban terrorists, spread throughout the colonial world. Their methods and organization were derived largely from those of the European resistance. These movements received support from Communist Eastern Europe and a number of newly independent states; their strategies often involved convoluted and protracted wars of attrition, leading to the negotiating table. Palestine, Indochina, Malaysia, Kenya, Algeria and Cyprus were places where this occurred.

19. The Algerian experience between 1954 and 1962 was a milestone; for the first time, indiscriminate and generalized terrorism was successfully used in a war of national liberation and social revolution. Ever since, Algeria has become a Third World model for the "creative use of violence." The passionate writings of the Martinique-born psychiatrist Frantz Fanon (*The Wretched of the Earth*) argued that violence performed a liberating function for the colonized peoples by restoring their dignity and self-respect. The Algerian experience was influential in the Middle East, in Latin America, in Europe and even in North America (the Weathermen, the Black Panthers, the FLQ). Although the Algerian revolution was an inspiration for would-be revolutionaries, it involved a good deal of myth. The fact is that by 1960 the FLN terrorists of Algiers and Oran had been defeated in the military front. What happened was that the repression exercised by French forces crystalized

Algerian opinion against the military, and this played a vital role in the emanicipation. The military overreaction almost destroyed France in 1958 and again in 1961 through the operations of the right-wing Secret Army Organization. But independence was granted to Algeria in 1962. Terrorism was successful even in defeat.

20. There is no single explanation for the spate of terrorism that has occurred in the last decade. There is no unified "terrorist international." The explanations have to be found in the motives of the three kinds of terrorist organizations that have been in existence since the beginning of the terrorist boom in the late '60s — the nationalists, the New Left and the neo-fascists.

21. Nationalism motivates the separatist and irredentist groups seeking either territorial autonomy or a homeland of their own. An example is the takeover of the IRA by its ultra-nationalist Provisional Wing or *provos* following the collapse of the civil rights movement of 1969 in Northern Ireland. Other examples are the radical Basque and Quebecois nationalists of the ETA and FLQ. The most dramatic expression, however, has been the emergence of the Palestinian *fedayeen* (martyrs); it is also the one with the broadest international implications. IRA, ETA and FLQ terrorism have been mostly confined to the homeland, seeking to redress ethnic, linguistic, religious or economic grievances. *Fedayeen* terrorism, on the other hand, has altered the very fabric of world politics. After 1967 an unprecedented cycle of terror and counter-terror opened the road to Yasir Arafat's triumphant address to the United Nations in November 1974. From that point on it has been inconceivable to think of an effective Middle East peace without the Palestinians. The lessons of the *Irgun* and FLN have been learned all too well.

22. New Left terrorism has been a recent mutation of the militant student movement of the 1960s. The failure of the student movement in Europe and the United States, the growing frustration with "politics as usual" and official repression are at the root of the Weathermen in the United States, the West German Red Army Faction (Baader-Meinhof gang) and to some extent the Italian Red Brigades. These groups have evolved from small, radical, though relatively peaceful organizations, into more complex secret societies engaged in an open war against the "capitalist state." In all of these cases, confrontation and escalation have resulted in an increased radicalization of the ultra left.

23. The consequences of New Left terrorism are yet to be seen. The chances of these movements bringing about revolution are insignificant. The danger is not terrorism itself but government overreaction. Total security can exist only in a totalitarian state. In a

sense, New Left terrorism, like the 19th century *narodniki*, sees itself as a detonator of the revolution: by forcing the state to become repressive, thus showing its "true colors," the parliamentary "illusion" would vanish and the "objective conditions" for a future revolution would be created. The trends toward legal repression in Italy and Germany, while effective in the short run, could prove to be a far worse remedy than the disease. A police state offers protection against terrorism, but transforms the state into a super terrorist.

24. This trend is closely related to the third strain of contemporary terrorism: neo-fascism. In reaction to liberal "permissiveness" and the '60s protest movement, the world now has such organizations as the Spanish *Fuerza Nueva* (New Force), *Ordre Nouveau* in France, *Ordine Nuovo* and *Ordine Nero* in Italy, the (300,000 strong) *Bozkurtlar* (Grey Wolves) of Colonel Türkes in Turkey, MANO in Guatemala, the anti-Castro CORU, the Argentinian Anti-Communist Alliance (AAA) and the ubiquitous "death squads."

25. Latin America is an outstanding example of the failure of leftist insurgency. It is also the region of the globe exhibiting some of the most repressive forms of state terrorism. Some urban guerilla movements, such as the Venezuelan FALN in the early '60s and, more recently, the Argentinian Montoneros and ERP, have resorted to terrorism. Despite numerous spectacular capers, terrorism has proven unsuccessful for all these groups. On a continent where the establishment retains a monopoly on terror, there is little opportunity for private entrepreneurs unless they are supported by the state and its foreign allies. In Chile, Brazil, Guatemala, Nicaragua, and other states, terror is a form of government. Official "counter-insurgency" by the police and the special forces has been encouraged since the early '60s by the United States through military assistance and by AID public safety programs. The security forces are helped by a myriad of private vigilante organizations: the *Tontons Macoutes* of the late "Papa Doc" Duvalier in Haiti, *Ojo por ojo* (an Eye for an Eye) in Guatemala, Motherland and Freedom in Chile, *La Banda* in the Dominican Republic and the Falcons in Mexico. All of these at different times have acted as self-proclaimed "antibodies to combat red infestation." There is also a "mixed economy" of terrorism in the death squads. These are semi-official killer gangs made up of volunteers from the military and the national police. They have been active in Brazil and to a lesser degree in Uruguay, Bolivia, Guatemala, Paraguay, Argentina, Chile, Nicaragua, Honduras and El Salvador. The functions of private vigilantes and those of the death squads are not too different from those of the German

Geheimbündler of the '20s: the intimidation and elimination of opponents.

26. Outside Latin America, vigilantism is one of the fastest growing forms of contemporary terrorism. In Germany alone, the Federal Office for the Protection of the Constitution reported that in 1972 "New Right" organizations had committed at least 428 various criminal "outrages". (This is almost 50 percent of all terrorist acts for that year.) In Italy last year, death squads staffed by off-duty policemen started operations against "terrorists and other radicals." As states move to stiffen legislation to cope with leftist and separatist terror, more links between vigilante groups and law enforcement agencies are likely to develop.

27. One of the factors contributing to the spread of terrorism is modern communications, which enable new groups to learn from each other. Demonstration, imitation and experimentation play a vital role in the development of terrorism. Thus the international scope of contemporary terrorism results from global communications rather than from any global aims on the part of the terrorists. By and large, the aims of terrorists have remained national in scope, although the Cold War has contributed to the spread of terrorism. Penetration of the adversary's camp through terrorist organizations has become an attractive alternative to nuclear confrontation for the USA, USSR and China alike. There is no mystery about Soviet support for the PLO and other "liberation movements," nor about American commitment to vigilante organizations in Latin America and elsewhere. All of this raises serious doubts about the sincerity of many nations to control terrorism.

28. The impressive raid at Entebbe by Israeli troops in 1976, at Mogadishu by the German GSG-9 in 1977 and at Essen by Dutch marines in 1978 suggest that individual western countries have the military capability to deal with terrorism. Political containment, however, is as flimsy as it was at the time of the League of Nations Convention in 1937. Military or police action at times can deal with the symptoms of terrorism, but never with its causes. Oppression, lack of political expression, unbearable living conditions and displaced populations are common denominators of almost all violence and terrorism. The most fundamental justification for group violence—nationally or internationally—is self-preservation, and this applies to revolutionaries, separatists and reactionaries. As long as there are inequalities, discrimination and nations without states, there will be radical or nationalist terrorism. As long as ruling elites feel threatened by rebellion or insurrection, there will be official and vigilante terrorism. And there will be no end to terrorism as long as the individual nation-state remains the sole arbiter of international morality in an anarchical and violent international system.

29. There is an alarming psychocultural aspect to contemporary terrorism. This is the growing acceptance of violence as inevitable and legitimate. Violence has been glorified in the collective machismo of our global culture, becoming a virtue both for the Right and the Left, for advanced nation-states and backward ones, for the "people's democracies" and "the Free World." In an echo of "the war to end all wars," we have even glorified violence as the solution to violence. It is this trend in our culture that makes the human tragedy of terrorism acceptable—tactically expedient in the short run, morally justifiable in the long run. For a generation who witnessed Hiroshima and My Lai, terrorism holds no horrors—providing it serves a "noble" purpose.

Style and Structure

1. The thesis statement seems to be divided into two parts (the opening sentences of paragraphs 3 and 4).
   (a) Underline the thesis statements.
   (b) What effect does Nef create by dividing the thesis into two parts and presenting them in the order he does?
   (c) Write a single thesis statement for the article combining the two thesis statements above. Which approach to the thesis statements do you find most effective?
2. Reread the illustrations which open the article (paragraphs 1 and 2). Why would the writer have selected these two particular illustrations?
3. Reread paragraphs 5, 13 and 20. What is their function in the organization of the article?
4. The writer could have reduced his article to one page and still have conveyed his thesis to the reader, if he had omitted his descriptions of individual terrorist acts. For what reasons did he include these descriptions? What effect do these descriptions have on the reader?
5. The writer builds paragraph 2 around two sets of parallel structures. Underline them. How does the use of parallel structures increase the impact of the material presented in this paragraph?
6. For what other purposes, in addition to recapitulating his thesis, does the writer use his conclusion?

Thinking and Writing

a. Write a precis of this article. (A precis is an essay which condenses the material of the original work down to about one-third of its length while maintaining the essential ideas of the original.)

Audience:

an "average" newspaper reader who has not read the original article.

b. In paragraph 5 Nef states: "But condemnation without comprehension is of little practical or even moral value. How can we devise a strategy of containment without trying to understand the nature of the beast [the causes of the terrorism]?"

Research the grievances and objectives of *one* of the terrorist groups named in the article. (The information should be available in your library: use the newspaper indexes, *Reader's Guide, Canadian Index, Facts on File,* etc. If you encounter any difficulty, contact the research librarian.)

Write an essay in which you examine the grievances, objectives, and methods of the terrorist group chosen and suggest practical means by which the conflict could be ended. (Try to be realistic and fair in your suggestions.)

Audience:

the "average" newspaper reader who is probably not familiar with your terrorist organization beyond knowing of its most publicized acts, and, as a result, is likely to possess superficial and unrealistic opinions about how the problem should be resolved.

Send a copy of your paper to the editor of a newspaper in your area.

Passenger pigeon, bird of yesterday

by Alan Devoe

1. On the first day of September, 1914, a slim-winged bird of delicate blue and fawn plumage which had been on exhibition in the Cincinnati Zoological Gardens toppled from its perch and fell dead on the floor of its cage. The incident attracted wider attention than the passing of zoo captives customarily receives. The bird was a passenger pigeon. Precisely, it was *the* passenger pigeon. It was the sole surviving member of that race of "wild blue doves" which once had inhabited our country in such multitudes that the migrating flocks darkened the noonday sky, and the vibrance

of rushing wings had the sound, said Audubon, of "a gale passing through the rigging of a close-reefed vessel". What happened on that fall day in 1914 was a good deal more than the dying of a bird in a zoo. What happened, in the eloquent words of the zoologist Hegner, was that "another of our 'inexhaustible resources' had come to an end".

2. The vanishing of the passenger pigeon is often enough alluded to, and its extinction deplored, but the manner of that vanishing is not often told. Occasionally it is hinted that there was some "mystery" about it—that an unprecedented storm on Lake Michigan wiped out the birds, or that a baffling plague came upon them so that they were extirpated over night. The actual story of the passenger pigeons—the part they once played in the American wild scene, and the reason why now they are gone forever—has been infrequently set down. It is a tale worth telling. There is no mystery about it. There is only a considerable melancholy—the melancholy that attaches to any record of stupid human avarice and gluttony and blood-lust. It is worth thinking about.

3. When Champlain was on the coast of Maine in 1605, he observed delightedly the presence of a species of soft-feathered blue-grey doves. There were, he recorded, an "infinite" number of the birds. They passed over the heads of his party with that curious soft sweet whistling of wings that is characteristic of pigeon-flight and settled numerously, with low murmurous voices, in the nearby evergreen trees. No less delightful to Champlain than the "infinite" numerousness of these delicately plumaged wild pigeons was their singular trustfulness. For all that they were remarkably fleet of wing when they chose to fly, they appeared to be as unsuspicious of human beings as were the clumsy flightless dodos which had been discovered a few years before on the island of Mauritius, and which were currently affording amusement to Portuguese sailors who walked up to the waddling birds and clubbed them to death with barrel-staves. Champlain sent his men among the roosting pigeons, and, as he puts it, "took a great quantity".

4. That is one of the earliest records of the Europeans' experience with the passenger pigeons, and it well sets the tone for subsequent events. The Jesuits, exploring Nova Scotia a decade later, also found the pigeons to be "infinite", and also, in the same grim phrase, "took great quantities". In the Plymouth Colony, by 1643, the colonists had become so fascinated by the possibilities of limitless slaughter among the pigeons that Winthrop has a phrase about "it being incredible what multitudes of the doves were killed daily". In Carolina, by 1702, the ingenious settlers had devised such efficient methods of grain-baiting for the legions of birds that one particularly expert hunter was able on a notable day to record securing

seventy-one pigeons with two shots of a flintlock. From Nova Scotia to Florida, in every part of the Atlantic region where the colonizers came, there were discovered the same gratifyingly "limitless" numbers of pigeons, and there took place the same kind of enthusiastic and enormous killings among them.

5. The passenger pigeons were migrants. They fed on acorns and hemlock seeds and a variety of nuts and berries, as well as on beetles and caterpillars, and in seasonal pursuit of their food they banded together in flocks so huge that the watching settlers could hardly credit their senses. There were pigeon-flocks five miles wide and more than two hundred miles in length, great whistling-winged throngs that required three days to pass a given observation-point, hordes of pigeons that were reckoned by careful calculators to contain more than two billion birds.

6. When the great flocks were passing, the air was heavy with the pungent scent of them and the light of the sun was obscured as by an eclipse, and at night, when the birds came down to roost in the forest, the branches of massive oaks and pines were broken down by the weight of their numbers. "From right to left, as far as eye could reach," wrote Alexander Wilson, "the vast procession extended", and other observers recorded how in the pigeons' winter roosting-places the constant crash of breaking limbs was like the sound of gunfire in the night, and how once, between Hardensburgh, Ohio, and Louisville, Kentucky, the sporting citizens lined the banks of the Ohio and fired broadsides incessantly into a flock of passing pigeons for eight successive days.

7. The pigeons' nesting was communal like their feeding and travelling. By tens of thousands they massed together in the woods to build their frail twig-nests, often a hundred nests to a single tree. Each female customarily laid only one egg or occasionally two, and the male and female pigeons, after the devoted fashion of most doves, took turns in the eggs' incubation and later in the rearing of the squabs. The young were fed on the "pigeon's milk" from the parents' crops, and later on insects and caterpillars and finally small nuts and grain; and for miles around a nesting-place there could be heard the soft cooing of the countless parents and fledglings. Ever unsuspicious of humans, the pigeons at nesting-time became almost wholly heedless of their presence. One could walk among the nest-laden trees and cause no disturbance beyond a little momentary rustling of soft-feathered wings, a little puzzled scrutiny by scarlet-irised eyes that watched with mild wonderment.

8. The early colonists, finding available a bird so numerous, so communal, and so trusting, accomplished as much depredation as they could with their limited instruments, but it was in the nineteenth century that pigeon-killing became efficiently organized on a large

scale. It was apparent that in pigeon-meat there could be profit, and the commerce-minded developers of the country undertook to realize it. The old methods of the hunter were replaced by the new methods of the professional fowler—replaced so expertly that a fair day's haul in pigeon-netting came to be reckoned as two hundred and fifty dozen birds.

9. By the time of the American Civil War there were upward of a thousand fowlers giving all their time to the capturing and killing of passenger pigeons. The fowlers' numbers were augmented by the helpers who went into pigeon-roosts at night, firing half-a-hundred charges of bird-shot simultaneously, so that the dead pigeons fell to earth like rain around them, and by the squab gatherers who went into the birds' communal nesting-places and carried off the plump young birds which were as yet unable to fly. It was all extremely profitable, while it lasted. The markets of the city of New York alone took a hundred barrels of pigeons every day, and the markets of every other great city were similarly good customers.

10. It seems to have occurred to no one that the supply of even the "limitless" wild pigeons would not withstand such intensive pillage indefinitely. It seems to have occurred, at any rate, only to the native people. They had lived on pigeons for centuries, pitching their camps near the sites of the great roosts in order that there might always be game available, but there was a law in the tribes that young pigeons must never be molested before they could fly, and a law likewise that no more pigeons must be killed at a time than could properly be smoked for food. The native people brought these matters to the Europeans' notice and remonstrated with them. A chief of the Potawatomi uttered a long grave plea that had in it a good deal of simple eloquence and a great deal of sound conservation-sense.

11. But to the native peoples' representations and threats in the matter of pigeon-killing, as to their threats and representations in most other matters, the continent's exploiters gave no heed. Towards the end of the century the pigeons were so scarce in the east that few were to be found for the New York market except in the wooded Catskills, but even then—in that same era when Western railroads were advertising that passengers might amuse themselves, without charge, by shooting at bison from the observation-platforms of the moving trains—the dwindling flocks were being unabatedly trapped and shot.

12. The end came quickly. By the 1880's the once-great flocks of the middle west had become only occasional stragglers; by the nineties a great migration-flock was nowhere to be found in the country; by the turn of the century the last of the professional fowlers,

who only a few years before had found their trade so rewarding that they communicated flock-locations to one another by telegraph and travelled all over the country by train in pursuit of their game, had had to turn to other ways of livelihood. Fourteen years later, when a solitary pigeon fell dead in the zoo cage where it had been on exhibition as a unique curiosity, the race of "wild blue doves" that once darkened the American sky in their myriads was vanished forever from the earth.

13. That is the story of the going of the passenger pigeons. That is the story of why the word "pigeon"—that once meant hordes of shimmering wings, and a rushing murmurous music in the American wild places—means now only a dingy fancier-bred bird that creeps on soot-stained feet around the grimy cornices of office buildings.

Style and Structure

1. What is the average reader's reaction to the first sentence in paragraph 1? What is the reaction by the time he/she has read the last sentence in paragraph 1?
   How does the writer bring about this change? Why does he employ this device?

2. In paragraph 2, identify the thesis statement and the indication of how the body of the essay is organized.

3. Draft a plan of the essay's organization. What principle behind the ordering of the information gives the essay unity?

4. Examine the words and phrases in quotation marks in paragraphs 3 and 4. How does the relationship between the quotations in each paragraph fit in with the thesis of the essay?

5. Paragraphs 5 to 7 describe the passenger pigeons and their habits.
   (a) What does the information included in these paragraphs tell us about the intended reader of this essay?
   (b) Instead of giving bare statistics on the number of birds, the writer describes "pigeon-flocks five miles wide and more than two hundred miles in length". Identify any other such descriptions. Is this descriptive technique more effective than the statistical for the intended reader? Why?
   (c) Underline the words and phrases in paragraph 7 that are calculated to engage the reader's sympathy for the birds.

6. Why does the author juxtapose (place side by side) the information contained in paragraphs 10 and 11 with that of paragraphs 8 and 9? How does this organizational technique reflect the writer's thesis?

7. How does Devoe's sentence structure in paragraph 12 emphasize the topic sentence, "The end came quickly."

8. What contrast does the writer present in paragraph 13? What feelings about our "civilization" does the contrast evoke?

Thinking and Writing

a. Do research in the library about another North American species that is now extinct or on the endangered species list. Write an essay outlining the cause of its decline.
    Audience:
    someone who does not know the story of your chosen species and who may not realize the importance of conservation.

b. Read a number of the essays written by other members of your class for section a. They will probably describe a number of species that were not exterminated through hunting but disappeared because their natural habitat was destroyed by expanding "civilization".
    Write an essay in which you take a stand for or against the statement "Modern industrial society cannot be asked to restrict its development simply to preserve one or two relatively insignificant species."
    Audience:
    someone who knows little about conservation.
    Send a copy of your essay to a conservation group in your area.

The eyes of God

---

by Banesh Hoffman

1. Considering that Albert Einstein was one of the greatest scientific geniuses of all time, some of the facts of his early years seem quite unbelievable. He did not learn to speak until the age of 3. He hated school; one of his teachers told him he would never amount to anything, and at 15 he dropped out. At 16 he wrote the entrance examination for the Polytechnic Institute in Zurich, and failed.
2. There is, however, another side to the story. At about the age of 5 he was given a magnetic compass by his father, and when he saw its needle in the grip of a mysterious, invisible force he was filled with a sense of awe and wonder that never left him. At 12 he came upon a geometry textbook that utterly fascinated him; he spoke of it as

"the holy geometry book" and cherished it all his life. What he hated about German schools was their rigid, oppressive discipline and their emphasis on learning by rote (he had a poor memory for words). He taught himself calculus and read about science with intense excitement. Although he failed the entrance examination at the Polytechnic Institute, his performance in mathematics and physics was impressive, and ultimately he was permitted to enrol.

3. Einstein was a strong-willed student with ideas of his own about what to study. He attended lectures only occasionally, preferring to spend his time performing experiments and studying the writings of great scientists. This was an ideal way for a genius to study, but it caused a serious problem when examination time arrived. Luckily his friend Marcel Grossmann had taken superb lecture notes and allowed him to study them. Without these notes he might have failed. Cramming for the final examinations was so distasteful to him that for a year he lost all interest in science. He antagonized his professors and as a result was unable to obtain an academic position anywhere. After bitter, despairing years of temporary teaching jobs, he managed, with Grossmann's help, to obtain a position in the Swiss patent office in Berne. There his genius burst into flower.

4. The year 1905 would have been memorable in the annals of science even if Einstein had produced only his paper "On the Electrodynamics of Moving Bodies," in which he presented what we now call the special theory of relativity. But he made other major contributions; in those days there were outstanding scientists who still doubted that atoms existed, but they could doubt no longer when predictions in another of Einstein's 1905 papers were verified experimentally. Then, too, there was a momentous paper, only three pages long, in which he showed that energy has mass according to his famous formula $E = mc^2$ — that is, energy equals mass times the speed of light squared. (Two years later he realized that this formula also showed that mass is a reservoir of colossal amounts of energy.)

5. Perhaps his most remarkable and certainly his most revolutionary paper, the first of his 1905 papers, argued that we should think of light as particles even though overwhelming evidence suggested that light consists of waves. Five years earlier the great German physicist Max Planck had introduced a new concept, the quantum, an idea so revolutionary that not even Planck believed in it; what Einstein did was to take the quantum seriously and apply it to light. In 1913, when some of the greatest German scientists wanted to offer Einstein a prestigious position in Berlin, they spoke glowingly to the authorities of his accomplishments and apologized for his idea of particles of light. But Einstein had found a surprisingly

simple mathematical formula for the photoelectric effect, which is used today by television cameras to convert light into electricity. About the time of the invitation to Berlin, the American physicist Robert Millikan began a long and difficult experiment to show once and for all the falsity of Einstein's photoelectric formula. The experiment took some two years. To Millikan's surprise, he found that the photoelectric formula was in precise agreement with the experiment, and he published the results with enthusiasm. When Einstein received the 1921 Nobel Prize in physics, his photoelectric formula was the only one of his achievements specifically mentioned in the citation.

6. Einstein knew that people were in awe of him, and he had an extraordinary gift for putting them at ease. My own first meeting with him remains vivid in memory. In fear and trembling, I knocked on his door at the Institute for Advanced Study in Princeton, New Jersey, hoping to ask him about some ideas in relativity that I had been working on. When I entered I found him sitting in a comfortable chair smoking a pipe, sloppily dressed, hair unruly, with papers on his lap on which he had been making calculations. He smiled and asked me to write my equations on the blackboard. "Please go slowly," he said. "I do not understand things quickly." At once all my fears vanished. I felt as if we had known each other for years. He asked me penetrating questions, many of which I had not thought of, and he did it without making me feel stupid. It was as if we were partners and even fellow conspirators looking at an idea from all sides. Other people had analogous experiences on meeting Einstein: fear was replaced by a feeling of friendship. A natural modesty, sensitivity and kindness shone through his every action.

7. What of the millons of people who never met Einstein? By what magnetism were they captured? Such questions are important, considering the attitude toward scientists that many people have today. Forgetting the good that has come out of science, they recall such things as the thalidomide tragedy, the chemical defoliation in Vietnam, the manufacture of poison gas, the dangerous radioactive residue from nuclear power plants, and the enormous sums spent on space research.

8. Einstein, like Isaac Newton with his law of gravitation, found sublime simplicity in the universe, and this was the secret of his enduring fame. Throughout his life he looked primarily for beauty in the laws of the universe. He said that in evaluating a scientific theory, his own or someone else's, he asked himself whether he would have made the universe in that way if he had been God. This he did to arrive at his general theory of relativity. One of the basic principles of his 1905 theory was that uniform motion is relative: if we are in a closed, windowless vehicle that is moving uniformly we

cannot detect its motion by any experiment we make inside it. Einstein felt it was inartistic that only uniform motion should be relative. God would not have made the universe in so clumsy a way. The trouble was that non-uniform motion is detectable: when a train suddenly speeds up or slows down the passengers have to hold on tightly. But Einstein's artistic feelings were strong. He studied the facts and saw to his joy that it was indeed possible to regard all motion as relative. For the passengers in the train, the effects of the acceleration or deceleration could be thought of as gravitational, and with this insight Einstein was on his way to a new theory of gravitation.

9. Einstein was working on his general theory of relativity in Berlin when the First World War broke out in 1914. Having been for some time a Swiss citizen, he was able to devote himself to his work, and in 1915 he presented his general theory of relativity. In it he found himself building on such concepts as curved, four-dimensional space-time; one of his basic predictions was that light rays would be found to be bent by gravitation. British scientists had no direct communication with Germany, but the Cambridge astronomer and physicist Arthur Stanley Eddington, who was a Quaker and pacifist, obtained details of Einstein's new theory of gravitation through scientists in neutral Holland. He was fascinated with its extraordinary beauty. In the midst of war, an expedition was mounted to test the bending of light rays during an eclipse of the sun that was to occur in 1919. It was carried out after fighting had ceased but with the war still not ended. Eddington was delighted to find that the eclipse observations agreed with Einstein's prediction. The British put aside their strong anti-German feelings and announced the results enthusiastically at a special joint meeting of the Royal Society of London and the Royal Astronomical Society. It was clear to the scientists in the crowded hall that Newton's theory of gravitation, which had held sway for 250 years, must now yield to the theory perfected in enemy Berlin. The newspapers eagerly reported the event and almost overnight Einstein became world famous.

10. With fame came responsibilities that Einstein did not shirk. He knew his name carried weight, and he spoke out boldly in the cause of peace and freedom and human rights. Having himself experienced anti-Semitism and seen its devastating effect on less fortunate Jews, he gave his support to Zionism and helped to raise funds for the construction of the Hebrew University in Jerusalem. In Germany, envy and his being a Jew led to sharp attacks on his theories, and even threats to his person. When the Nazis seized power in 1933, they confiscated his savings and brought an action against him accusing him of treason. There were rumors that they

had put a price on his head. Luckily, he was outside Germany at the time. He never returned. Instead he became a professor in Princeton, New Jersey, at the newly created Institute for Advanced Study. There he spent the rest of his days, continuing his long search for a way to link gravitation and electromagnetism in a single unified theory while speaking out as boldly as ever against both foreign and domestic threats to freedom.

11. Many people, Jews and non-Jews, tried to escape from Nazi tyranny, but it was not easy for them to find a haven. To get permission to enter the United States, for example, they had to have not only visas, which were hard to come by, but also financial sponsors who would guarantee that they would not become public charges — an incredible rule given the desperate circumstances. Einstein used his influence with rich Americans and also staked his own small resources many times to provide the necessary guarantees. He saved many people from almost certain death in the Nazi gas chambers.

12. In early August 1939, with the world on the brink of the Second World War, Einstein sent a letter to President Franklin D. Roosevelt, alerting him to the alarming possibility of an atomic bomb being made out of uranium and pointing to the ominous fact that the Nazis had already stopped the sale of uranium from the extensive mines in conquered Czechoslovakia.

13. Einstein has sometimes been called the father of the atomic bomb. But a father is likely to cherish his offspring, and Einstein certainly did not cherish the bomb. To what extent does the title fit? Einstein's formula $E = mc^2$, told that in a small amount of matter there is entrapped an enormous amount of energy; the mass of a grain of sand is equivalent to the energy given off in burning thousands of tons of coal. But the formula gave no method of releasing the energy, and at the time there seemed no possibility of ever doing so. As we now know, a fraction of this energy can be released from uranium by means of nuclear reactions; it was Ernest Rutherford who discovered the atomic nucleus, but people do not speak of him as the father of the atomic bomb. It is easy to think of other candidates for the title of father, including physicists like J. Robert Oppenheimer who actually developed it. Einstein took no part in the work; it was done in secret and he had no security clearance for it.

14. As for the letter to Roosevelt, it took 10 weeks to reach the president and by then the war had already started. Moreover, except for an initial flurry, the letter turned out to have very little effect. Serious work on the atomic bomb by the Allies did not begin until two years later, and then only after the urgings of scientists in embattled Britain. These scientists — chiefly refugees from Nazi

Germany—made experiments and calculations that demonstrated that an atomic bomb was frighteningly possible. Its development was carried out in the United States to avoid interruption by air raids.

15. When Einstein wrote his letter to Roosevelt he had been afraid, with good reason, that the Nazis would develop the bomb first and with it impose their dictatorship on the world. When the United States dropped atomic bombs on Japanese cities he was horrified, and on learning that the Nazis had not done any major work on the bomb he said that if he had known it at the time he would not have sent the letter to Roosevelt. Fate plays strange tricks. No one would have expected a gentle, unworldly, peace-loving man like Einstein to find himself caught in such a web.

16. Einstein's fame arose in 1919 because men saw in him a way to honorable, unselfish, brotherly behavior in a world too long torn by the bitter hatreds of war. But the fame also was based on Einstein's personality and the very nature of his ideas. The artistic quality and cosmic simplicity of Einstein's thought came across to the general public. Though his theory of relativity spoke of strange new ideas, it referred to familiar concepts like time and space, and the man in the street realized that something momentous was being said even if he was not sure what it was. Its seeming paradoxes were especially intriguing. For example, time seems to slow down as relative speed increases: imagine one twin staying at home while the other twin goes via spaceship to a star and back at a speed that, relative to Earth, is close to the speed of light; at journey's end, the traveling twin will be much younger than the one who stayed at home. The effect has been verified experimentally: an atomic clock on the ground was compared to a second one that had circled the earth in a jet; the stationary clock showed a later time. The fact that Einstein's theory leads to such surprising results is a tribute to its originality. The predictions were made by a gentle, unworldly scientist whose tools were pencil and paper.

17. Einstein showed us that science at its most profound is one of the creative arts. If we do not begrudge the money spent on music, ballet and theatre, we should try not to begrudge the money spent on space research and other branches of science. The universe stands before us in awesome mystery. Who knows what will emerge as we turn our eyes to the heavens using all the tools that technology provides? If the past is a guide, extraordinary discoveries are almost inevitable, and one day a future Einstein will find an unsuspected new beauty in the heavens that will gladden the hearts of men and lift up their souls. This vision of the scientist as artist and prophet is what keeps Einstein's memory vividly alive. It is his enduring monument, and the one that he would have preferred above all others.

Style and Structure

1. Interpret the meaning of the title in terms of the essay. Why is this a good title?
2. Instead of opening with a formal introduction the writer moves directly into Einstein's biography. Write a formal introduction containing a thesis statement appropriate to this article. Does the addition of a formal introduction improve the essay?
3. Why does the writer select the biographical details he does in paragraph 1? What is the reader's immediate reaction to them? Why does the writer select the biographical details he does in paragraph 2? How do these two paragraphs serve as a good informal introduction?
4. What is the function of the last sentence in paragraph 3? Can you locate any other sentences in the article which perform the same function?
5. Generally speaking, what organizational principle does the writer employ?
6. Why does the author go to so much trouble in paragraphs 12 to 15 to disassociate Einstein from the development of the atomic bomb? What arguments does he use to vindicate Einstein's reputation? How is the writer's attitude toward Einstein in this section typical of his presentation of Einstein throughout the article?
7. How does the concluding paragraph build upon the example provided by Einstein's life?

Thinking and Writing

a. Write a precis of this article. (A precis is an essay that accurately presents the main ideas of a longer piece of writing, but does so in approximately one-third of the length.)
   Audience:
   the same "non-scientific" reader for whom the original article was written.

b. In the last paragraph of the article, the author tries to argue that more money should be spent on space research and other scientific projects. He is reacting against a very strong movement in recent years that maintains that the vast amounts of money that have been spent on space research should have been used to solve much more practical problems here on earth, problems such as poverty, starvation, pollution, unemployment, education, and so on.
   Write an essay in which you take one side or the other in this debate and produce logical arguments and concrete data to support your stance.

Audience:
a reader who is very interested in the sciences and who has
opinions on the topic that are completely opposed to yours.
Send a copy of your paper to the editor of a science magazine, or
the National Research Council.

Let the punishment fit the crime

by Philip Brickman

1. When a thief in Chicago stole a motorcycle, the press reported, the
   victim, who knew the thief, was not particularly interested in
   seeing the thief punished, just in getting his motorcycle back. By
   the time the police caught the thief, he had sold the motorcycle. He
   received a suspended sentence. The victim was told he would have
   to sue the thief if he wanted his money back.
2. What is wrong with this story? It does not satisfy our sense of
   justice because justice means that everyone gets what he deserves.
   Justice should mean helping victims as well as punishing offenders. This story and our criminal justice system ignore the problem
   of restoring fairness for victims as a principle of justice.
3. We set two primary goals for our criminal penalties. We want them
   to deter crime and we want them to rehabilitate criminals. In
   theory these two goals should go together, since they amount to
   saying that we want to keep crime from happening in the first
   place, through deterrence, and to keep crime from happening
   again, through rehabilitation.
4. In practice these two goals seem incompatible, since the harsh
   penalties that might work a deterrent offer little hope for
   rehabilitation, while the supportive treatments that might work
   as rehabilitation seem inadequate as deterrents.
5. Curiously, however, neither deterring crime nor rehabilitating
   offenders are principles of justice. Our sense of justice requires that
   penalties be proportionate to their crimes.
6. Suppose we took restoring fairness as the first principle of our
   criminal justice system instead of either deterrence or rehabilitation. What would such a system look like?
7. Simply put, offenders would be given sentences whose purpose, in
   the end, was to restore both the loss that the victims had suffered

and the loss that society suffered through its investment in preventing, detecting, and punishing crimes. Where possible, this could involve labor directly related to recovering property, repairing damage, or making streets safer. More generally, it might involve contributing earnings from specified tasks to a general fund whose purpose was to compensate victims.

8. In informal systems, where victims and offenders are known to one another, restoring fairness is the common penalty that satisfies all concerned and preserves the social bond. It is typical of penalties that are meted out in healthy families.

9. Restitution as a principle of justice appeals to both liberals and conservatives. Liberals like the idea that the penalty involves something more meaningful than just going to prison. Conservatives like the idea that the penalty involves holding offenders responsible for their actions and making them pay for their crimes. It appeals to people on moral and emotional grounds. It appeals to people on practical grounds, in that it offers some hope of helping both the victims and the offender, and also society.

10. Restitution can work in the service of both deterrence and rehabilitation. The cost of making restitution should substantially outweigh the potential gain of the crime, since both the victim's pain and suffering and society's costs of enforcement may be included. At the same time, the act of making restitution should serve not only to restore the offender's sense of himself or herself as a worthwhile member of society but, even more crucial, society's sense of the offender as well, in a way that punishment alone could never do. The penalty can and should involve real cost for the offender, but the novel and critical feature is that it should also involve creating something of value in both society's eyes and the offender's own eyes.

11. The idea of compensating victims can be distinguished from the idea of restitution by offenders. There are many crimes with victims needing help where offenders are unknown. Even if an offender is caught and convicted, restitution at best takes time while the victim's needs are immediate. The solution is to use state funds to compensate victims while offenders either replenish these funds or provide other services.

12. To be successful, the principle of restitution must be implemented in a way that is not seen as exploitation of offenders in the service of existing class interests. Most offenders are poor and many victims are rich. It is doubtful that making restitution to a corporation like an insurance company will have much meaning for people who do not see the corporation as a victim in the first place. It is certain that chain gangs and corrective labor camps do not supply work from which either victims or offenders derive any sense of

meaningful restitution. They are merely punishment, and should be plainly so named. Restitution that is psychologically valuable will have visible and tangible effects that can be seen by victims, offenders, and society.

13. Although not widely known, laws for victim compensation have been enacted in a number of countries (including England and New Zealand) and a growing number of states (including New York and California), while experimental programs for offender restitution are underway in Georgia, Iowa, and Minnesota. Preliminary results are encouraging, but they represent only a beginning. Much remains to be learned about tailoring sentences to both society's needs and offenders' capacities, and we have yet to work out how to allow prisoners to work without threatening jobs for anyone outside prison. These are reasonable tasks for social science and social policy. It is unreasonable to leave the field of criminal justice to the bankrupt debate between deterrence and rehabilitation.

Style and Structure

1. For what reasons does Brickman open his article with the particular illustration that he chooses?
2. Underline the thesis statement and draft a plan of the article's organization.
3. Trace the development of the writer's argument in paragraphs 3 to 6. Show how this development is logical.
4. What is the relationship of paragraph 7 to paragraph 6? How do paragraphs 8, 9, and 10 relate to paragraph 7? How do paragraphs 11 and 12 relate to paragraph 7?
5. In what ways does paragraph 13 function as a good conclusion for the article as a whole? How does the author by his choice of words in the last two sentences attempt to win the reader over to his point of view?

Thinking and Writing

a. 1. The benefits which Brickman outlines for the victim, the criminal, and society are needed nowhere more than in dealing with the crimes of murder and rape. However, no crimes offer greater difficulties to the judge who has to determine the sentence for a particular offence and to convince the general public that his/her sentence is "just" to all those concerned. Write an essay in which you assume the role of a judge who is sentencing a person for one of the following crimes; outline the sentence that you would give in accordance with Brickman's "restitution" and justify this sentence to the general public who may, at present, prefer punishment or revenge:

(a) A woman with three children who has killed her husband in a fit of rage during a domestic quarrel.

(b) A man who has no previous convictions and has before this offence been considered to be an ideal "family man", who has been convicted of raping a woman whom he had never met before.

Audience:
the "average" newspaper reader.

b. 1. Write an essay in which you outline and present evidence to substantiate your personal point of view on the value and effectiveness of basing our system of criminal justice upon a theory of restitution such as Brickman proposes. Use concrete examples and logically developed arguments to support your thesis.

Audience:
someone who works in a field related to criminal justice (e.g., lawyer, judge, police person, or social worker).

Send a copy of your essay to a person employed in one of the positions listed under "audience", or your MP or MPP.

Sceptics and optimists debate nuclear power

by John Pepperell

1. A new set of contestants is taking centre stage in the debate on energy supply. Where nationalists and multinational oil companies once fought, the pro and anti nuclear forces now square off.

2. At the extremes, nuclear power supporters see their opponents as well-meaning but paranoid alarmists who should spend more time learning the facts. In return, opponents view the pro-nuclear group as technological optimists blind to the risks of radiation poisoning.

3. This mutual vilification, indicative of a larger disagreement, sharply contrasts with earlier widespread support for the development of nuclear power.

4. Recoiling from the horrors of Hiroshima and Nagasaki in 1945, nations pledged themselves to "atoms for peace". In the same way that awesomely powerful bombs had been devised, so awesome electrical power stations would be developed. And so they were.

5. The Canadian nuclear establishment at Chalk River, Ont., developed a new reactor, the CANDU, which promised ease of operation and less toxic wastes than other reactors. Our nuclear industry was a world leader, a jewel in the rather limited range of Canadian high technology.

6. The maturing of the CANDU coincided with the sudden vulnerability of our oil supplies in the early 1970s. A logical matching was made between energy demand and nuclear energy supply of massive potential.

7. Nuclear energy in Canada was projected to grow from supplying 1.4% of total energy in 1975 to 8% in 1990, and a higher proportion as more generating stations came into operation. Of federal government research and development expenditures on energy in the 1975-76 fiscal year, 75% went to nuclear and uranium activites.

8. For many, the first notable doubts about the wisdom of this course came after India detonated a nuclear device using spent fuel from an experimental reactor supplied by Canada. India had not signed the nuclear non-proliferation treaty.

9. Soon after, it became clear that Canada had been trying to sell CANDU reactors abroad without great concern for the political stability of its purchasers — we had sold reactors to Argentina and South Korea as well. The dubious nature of these transactions served to underline other growing uncertainties about nuclear power.

10. If other countries could make bombs from a "safe" reactor's nuclear waste, how safe was that waste? It was then that many heard for the first time the term "radioactive half-life" — the time it takes for half the atoms of a substance to discharge their radiation. In the case of CANDU wastes it was up to 25,000 years.

11. By the year 2000, Atomic Energy of Canada Limited estimates that we will have between 80,000 and 100,000 metric tons of this waste to deal with in Canada.

12. How does one lock up these wastes safe from terrorists and accidents for 25,000 years? It turns out that there is no universally agreed upon method. In the meantime, the wastes are kept in temporary storage. The government is studying the question.

13. One possible technique is to bury the wastes deep underground in salt formations that have been stable for millions of years. The federal and Ontario governments have just launched a study program of site selection. Nuclear opponents say theft or escape of the wastes through underground water flows or geological shifts are still possible.

14. Another possibility is to recycle the waste as fuel in another form of reactor, thus reducing the amount of CANDU waste to worry about but increasing the operating dangers in a reprocessed fuel reactor

which creates a smaller and more controllable quantity of a much more lethal form of waste. Many are horrified by the risks attending this proposal.

15. At the same time, the dangers of uranium mining should not be overlooked, say the critics. Not only is there a relatively high incidence of cancers among uranium miners, but the mine tailings are themselves dangerous. The federal government is still cleaning out radioactive landfill from uranium mine tailings used in housing developments in the Ontario towns of Elliott Lake and Port Hope many years ago. Several streams and rivers in the vicinity of the Elliott Lake mine contain an eerie color instead of fish, thanks to leaching of uranium mine tailings into the local watershed.

16. The half-life of these mine tailings is shorter than for reactor waste — "only" 2500 years. But these tailings will require monitoring constantly over that period. No problem, says the industry.

17. The safety of the reactors themselves is also a target for nuclear critics. Reactors invite terrorist blackmail or theft, they say, and the reactors are not that safe anyway. They point to a recent British study showing a relatively high incidence of cancers among reactor workers exposed to supposedly safe levels of radioactivity over a long period.

18. The Atomic Energy Control Board recently acknowledged safety flaws in the design of the experimental reactor at Rolphton, Ontario, the key to the nuclear training program in Canada.

19. The nuclear proponents counterpunch by saying that the incidence of radiation from reactors is much lower than that from other sources in the environment, and that the dangers of the design flaw in the CANDU have been greatly magnified, but will be remedied just the same. Based on experience to date, an individual is over one million times more likely to die from an automobile accident than a nuclear accident, they say.

20. Quite apart from safety, say the critics, the ultimate irony is that nuclear power is uneconomic. Reactors are highly subject to cost overruns in construction and to operating shutdowns for repairs. They will also be expensive to decommision at the end of their utility.

21. In the U.S., reactors have been operating at less than 60% of capacity and have been suffering construction cost overruns of about 35%.

22. In Canada, reactor operations appear to suffer less down-time for repairs, but the price tag is still high. Cost overruns, particularly in heavy water plants, have already run to several hundred millions in Nova Scotia and Ontario.

23. The bugs are being worked out, and nuclear energy is still cheaper

than imported oil, or coal or solar, according to the industry, disputed by the critics.

24. It is not surprising people are confused. Each major political party appears split on the issue. Québec has declared a two-year moratorium on new nuclear developments while it studies the question, a clear about-face by the Parti Québécois from its strongly pro-nuclear position when in opposition. Ontario, the most pro-nuclear province, with nearly 40 reactors on the books for completion by 1999, is hearing anti-nuclear arguments through its royal commission on electrical power planning. Saskatchewan will allow development of a considerable uranium deposit, but for use only outside the province so far.

25. Even the federal government has started to make bows in the direction of the anti-nuclear side, despite major involvement in all phases of the nuclear cycle and reliance on nuclear power generation in long-range energy forecasts. Funds have finally been released to encourage various forms of renewable energy, believed by exponents of nuclear energy the best alternative. The government has also been constrained to include nuclear opponents in the staff of its nuclear information program.

26. The debate goes on internationally, in Europe, the U.S., Japan. Meanwhile, more reactors are sold and planned.

27. The divisions are reflected within the scientific community itself, as witness the range of opinion in the journal *Bulletin of Atomic Scientists.*

28. The growing fears about the safety of nuclear energy are part of a revived popular division over the value of modern technology. The longstanding western view of technology as a beneficent tool for universal good has been battered by the realization that our practices are rapidly poisoning our air and oceans, that we cannot explain how cancers are rapidly increasing and how they are environmentally caused.

29. Some believe the remedy will come only from changing our lifestyles; others believe that science will find a way, that we can continue to live pretty much as we are.

30. These attitudes of scepticism and optimism towards science are central in the debate over nuclear energy. Nuclear opponents fear human error, sabotage, and health risks. They tend to favour the "sound and decentralized technologies of wind, sun, and biomass energy. They emphasize conservation of resources above all else; they quote from E.L. Schumacher's "Small is Beautiful".

31. Nuclear proponents recognize that nuclear energy poses grave potential risks, but they are confident science can anticipate and control them. They maintain that renewable energy resources are insufficiently developed to justify a leap of faith in their technological feasibility.

32. The debate is sharpened by another question. The science of nuclear physics is less than 100 years old. How do we know when a subject matter has received sufficient attention? How, by definition, do we know how much we have yet to know? Despite the billions spent, is 100 years enough time for scientists to determine all the long-term hazards of a highly dangerous substance?

33. The question that preoccupies professors of the philosophy of knowledge has become crucial for everyone in the face of nuclear risks.

34. We cannot answer the question factually. We answer it only through our more general attitudes towards science: cautious, sceptical, or optimistic. The nuclear debate itself will have a long half-life.

Style and Structure

1. Underline the passage which introduces the topic to the reader.

2. How does the organization of the information in paragraph 2 into two sentences prepare the reader for the organization of the material in the body of the essay?

3. Make a list of the points in the body of the essay for which the writer presents "pro and con" arguments. What are the advantages of dealing with the "pro and con" arguments one point at a time, as the writer does in this article, over dealing with all of the "pro" arguments in one section and all of the "con" arguments in a separate section?

4. Compare the author's choice of words in this essay with the choice of words in "Nightmare in Niagara". How are the word choices in each intended to affect the reader?

5. Can you detect anything in Pepperell's word choice that would indicate that he is being anything but objective in this essay?

6. Re-examine your list of "pro and con" arguments. How much space does the writer devote to the "pro" arguments? How much space does he devote to the "con"? Does this imbalance indicate a bias on the part of the writer?

7. Why is the conclusion (paragraphs 32 to 34) appropriate for this article?

Thinking and Writing

a. Write an essay in which you either support *or* oppose the proposition "Nuclear energy is the only *feasible* source of energy for the immediate future."
   Audience:
   an "average" member of the general public who knows very little about nuclear energy other than what he/she has read in newspaper accounts.

b. Write an essay, in the form of a letter to the editor of a newspaper, in which you outline and justify your personal attitude toward the future development of nuclear power in your province.

Audience:

an "average" member of the general public who knows very little about nuclear energy other than what he/she has read in newspaper accounts.

Send a copy of your essay to the editor of a local newspaper.

Heart attacks: delay can be fatal

by Oscar Roth, M.D.
with Lawrence Galton

1. What happens when you have a heart attack? What are the symptoms? What happens to the body? If you suffer — or suspect you may be suffering — an attack, what should you do? What can be done for you? What will happen — what will your minutes, hours, days be like?

2. In this first part of a three-part series, heart specialist Dr. Oscar Roth, clinical professor at Yale University School of Medicine, answers your most pressing questions about heart attacks. Lawrence Galton is a medical writer.

   Are there particular times of day — and special circumstances — under which heart attacks occur?

3. No. They can occur at any hour and under varying circumstances — in the midst of a hard set of tennis, while running to catch a bus, while shovelling snow, in the middle of a heated argument, but also while you're having a pleasant dinner or resting or sleeping.

   Is it possible to have a mild heart attack without realizing it?

4. Yes. What are called "silent" heart attacks do occur occasionally.

5. Sometimes, during a routine examination, a physician will find evidence of a past heart attack in an electrocardiogram. Yet, the patient has no memory of an attack. And, in fact, the episode may have been relatively minor and the heart muscle so little affected, that no symptoms at all occurred.

6. Some so-called silent attacks, however, are not really silent. They

do produce symptoms but the symptoms may be mild or may be misinterpreted.

7. But such attacks are not common. Usually a heart attack makes itself known by its symptoms.

How can a heart attack usually be recognized?

8. Chest pain is by far the most common symptom. At times, it may be localized in the upper-mid abdomen.

9. The pain can vary greatly. On the one hand, it can be a slight feeling of pressure, of oppression in the chest. At the other extreme, it can be very severe, crushing, viselike, sometimes spreading into the throat, the shoulders, the arms, even the back.

10. Some people are prostrated immediately. Others walk around trying to find relief.

11. If a person has had anginal pain in the past and then experiences a heart attack, he or she may think at first that the chest pain of a heart attack does not stop, does not respond to rest or nitroglycerin. Often, it may radiate to the neck, jaw, right or left shoulder or arm, or to the region between the shoulders in the back. Occasionally, the pain will not be in the chest, only in the area of radiation.

Are there other symptoms with the pain?

12. Commonly there is a feeling of great anxiety, even of impending death. Also, there is often a cold sweat and the face turns almost gray.

13. There may be retching, belching, or vomiting and sometimes these may cause a heart attack to be confused with a stomach upset.

14. Shortness of breath is not inevitable, but it is common. Sometimes a patient will gasp for air during an attack. In some cases, there are palpitations—sensations that the heart is beating abnormally hard and fast.

Why is immediate medical attention so important?

15. There is only one safe way to tell what is causing your chest pain or other symptoms: have a physician check right away.

16. Medical attention without delay can be absolutely vital. In some cases, a few minutes have meant the difference between life and death—which is why most physicians urge patients to go immediately to the hospital rather than wait for medical help at home.

17. Heart attacks don't have to be fatal. Many who die from an attack die needlessly. They die, even though, despite their attack, their hearts are too good to die—that is, the damage to the heart muscle is not enough to cause death.

18. More than 80 per cent of heart attack deaths occur within the first twenty-four hours, many within the first hour. You might expect that extensive damage to the heart accounts for the deaths. But in many victims of a fatal heart attack, the heart is only minimally damaged. Sudden death after a heart attack is somewhat compara-

ble to the way a clock sometimes stops ticking even though its mechanism is still in good working order.

Why does a heart that is still basically sound and too good to die stop?

19. Electrical failure.

But let me make this point: Electrical failure of the heart can often be prevented — and, if it should happen, can often be overcome — if the patient gets immediate medical attention.

20. So if you know you're experiencing a heart attack, or have only the slightest suspicion that you may be, get to an emergency room. At once.

21. Once you're there, waste no time in saying that you may be having a heart attack. That will get you immediate and appropriate attention.

22. Delay by heart attack victims in getting medical attention is awesomely common. The following information will help show how important prompt action is.

23. More than half of the people who die of heart attacks succumb before they reach a hospital, where their chances for survival would have been greatly improved.

24. When University of Rochester cardiologists did a special study of coronary patients to find out how much time had elapsed between the onset of symptoms and hospitalization, the average interval turned out to be $3\frac{1}{2}$ hours. In some cases, the delay stretched for as long as five days. Transportation time to the hospital accounted for only a tiny fraction of the delay — 20 minutes on average.

25. The trouble was that patients were slow to seek help even when symptoms should have been unmistakable. Eighty per cent had experienced intense chest pain, yet had delayed seeking help.

26. At a special American College of Cardiology conference on the delay problem, experts agreed that heart attack victims often hold off seeking help — and even deny to themselves and others that they have symptoms of an attack — because they believe that a heart attack is a completely incapacitating condition from which they will never truly recover.

27. But that is wrong. A heart attack victim reaching a hospital quickly after an attack begins not only has an excellent prospect of leaving the hospital alive but also a very good and constantly improving likelihood that he or she will be able to return to a full life, including work, sex and play.

Style and Structure

1. Why does the author choose to open with a series of questions?
2. Paragraph 2 does not contain a very effective thesis or topic

statement. Write a paragraph which introduces the writers and states the topic more effectively.

3. The body of the article is arranged around six key questions. Why is this a more effective format than a straightforward explanation? Why has the author chosen to arrange the questions in this particular order?

4. Repetition of a key point in a variety of ways is one of the devices used by writers to make that point stand out in the reader's mind. What point does the writer use repetition to emphasize in this article?

5. Does the final paragraph serve as an adequate conclusion for the essay as a whole? Give reasons for your answer.

Thinking and Writing

a. Conduct an informal survey, based on the information in the article, amongst your friends and relatives to find out how many people know the symptoms of a heart attack.
Write an essay based on your findings.
Audience:
a member of the health services professions who would find such information helpful in improving his/her ability to communicate with the general public.

b. Write a brochure aimed at educating the general public on how to avoid, recognize and react to a heart attack. Aim this paper at the type of reader who knows least about heart attacks according to your survey.
Audience:
as indicated in the assignment.
Send a copy of your essay to a member of the segment of the population that your survey has identified as knowing least about heart attacks, or the Heart Association or a member of the medical profession (enquire whether your paper would be of any use to the recipient in an educational program for the general public).

Coiled collector

by Katherine Griggs

1. Gary Jensen has met the challenge of putting the sun to work as inexpensively as possible. His no-frills solar collector for heating water costs less than $40 in readily available materials and can be built at home as a weekend project.
2. "I use this system exclusively on my summer cabin in central Washington," says Jensen. "I find that two to three hours' exposure to the sun (65° to 75° F outside temperature) will deliver water at 120° to 130° F."
3. Jensen's device is certainly simple: a four-ft.-square wood platform that supports 100 feet of coiled one-inch polyethylene pipe. He attached the structure to his cabin's roof, but any surface with good exposure to the sun will do. Connected to a cold-water main at its inlet in the center of the coil, the pipe delivers approximately five gallons of solar-heated water through its upper outlet. In the house, the hot water is tempered with cold in the shower or at the sink.
4. When Jensen closes his cabin for the winter, he uses a clever draining method to prevent the water heater from freezing. After disconnecting the inlet and outlet fittings at the hose coil, he simply rotates the hose reel on the base in the direction opposite that of the hose winding. This action "unwinds" the remaining water out of each coil.
5. Undoubtedly, this unit's simplicity confines its practicality to use in the summertime — or in frost-free areas. But Jensen has suggestions for increasing the system's efficiency. He recommends, and offers plans for, construction of a cover, which, he says, provides hotter water. In addition, he claims you can get greater quantities of hot water by building two, three, or more units and connecting them in series.

Caveat

6. One caution concerning the use of polyethylene pipe: Sears approves its PVC pipe for cold water only, and strongly discourages its use for water that reaches 160° or higher. Although Jensen maintains that the polyethylene pipe functions successfully during summer weekends at his cabin, we'd recommend flexible polybutylene (PB) pipe as the longer-lasting material.
7. Jensen offers complete plans and instructions for $7.95 ppd. To ask

a specific question, send a stamped return envelope to Gary I. Jensen, 15800 9th Ave. N.E., Seattle, Wash. 98155.

Style and Structure

1. Underline the topic sentence of the article and draft a plan of its organization.
2. What type of reader is this article aimed at? How does the writer try to attract this type of reader in the introduction?
3. Why does the writer use direct quotation in paragraph 2? Although direct quotation might be appropriate in this type of writing, would it be appropriate in a technical report? Give reasons for your answer. Rewrite this paragraph so that it presents the information in a way that would be more acceptable in an "on the job" situation.
4. Paragraph 7 is not a particularly good conclusion to the article. Write a conclusion that more effectively deals with the complete article.

Thinking and Writing

a. The author of this article not only intends to give the reader information about a particular type of solar collector; she is trying to convince the reader to buy copies of the plans.
   Select another form of solar energy collecting (either active or passive) and write a short essay in the form of a sales brochure for that device. There is such a wide range of information available on solar energy that a brief trip to the library should enable even someone who knows nothing about the subject to become familiar with it very easily.
   Audience:
   someone who is just becoming interested in solar energy but is not yet knowledgeable about the technology involved.

b. By reading copies of as many of your classmate's sales brochures as possible and by doing further research on the topic of solar energy in newspapers, magazines and books, prepare an essay on the feasibility of using solar energy on a large scale to meet future energy needs.
   Audience:
   a reader who already knows something about solar energy, but whose opinion on its future feasibility is opposed to yours. Send a copy of your essay to the public relations officer of a major electronics corporation that is experimenting with solar energy (if you do *not* think that solar energy is a feasible alternative), or the public relations officer of a major gas or oil company (if you think that solar energy *is* a feasible alternative).

uraza, oburzenie, obraz

Middle class resentment's base is envy
zawiść, zazdrość

by Robert Fulford

1. I know a man who has millions and millions of dollars and can't stop complaining. He makes more money just by living through the day than most people make by working for a year. But he talks endlessly about high taxation, government interference in his business, "welfare rip-offs" and people who get "a free ride."

2. If you listened to his conversation, and didn't know anything about his net worth, you'd believe that somehow the world had conspired to keep him from earning a proper living. He's mad as hell and he's not going to take it anymore!

3. In my mind he stands as a symbol—though of course a particularly outlandish one—of the late 1970s and their very peculiar mood. In recent years a dark cloud of bitterness and meanness has risen over the North American middle classes. By now it has saturated our political life and tends to dominate much of our culture, particularly print and television. The people who express themselves loudest in this historic period may eventually be known not as the Me Generation but as the Mean Generation.

Rich and unhappy

4. How is it possible, logically, to reconcile these two facts:
   (i) Our middle classes are richer by far than any similarly large group in the history of humanity. They have what their parents and grandparents dreamed of having. For whatever reasons, society has so arranged things that these millions of people are now — by any reasonable standard based on historical or global comparisons—extremely rich.

5. (ii) Our middle classes are desperately unhappy with their position in life. They believe that government, far from helping them, has damaged them, through cruel taxation and other means. They also believe they have been cheated by other parts of society, notably the poor.

6. In the recent local elections in Toronto, David Lewis Stein detected what he called "bitter, selfish ideas" beginning to surface. There were aldermanic candidates who came up with preposterously narrow positions, such as the notion that people who don't have children shouldn't be taxed for education—and they were applauded.

7. This isn't limited to Toronto. Douglas Fisher noted a few months ago that across Canada, "the economic troubles of the country are increasingly laid to bad government leadership...and (among other things) an over-extensive set of educational, health and welfare systems."

Poor taxpayers

8. The health-care system of Canada, whatever its flaws, is one of the great accomplishments of our social order, and our education system is another. Yet it has now become commonplace to say that we have gone too far with them, they cost too much, they are "soaking" the taxpayers, etc.

9. In the recent Toronto Rosedale by-election, canvassers noted — according to a report by Christina McCall Newman — that the voters in the best districts, with the best houses, were the loudest in their complaints about the government. This accords with my own observation: Those who benefit most by the system also resent it most.

10. Doctors, for instance, who have been made rich by government health-care, tell me that taxes are driving them out of the country. They may have to move to Houston to make a decent living. Then they go off to their beautiful houses in their expensive cars, or sail their lovely boats, or get on the plane to ski in Europe. They aren't aware, perhaps never will be aware, of the comedy that lies in the contrast between what they say and what they are.

11. It will do you no good to tell such people that they've never had it so good; that's probably true, but it doesn't help. Middle-class resentment isn't based on logic. It's based, so far as I can tell, on envy.

12. For some people, envy is the only belief-system left. Envy provides a reason to work, a reason to achieve, and a reason to get mad — all things that religion or the family once gave us. Envy fuels the energy of the truly ambitious.

Welfare bums

13. And in our historic period the most prominent institutions of society are ready and eager to feed and heighten envy. Television, the movies, the magazines — all of them tell us, all day, every day, about a world where people are richer, more beautiful, more interesting, a world where someone (unlike us) is having a good time.

14. At the same time, envy produces a permanent sourness of the spirit, a lack of generosity, that spills over into public life. It makes us suspicious and narrow. It makes us believe Quebec is taking over the country ("and ramming French down our throats") or the welfare bums are milking us, or schoolteachers are making too much money. It makes us wildly illogical when we talk about

mundane issues like taxes or welfare. It creates, alas, the public mood within which the country must live in this difficult season.

Style and Structure

1. How does Fulford present his illustration in the opening two paragraphs in such a way as to get the reader on his side? Why does he choose this particular illustration even though he calls it "outlandish" in paragraph 3?
2. Underline the thesis statement and draft a plan of the article's organization.
3. Why does the writer use clichés in the concluding sentences of paragraphs 1 and 2? How does he use a cliché in the last sentence of the third paragraph to emphasize his thesis?
4. What is the purpose of paragraphs 4 and 5? What is the relationship of paragraphs 6 to 10 to paragraphs 4 and 5?
5. What persuasive techniques does the writer use in paragraphs 6 to 10?
6. At which point in the article does the writer resolve the logical inconsistency summarized in paragraphs 4 and 5? What is the effect of the author's use of the words "logically" and "logic" in these two situations?
7. A conclusion may have a number of functions; the most common is a restatement of the thesis. In this essay, however, Fulford uses his conclusion for another purpose. What is this purpose and is it consistent with his thesis and the body of his article?

Thinking and Writing

a. Write an essay on the Welfare System *or* the Unemployment Insurance System in which you reveal some of the following information:
    (i)   How does one qualify for benefits?
    (ii) How can one be disqualified from benefits?
    (iii) Who administers the system and where do the funds come from?
    (iv) How much money does a recipient receive?
    (v)   What controls exist to prevent cheating?
    (vi) Any other information that seems pertinent.
    Audience:
    someone who maintains the popular notion that Welfare and Unemployment Insurance are "rip-offs".

b. Based on your research in question a. write an essay on how the Welfare System *or* the Unemployment Insurance System could be improved to make it fairer to both the recipient and the taxpayer.

Audience:

someone who already knows something about these "systems" and is in a position to make changes in them.

Send a copy of your essay to your Member of Parliament (if you have written about Unemployment Insurance); or the Welfare Board in your community (if you have written about the Welfare System).

The liberation of Canada's writers

by George Woodcock

1. Canadian writing has flourished in the Sixties and Seventies as never before. It has taken on form as a national literature we can seriously compare with other English-speaking countries. In fact, there are more good poets in Canada today than there are in Britain. You are skeptical, perhaps even deny what I say. If you do, I suggest you deny the evidence of history and—more to the point—the evidence of those shelves heavy with good Canadian books in a way nobody imagined 30 years ago.

2. Don't you remember what it was like to be a writer in Canada 30 years ago? Writers were few and scattered and not greatly respected; they didn't fit in with the Canadian image, which was still manly and open-air. Hugh MacLennan in those days wrote a novel about the Canadas of the French and English which he called Two Solitudes, but if he had then written a novel about Canadian writers he could easily have called it Many Solitudes.

3. When I returned to Canada in 1949 there were precisely three anglophone literary magazines functioning, one in Montreal (John Sutherland's Northern Review), one in Victoria (Alan Crawley's Contemporary Verse) and one in Fredericton (Fiddlehead); there were none in Toronto or Winnipeg or Vancouver. Most publishers were mainly in the business of selling foreign books, and were very conservative about publishing Canadian books.

4. I met nobody in 1949 who lived by writing. Most writers had to rely on univeristy teaching or CBC work or some unliterary occupation to make up a real income. Even those who were and still are great

names in Canadian writing either taught or broadcast to keep alive. We were a country of Sunday writers. Real literary professionalism hardly existed.

5. Today the situation is vastly different. The latest edition of the Literary History of Canada comes in three volumes. Two include Canadian writing for the whole three centuries from Robert Hayman in seventeenth-century Newfoundland down to 1960. The third volume is devoted entirely to the 13 years between 1960 and 1973. A vast literary explosion has affected every kind of writing — poetry and drama and fiction as well as biography and history. I wrote the section on poetry between 1960 and 1973 for the LHC. I found in that 13 years, 1,100 books of poetry were published, an average of 80 a year, whereas only about 20 a year were being published as recently as 1959. Canadian books of every kind occupy far more shelves in our bookstores and libraries than ever before.

6. It isn't just a matter of quantity. The 1960s and 1970s have fostered many fine new talents, like Margaret Laurence with her splendid Manawaka quartet and Margaret Atwood in poetry and prose, and the later Al Purdy, and Matt Cohen, perhaps the best of younger novelists, and Alden Nowlan and Marian Engel, and a whole company of young playwrights appearing in response to the new theatres. As many good writers have emerged in Canada during the past 20 years as in the whole previous history of our literature.

7. Perhaps an even more striking fact is that the infrastructure of a real literary world has grown up at the same time as these writers emerged. As a literary historian, I've always found that a steady output of good writing depends largely on the kind of sustained and sustaining interest that draws writers together, gives them organs of expression and provides ways for their books to be published and criticized.

8. The literary world, with its population of interested but not always very creative people running magazines and presses, is really the kind of undergrowth out of which the trees of creation rise in any culture. It has its own kind of ecological balance, and what I feel has happened in Canada over the past 20 years — partly though not entirely through the judicious support given by the Canada Council, the Ontario Arts Council and similar bodies — is precisely the creation of this necessary balance, of this kind of responsive infrastructure.

9. Now we have not three precarious literary magazines, but several dozen scattered over the country which flourish year after year. There are many more publishing firms, and the trade has moved to a great extent out of the old centre of Toronto, so that there are adventurous and important regional houses like Hurtig in Edmonton and Douglas & McIntyre in Vancouver. The writers are no

longer isolated as they were in the past. They wander between St. John's and the Queen Charlottes, reading their work, meeting each other, and working together in their recently founded organizations, the League of Canadian Poets and the Writers' Union of Canada. The old Canadian Authors' Association survives, but mainly as a memento of the days when authors were amateurs; the Writers' Union is an organization of professionals, and it makes clear the shift from the old days of the Sunday writers to the new days of those who can afford to make writing a full-time occupation. I do not say there are even now many writers who make a living from books alone, but a surprising number do live very well by combining books with periodical writing. No longer is it necessary to depend on the CBC or some teaching post in an English department.

10. The Canadian writer, then, has been largely liberated because now he no longer pegs away in isolation, but is part of a real literary world like those of London and Paris and New York; it has its Canada Council and its varied publishers, its magazines and writers' organizations (though it no longer has the CBC); most important, it offers the chance to live by doing what a writer does best, which is not to teach or to broadcast, but to write.

11. I believe that Canadian writing has never been so good as it has become over the past two decades, and Canadian writers have never been so well off as they are now. If you don't believe it, read the letters of Frederick Philip Grove, a writer who in a past generation did try to make it under his own steam. He endured a life of frustration and bitterness that warped whatever talent in the beginning he had.

Style and Structure

1. Underline the thesis statement and draft a plan of the essay's organization.
2. What effect does Woodcock hope to achieve by presenting the claims for Canadian literature in the particular order that he does in the thesis statement?
3. How do sentences 4 and 5 in the opening paragraph prepare the reader for the writer's argument in the body of the essay?
4. Underline the problems faced by Canadian writers thirty years ago as outlined by Woodcock in paragraphs 2, 3, and 4. Identify the corresponding references to those problems in paragraphs 5 to 10. Based on your observations what organizational principle has been used in this article?
5. Examine two or three of the writer's paragraphs. In each does the author
   (a) introduce his paragraph with a topic sentence?

198

    (b) incorporate only those ideas which relate directly to the topic sentence?

    (c) provide a concluding sentence which summarizes or comments upon the material in the body of the paragraph?

6. How does the conclusion reflect the organization of the body of the essay?

Thinking and Writing

a. Select a Canadian writer whose work you find particularly interesting, and write an essay in which are outlined the qualities of the writer's work that are interesting and relevant. The essay should be aimed at someone who is not familiar with the author's work and should attempt to interest this person in reading something by that author. Remember to give impact to your essay by using a central organizing principle that will give a focus to your individual points.

Audience:
as outlined in the assignment.

b. Woodcock maintains that things have changed in Canada from 30 years ago when "writers were few and scattered and not greatly respected; they didn't fit in with the Canadian image, which was still manly and open-air."

Write an essay in which you consider just how much contemporary Canadian writers are respected by the general public and how they fit in with the modern "Canadian image" (*i.e.*, fit into the mainstream of Canadian society). Try to use specific information and well-reasoned arguments to support your position.

Audience:
someone who has read a few Canadian novels, but whose opinion on the topic, if he/she has ever thought of it, is opposed to yours.

Give a copy of your essay to friends and family members. Before they read the essay, ask them what they think about the importance of writers in our society. After they have read the paper, question them to find out if their opinions have changed as a result of what you have written.

A better way of dying

1. For many months, the 35-year-old man has been receiving chemicals to halt his cancer. But now, emaciated and racked with pain, he can no longer tolerate the powerful drugs. Everyone, including the patient, realizes that the chemotherapy is not working. The cancer has spread, and treatment is being stopped. Even before the notion of death can be fully accepted by the man or by his family, a hospital official calls aside the patient's wife. He tells her that since the hospital can do nothing more for her husband, he must be discharged and she must find another place for him to die.

2. In one form or another, such harrowing scenes are played out again and again each day across the U.S. Imbued as the medical establishment is with the idea of fighting at all costs for the prolongation of life, it is naturally geared to hope of success rather than the fact of failure. Once it becomes apparent that an illness is terminal, conventional medicine often seems unequipped, untrained and even unwilling to deal with death. It is mainly nursing homes—which are often dreary, costly and isolated from the rest of society—that seem ready to shoulder that inevitable human burden. As British Historian Arnold Toynbee once noted, it is almost as if "death is un-American."

3. Today, in a remarkable turnabout, a growing number of Americans have begun looking for a better way of dealing with the dying. In their search they have reached back to the Middle Ages, when religious orders established hospices (derived from the Latin word for guest) to care for travelers as well as ailing and dying pilgrims. Within the past few years, 130 groups have organized hospice programs, and about 20 institutions recognized by the newly formed National Hospice Organization (N.H.O.) are operating in the U.S. Unlike the way stations of the past, the present-day hospices provide more than attentive, sympathetic care for the dying. They do pioneer work in such neglected medical areas as the easing of pain and other symptoms of terminal illness and deal in psychological counseling for both patients and their families.

4. Most hospices in the U.S. take as their model London's St. Christopher's Hospice, founded a decade ago by Dr. Cicely Saunders. The primary goal of the London hospice and its North American cousins is to help people die with as little discomfort and as much serenity as possible and live as individuals during the weeks and months left to them.

5. Such care is often best given at home with the support of family

and friends. Indeed, the first U.S. hospice, established in New Haven, Conn. in 1971, is only now erecting its own 44-bed building as a backup for its home care. It will continue to rely largely on home visits by staff nurses and dedicated volunteers. That home technique has been widely and successfully emulated. Says Dr. Walter Norley, 62, who is dying of bone cancer and is being cared for at home by Riverside Hospice in Boonton, N.J.: "I don't know whether it's because I'm a physician or not, but I have no desire to spend more time in a hospital than I must."

6. Other hospices, like the one at Manhattan's St. Luke's Hospital Center, now flourish within existing medical institutions. In fact, at St. Luke's, the hospice patients are not kept in a "death ward," but are scattered throughout the hospital, where they are regularly visited by special doctors, nurses and counselors attached to the hospice program. Members of the regular hospital staff report that watching the way hospice people treat the terminally ill has helped them modify their own behavior. "When a patient knows he's dying," one doctor notes, "you can't just smile and ask your usual 'Good morning, how are you?'"

7. Whatever the setting, an immediate priority of hospices is the relief of chronic pain and fear, which can be particularly severe when patients are dying of cancer. Unlike traditional hospitals, where terminal patients are often so heavily doped that they are virtually in a stupor, hospices usually administer methadone or a special mixture that may include morphine, cocaine, alcohol and syrup. Even before the pain begins to be extreme, the mix is given in relatively small quantities at various intervals around the clock. This helps allay the fear of pain and reduces the amount of drugging necessary to control it. One desired result: to keep the patient's mind as clear as possible.

8. Hospice personnel are trained to ease the social and emotional problems related to dying, doing everything from advising on the drafting of wills to caring for neglected pets. Jayne Murdock, a Ross, Calif., schoolteacher, recalls how her dying mother at first refused to see her grandchildren after she was brought home from the hospital. But when the visiting hospice team began reducing her pain and reassuring her and her family in other ways, a new tranquillity set in. Finally, the woman even let the youngsters give her medication and assist her about the house. Says Murdock: "I felt when she died that it was a victory for all of us. None of us had any guilt."

9. As the U.S. begins to cope more directly with the once taboo subject of death, the hospice idea is likely to spread even farther and faster. Sandol Stoddard's sympathetic new book, *The Hospice Movement: A Better Way of Caring for the Dying* (Stein & Day; $8.95), is

already in its third printing. Next October, at its first annual meeting in Washington, the N.H.O. will push for legislation that will allow insurance payments for hospice care. Zachary Morfogen, N.H.O. chairman, thinks enormous strides have already been made. Says he: "Ten years ago, it would have been impossible to persuade any corporation to include a hospice program under its health and medical plans. The reaction would have been, 'What are you doing, trying to create a death house?' Now people are willing to discuss such matters openly and candidly. <u>Death has finally come out of the closet.</u>"

Style and Structure

1. Instead of introducing his thesis in the opening paragraph, how does the writer begin his article and why?
2. What is the purpose of paragraph 2 in relation to the thesis statement in paragraph 3? What would be the effect on the article if paragraph 2 were left out?
3. Underline the thesis statement.
4. Paragraph 8 offers an interesting example of a writer's use of generalization supported by a specific illustration.
   (a) Distinguish between the generalization and the specific illustration.
   (b) What does the specific illustration contribute to the essay that the generalization does not?
5. A conclusion may have a number of functions, the most common being a restatement of the thesis. In this essay, however, the author uses his conclusion for another purpose. What is it, and is it consistent with his thesis and the body of his article?
6. Why does the writer conclude his essay with the quotation, "Death has finally come out of the closet"?

Thinking and Writing

a. Interview someone who is closely involved with the care or counselling of terminally ill patients. Inquire about the weaknesses this person sees in our handling of terminally ill patients and what recommendations he/she would make to improve the situation.
Write a report based on your findings.
Audience:
an "average" member of the general public who, like many of us, has never been personally involved with the subject.

b. Write an essay in which you outline your concept of the ideal method of handling the problems of death and dying in your community.

Audience:
a reader who is familiar with the problems and the present methods of handling them.
Send a copy of your essay to a member of the clergy, a medical professional or a social worker that you know.

Japan's robot revolution

by Katsuhiko Hirano

1. Industrial robots are becoming increasingly important in the marketing success of Japanese automobiles, electrical appliances, and other products. Robots work all day without demanding pay increases and liberate human workers from drudgery and poor working conditions. The day may not be far off when "blue-collars" are replaced on the production line by uncomplaining "steelcollars."

2. Toyota Motor Co. recently opened to the press the Tahara No. 2 Works, a new plant that uses robots in all production stages. The welding line has eighteen separate work processes, each of which takes only three minutes. Eighty welding robots work smoothly and appear ready to take up additional workloads if necessary. Ninety per cent of these welding lines are automated. The only human worker is the overseer stationed at one end of the line to check on the robots' work. Toyota claims it has successfully cut more than fifty workers through the use of robots.

3. Human workers are about to disappear from the painting factory of Honda Motor Co.'s Sayama Works. Each of two painting lines uses eight industrial robots, which snake into every cranny, applying paint deftly. In no other automobile plant in the world has the painting process been so perfectly automated.

4. At Fujitsu-Fanuc Co. robots are turning out other robots and NC (numerical control) machine tools around the clock. Only a hundred people are at work during the day, and at night the plant becomes completely automated with only one worker tending the shop. There are fewer than ten robots working in this plant; yet the monthly production is slightly less than $8 million. President Seiemon Inaba vows to boost this to $20 million, with a total workforce of 120.

5. It is not only to cut back on workers that Japanese automakers are increasing their use of robots. What makes their robot-oriented attitudes ominous for other auto-making countries is that they are primarily aimed at improving product quality and preparing

for the age of small lot demands for a wide variety of products. It requires only modification of the original program for robots to turn out different models of motor vehicles, thus reducing production costs and the chance for human errors.

6. The use of robots is by no means limited to big businesses. Small and medium-size operations now account for some 70 per cent of all the welding robots in use. Even cottage factories with only family workers are beginning to use robots. Because an average industrial robot costs only about $40,000, a cottage-level workshop can afford one and recoup its investment in a couple of years if it foregoes employing a human worker.

7. The "cleaning robot," developed by Automax Co. of Tokyo, not only cleans but does a nightwatch's job as well. With eyes, ears, and a nose of its own, the machine emits a warning sound when it senses unusual light, sound, or smoke, according to Executive Director Sueo Matsubara of Automax. The robot has a roller brush and a cleaning cloth in its belly and moves around on an automobile battery. It has five small "fingers" at strategic places that can sense walls and other obstacles and turn the robot another way. Automax claims that smaller robots will be ideal for home use.

8. Another new specialty model is the "secretary robot." In the hope of freeing busy executives from the daily chore of signing hundreds of papers, Fujitsu Ltd.'s Research Institute has recently come up with an experimental "stamp-applying robot," which stamps the executive's signature. (When he first saw this machine, Fujitsu's President, Taiyu Kobayashi, was reportedly heard to sigh that he would now have nothing to do.)

9. Nippon Electric Co. also has developed a secretary robot called the "Cybernetic Secretary." This robot not only writes letters but also formulates schedules and gives out warnings when departure or interview time comes around. Director Hiroshi Yamada of Fujitsu predicts that soon robots will do most office work.

10. Prof. Ichiro Kato of Waseda University is now developing medical robots, especially one for tactile detection of breast cancer. Equipped with twenty-five "fingers," Prof. Kato's robot relays its findings to a computer system that detects cancerous growths and other abnormalities.

11. The Nomura Research Institute predicted recently that Japan's robot industry will record $1.2 billion in sales in 1985 and $2.4 billion by 1990. Others believe that the industry will continue its 40 to 50 per cent annual growth in the next several years and that the total sales may reach $4 billion by 1990. This possibility is by no means remote, especially now that the use of robots is expanding from welding, painting, and other simple tasks to far more complicated jobs in homes, factories, offices, and hospitals.

Style and Structure

1. (a) Underline the thesis statement.
    (b) Many articles in popular magazines do not present the thesis statement in the first paragraph. Instead they strive to catch the reader's interest through more dramatic means, such as vivid examples. Hirano's article was written for the business section of *World Press Review*. Do you feel that his introduction is appropriate for its readership? Give reasons for your response.
2. What main advantage of robotics does the writer emphasize in the first part of the body of the essay (paragraphs 2 to 4)? What type of reader would this emphasis interest most?
    If the article had been aimed at union members, what aspects of robotics might the wise writer have chosen to emphasize in the first section?
3. What is the function of paragraph 5 in relation to paragraphs 2 through 4? What additional advantages of robotics are dealt with in the paragraph? Why does the writer devote only one paragraph (5) to these advantages but spend three paragraphs (2–4) on one advantage?
4. What new aspect of robotics does the writer introduce in paragraph 6? How appropriate to the topic announced there are the examples that he gives in paragraphs 7 through 10?
5. What aspect of the robot industry is emphasized in paragraph 11? Is this conclusion effective, given the audience identified in question 1? Give reasons for your answer.

Thinking and Writing

a. Using the information provided in Hirano's article, write an essay about the positive effects of introducing robots into industry.
    Audience:
    a factory worker.

b. Write an essay aimed at a business person who is considering the introduction of robotics into his/her company. Outline the negative effects such a decision would have. Be sure to include discussions of such issues as social responsibility, unemployment and welfare costs, and the effect on the market of workers' loss of income.
    Audience:
    as outlined in the assignment.
    Send a copy of your essay to the person in charge of the electronics program at your school.

"Mirror, mirror, on the wall..."

by John Leo

1. The poet may insist that beauty is in the eye of the beholder; the historian might argue that societies create the image of female perfection that they want. There has always been plenty of evidence to support both views. Martin Luther thought long, beautiful hair was essential. Edmund Burke recommended delicate, fragile women. Goethe insisted on "the proper breadth of the pelvis and the necessary fullness of the breasts." Hottentot men look for sharply projecting buttocks, Rubens favored a full posterior, and Papuans require a big nose. The Mangaians of Polynesia care nothing of fat or thin and never seem to notice face, breasts or buttocks. To the tribesmen, the only standard of sexiness is well-shaped female genitals.

2. An anthropologized world now knows that notions of what is beautiful do vary with each age and culture. One era's flower is another's frump. Primitive man, understandably concerned with fertility, idealized ample women. One of the earliest surviving sculptures, the Stone Age Venus of Willendorf, depicts a squat woman whose vital statistics—in inches—would amount to 96-89-96. This adipose standard stubbornly recurs in later eras. A 14th century treatise on beauty calls for "narrow shoulders, small breasts, large belly, broad hips, fat thighs, short legs and a small head." Some Oriental cultures today are turned on by what Simone de Beauvoir calls the "unnecessary, gratuitous blooming" of wrap-around fat.

3. The Greeks were so concerned with working out precise proportions for beauty that the sculptor Praxiteles insisted that the female navel be exactly midway between the breasts and genitals. The dark-haired Greeks considered fair-haired women exotic, perhaps the start of the notion that blondes have more fun. They also offered early evidence of the rewards that go to magnificent mammaries. When Phryne, Praxiteles' famous model and mistress, was on trial for treason, the orator defending her pulled aside her veil, baring her legendary breasts. The awed judges acquitted her on the spot.

4. Romans favored more independent, articulate women than the Greeks. Still, there were limits. Juvenal complains of ladies who

"discourse on poets and poetry, comparing Vergil with Homer... Wives shouldn't read all the classics—there ought to be some things women don't understand."

5. In ancient Egypt, women spent hours primping: fixing hair, applying lipstick, eye shadow and fingernail polish, grinding away body and genital hair with pumice stones. It worked: Nefertiti could make the cover of *Vogue* any month she wanted. For Cleopatra, the most famous bombshell of the ancient world, eroticism was plain hard work. Not a natural beauty, she labored diligently to learn coquettishness and flattery and reportedly polished her amatory techniques by practicing on slaves.

6. If Cleopatra had to work so hard at being desirable, can the average women do less? Apparently not. In the long history of images of beauty, one staple is the male tendency to spot new flaws in women, and the female tendency to work and suffer to remedy them. In the Middle Ages, large women rubbed themselves with cow dung dissolved in wine. When whiter skin was demanded, women applied leaches to take the red out. Breasts have been strapped down, cantilevered up, pushed together or apart, oiled and siliconed and, in 16th century Venice, fitted with wool or hair padding for a sexy "duck breast" look, curving from bodice to groin. In the long run, argues feminist Elizabeth Gould Davis, flat-chested women are evolutionary losers. Says she: "The female of the species owes her modern mammary magnificence to male sexual preference."

7. Still, a well-endowed woman can suddenly find herself out of favor when cultural winds change. The flapper era in America is one example. So is Europe's Romantic Age, which favored the wan, cadaverous look. In the 1820s, women sometimes drank vinegar or stayed up all night to look pale and interesting. Fragility was all. Wrote Keats: "God! she is like a milk-white lamb that bleats/For man's protection."

8. Victorians took this ideal of the shy, clinging vine, decorously desexed it, and assigned it to the wife. According to one well-known Victorian doctor, it was a "vile aspersion" to suggest that women were capable of sexual impulses. Inevitably that strait-laced era controlled women's shapes by severe compression of the waistline, without accenting breasts or hips.

9. Those womanly curves reasserted themselves at the turn of the century. During the hourglass craze, Lillie Langtry seemed perfection incarnate at 38-18-38. Since then, the ideal woman in Western culture has gradually slimmed down. Psyche, the White Rock girl, was 5 ft. 4 in. tall and weighed in at a hippy 140 lbs. when she first appeared on beverage bottles in 1893. Now, *sans* cellulite, she is 4 in. taller and 22 lbs. lighter.

10. In psychological terms, the current slim-hipped look amounts to a

rebellion against male domination: waist-trimming corsets are associated with male control of the female body, and narrow hips with a reluctance to bear children. Says Madge Garland, a former editor of British *Vogue*: "The natural shape of the female body has not been revealed and free as it is today for 1,500 years." W.H. Auden once complained that for most of Western history, the sexy beautiful women have seemed "fictionalized," set apart from real life. In the age of the natural look, a beauty now has to seem as though she just strolled in from Malibu beach, like Cheryl Tiegs.

Style and Structure

1. The opening paragraph offers an interesting example of a writer's use of generalization supported by specific illustrations.
   (a) Distinguish between the generalization and the specific illustrations.
   (b) What do the specific illustrations contribute to the introduction?
   (c) Would the opening be as effective if the specific illustrations were eliminated?
2. Underline the thesis statement and draft a plan of the article's organization.
3. What organizational principle does the writer employ in the body of the essay? Given the thesis, can you think of a more logical organizational principle?
4. Compare the description of Roman women in paragraph 4 with the other paragraphs describing female beauty. How could it be brought into line with the thesis?
5. The tone of an essay refers to the writer's attitude to his subject as reflected in his choice of words, selection of illustrations, etc. Is this writer completely serious about his topic? Use specific quotations from the article to prove your answer.
6. At first the final paragraph of the article does not seem to fulfill the requirements of a formal conclusion. It seems to continue the chronological development of man's idea of beauty into the present. How does the irony of the last sentence, "... a beauty now has to *seem* as though she just strolled in from *the beach at Malibu*" emphasize that the tyranny of a social rather than a personal standard of beauty still exists? Does this form an effective conclusion for the essay as a whole?

Thinking and Writing

a. "An anthropologized world knows that notions of what is most beautiful do vary with each age and culture."
   Write a short essay on what attributes your society declares

necessary in a woman for her to be beautiful, and try to outline the role of women that these attributes reflect (the author of the article points out, for example, that primitive man "idealized ample women" because he was concerned with fertility and child bearing).

Audience:

the same reader as aimed at by the author of the original article.

b. Write an essay in which you support or refute the proposition, "The predominant contemporary image of the ideal woman is limiting, shallow and degrading."

Audience:

someone who would argue against your stand on the proposition.

Send a copy of your essay to the editor of a "women's magazine" which champions the cause of women's liberation (if you argue *against* the proposition); or the editor of a "men's magazine" which devotes much of its space to presenting "beautiful" women (if you argue *for* the proposition).

Unaccustomed as I am...

by Andrew Weiner

You've been appointed area manager, an important promotion: there will be new responsibilities — some welcome, some not. For example, you've been invited to address the local Rotary Club in two weeks. But you're not accustomed to public speaking: in fact, you're terrified...

1. Making a bad speech, or not having the nerve to make any speech at all, is the biggest stumbling block facing would-be orators, a fear which has halted the careers of many budding speechmakers or at least made the process an agonizing exercise. And in the modern corporate world, where the ability to communicate effectively to large groups is a valuable commodity, an inability to do so can stunt the advancement of many otherwise promising executives.

2. Many aspiring orators, if they are fortunate to work for a larger corporation, can obtain counseling in the comfort of their offices. Imperial Oil, for instance, has set up communication training courses for their top executives to learn skills necessary to speak

not only at public meetings but also on TV, radio and at official inquiries. "Public speaking gives us a good opportunity to keep Canadians informed on energy issues," says Bob Landry, vice-president for external affairs at Imperial. And since what is said in a public meeting may also be repeated in newspapers across the country, the emphasis is very much on content as well as delivery.

3. Executives who don't have company programs such as Imperial Oil's usually turn to commercial schools. (Approximately 2,000 Canadians enroll in such schools each year.) Prices range from $120 for a 10-week course to as much as $2,000 depending on the amount of tutoring a novice elocutionist needs.

4. Dale Carnegie Courses, with branches scattered across the country, offers a 14-week program for executives and other interested would-be speakers. Carnegie spokesmen are tight-lipped on just what they charge students for their services, but they will say that most of their clients are executives or professionals.

5. "The first step towards effective public speaking is gaining the confidence to stand up and do it. After that, it's really a matter of organization," says Peter Lightfoot, a Toronto Dale Carnegie counselor. "But you can't have confidence unless you're organized —at least not unless you're a complete fool."

6. For many people, though, that first step is by far the hardest. If all the world's a stage, an awful lot of actors are suffering from stage fright. Fear of public speaking, according to Ken LeMaire, an instructor with Comm-Can Training, a public speaking school in Toronto, is "the most common fear in the world. I call it podiaphobia." An actor by profession, he says that effective speaking is really "acting—getting the words across, the way an actor does in a play."

7. Many people are "absolutely petrified of public speaking," agrees Lightfoot, "but they have to do it because of their jobs."

8. Using the tactic that it takes action to fight the fear of public speaking, Carnegie instructors push aspiring novices into the breach on their first outing. Students start with small exercises and work up to a full-fledged speech. Every student is called on to speak at least 29 times in the 14 weeks of the course, before a class of about 30. "If they can talk to that size gathering," Lightfoot says, "they can talk to any group."

9. A typical early exercise involves bringing in an object to talk about. Students have brought in everything from a car door to a live pig (although Lightfoot says that "we frown on firearms and snakes").

10. Once the student has gained self-confidence, he learns how to chart a speech. The key here is conciseness. "Learn to start at the beginning," says Lightfoot, "instead of *before* the beginning" and cut out

all extraneous details. He says that most ideas can be conveyed in as little as two minutes, and that a longer speech should be a succession of such ideas built up in a logical way.

11. The emphasis is on speaking *spontaneously* from a prepared plan. "You need a good memory to be a good speaker," Lightfoot says. "The worst thing you can do is get up and read something from a piece of paper. You can't get the same emotion into it. If you're going to do that, you might as well mimeo the thing and hand it out."

12. Ken LeMaire is also convinced that spontaneity is the key to smooth speechmaking. "Reading a speech is a different art." He concedes, however, that it is an art which it is sometimes necessary to master (for example: the danger of being quoted verbatim in the press).

13. LeMaire, who charges $120 for a 10-week course, urges his students to pay attention to other factors, namely their delivery. He teaches aspirants several acting tricks that succeed in winning an audience to their side; for example the rhetorical question followed by a pause. He also teaches them to be aware of their body language. When you give a speech your body is talking too, whether you know it or not. Stand with your arms folded and your audience will read you as defensive. Instead, LeMaire recommends an easy stance with arms open, and with every movement geared to "accentuate what you are saying at that moment. You should avoid any kind of repetitive and distracting mannerism that has nothing to do with what you're saying."

14. "More and more industry leaders are being asked to present their perspective in large public forums," says Mike Wilson, executive vice-president of Dominion Securities and one of Ken LeMaire's graduates. "And when they do, they've got to be able to present it in a meaningful way."

15. If a formal course in public speaking doesn't appeal, would-be speechmakers have an alternative. They can join what is virtually a self-help workshop in public speaking, a branch of the Toastmasters International Podium Club.

16. The first Toastmasters club was founded back in 1924 by Dr. Ralph C. Smedley. The first meeting was held in the basement of the Y.M.C.A. in Santa Ana, California. The club's avowed purpose was to "afford practice and training in the art of public speaking and the art of presiding over meetings, and to promote sociability and good fellowship among its members." Over the years this has evolved into the Toastmasters credo: that successful people can communicate effectively, and that the club can provide the setting in which to develop that skill. Sociability, though, remains an

important element, and the typical club newsletter is full of gossip about the doings of various members.

17. A non-profit organization, Toastmasters now has more than 3,000 clubs world-wide, over 200 in Canada. More than one million people have been through their programs since 1924. Initially, Toastmasters was an exclusively male preserve, leading to the development of a parallel Toastmistress organization. But these days, says Toronto-area governor Vince DaCosta "the great majority of clubs have opened their doors to the ladies," although a few bastions of male chauvinism do remain.

18. Each club has up to 400 members who pay $30 a year for the privilege of joining Toastmasters. Meetings are held weekly. Sometimes over dinner, sometimes over lunch, and sometimes with no refreshments at all. (Despite the name, there are few toasts at the typical Toastmasters meeting: in fact they are usually dry.)

19. Lunchtime in a specially reserved room in Simpson's Acadian Court restaurant in downtown Toronto: a meeting of the Toronto Business Club. Although this particular Toastmasters branch is co-ed, only two women are present today, along with twelve men. And while it is called a "business" club, those present include a housing planner, a university teacher, and the business manager for a union local.

20. On each place setting is the agenda for the day, which will be followed with almost military precision. The chairman calls the meeting to order and introduces the toastmaster of the day, who in turn introduces the leader of the day's table topics session: this is a ritual in which a member makes an impromptu two-minute speech on a topic he finds on a slip of paper beneath his bread plate (sample topic: how would you save the Canadian dollar?).

21. All of this introducing and speaking goes on against the background clatter of plates and cutlery, as the waitresses serve and the members work their way through the day's lunch. The meeting will run for 1½ hours, but hardly a moment will be wasted.

22. The prepared speeches begin: an insurance saleswoman gives an "ice breaker," a maiden speech so awesomely smooth you wonder why she is here at all. The housing planner talks about the joys of downhill skiing, and the teacher about misuses of vocabulary. All three are following exercises from the Toastmasters' training manual. If they persist with the club, they will ultimately gain certification as a CTM (competent toastmaster), ATM (able toastmaster), perhaps even a DTM (distinguished toastmaster).

23. These speeches are followed by what may be the most important item on the agenda: evaluation. A general evaluator of the day rates the chairman and toastmaster and table topics leader. Then

individual members rate particular speeches: the housing planner is told to use more gestures; the teacher to put more emphasis in his words. Finally the entire membership fills out ballots in which they evaluate not only the speakers but also the evaluators.

24. "We're all here," says president Dave MacKenzie, "to improve our communications ability." And while no great speeches are made on this occasion, nearly all the speakers appear confident and comfortable. The novice speaker is able to feel his way in what is obviously a very relaxed atmosphere: even the evaluations, while accurate, are gentle.

25. Toastmasters clubs, like most public speaking courses, make the assumption that you will deliver speeches which are entirely your own creation. But for the speaker approaching a really important engagement, yet occupied by other more pressing concerns, there is an honorable alternative: the professional speechwriter.

26. It may be absurd, but secrecy is almost invariably the rule when it comes to speechwriting for businessmen. It is, says Bernard Wheeler, "a very discreet profession." Together with Donald Davies, Wheeler runs a speechwriting service called Standing Ovation two days a week from a converted church manse on Toronto's Avenue Road. Wheeler and Davies who have extensive speechwriting experience from their years in advertising and public relations, charge executives between $1000 and $2,500 for their elocutionary expertise. A stiff price, but one which many executives are happy to pay for success in public speaking. In today's complex business world, what were once straight-forward business issues have become increasingly politicized. As a result, effective communication both inside and outside the organization is at a premium. Standing Ovation was born only after Wheeler had brought in Davies to collaborate on a rush job for an advertising client. "I expected a fair round of applause," the client told them afterwards. "But I didn't expect a standing ovation."

27. Davies and Wheeler then sat down and analyzed the process which had produced that standing ovation speech: once they had done so, they produced a booklet entitled *Standing Ovation or Polite Applause?* which they recently mailed to 300 senior Canadian corporate executives.

28. The standing ovation process breaks down, as they see it, into three main areas: the strategy; the message; and the actual delivery of the speech — each one critical in its own way. But it is in the area of strategy where they make the most novel proposals. Davies and Wheeler believe that the outcome of a speech is often determined before a word is written and that a bad speech is usually the result of a speaker making bad strategic decisions, even when he is not aware of making any decisions at all.

29. First, and perhaps most basic, is the decision to make a speech. In many cases, Wheeler says, the choice should be a *presentation* with visual aids instead. And the main criteria in choosing what the decision should be is "whether the information content becomes overloaded. There are so many executives who still believe that the purpose of a speech is to convey information."

30. If you want to reel off facts and figures, they suggest, give a presentation: you'll need visual aids to convey the information so that your audience retains it. And without them you'll just end up talking to yourself.

31. The proper function of a speech, as they see it, is to motivate, challenge and inspire. It should therefore appeal to the emotions of the audience as much as to their minds. As they point out in their booklet, "there is nothing logical about a standing ovation."

32. Strategy also extends to the choice of the kind of message you want to convey. Here Wheeler and Davies recommend another tried and tested advertising technique: "positioning." In searching for a subject, the executive should define the image of himself and his company which he wants to present: preferably one that will stand out from the crowd.

33. And just as the advertiser must know his consumers, so must the speaker know his audience. He should be aware of what they are expecting and wanting to hear, but he must also be prepared to confound those expectations to a certain degree if he wants to make a truly significant speech.

34. In working out a detailed speech strategy, the executive should use a small handpicked team of advisors, including a researcher and the writer or writers.

35. The fact that an executive has this team behind him, however, does not absolve him of all further responsibility: instead he must invest some of the time he has saved in polishing and practising the speech. Too many executives, Wheeler says, prepare only in the most cursory way — because in their experience, the investment of more time has not paid dividends in the past. Where the writer prepares the text, the executive must make sure that he is comfortable with it. And the key here is simplicity, in both words and the expression of ideas. Metaphors can help a great deal, as long as they are not overworked, in involving an audience. "All words are pictures," Wheeler says. They point approvingly to John F. Kennedy's inaugural address, a speech full of metaphorical zingers like "if a beachhead of co-operation may push back the jungle of suspicion..." In fact, they like this particular speech so much they send copies of it out to prospective clients.

36. Whether you decide to follow in the footsteps of John F. Kennedy, Franklin Delano Roosevelt or Pierre Trudeau and rely on the

expertise of a professional speechwriter, the time will come when, speech clenched in fist, you'll have to tentatively approach the podium. And while many tyro elocutionists take to the art like a boat to water, there are the rest of us, who struggle and squirm and thank our lucky stars that we can even *stand*, let alone speak in front of a live audience.

Style and Structure

1. Why does the author choose to open his article with the italicized paragraph? Why does Weiner use the second person singular subject "you" instead of the more common third person?

2. Underline the thesis statement(s) in the article and draft a plan of the article's organization.

3. Compile a list of the experts quoted either directly or indirectly in the article. How does quoting these sources affect the credibility of the article as a whole? How would this article have been impaired if the writer had not credited his sources of information and had tried to pass off his sources' ideas as his own (plagiarized)?

4. In many places throughout the article, Weiner presents information in direct quotations which could easily have been presented in the form of an indirect quotation. In paragraph 2, for example, the writer could easily have changed the direct quotation to the following:

   Public speaking gives their employees a good opportunity to keep Canadians informed on energy issues, according to Bob Landry, vice-president for external affairs at Imperial.

   How does this periodic use of direct quotation affect the readability of the article?

5. How does paragraph 36 function as a good conclusion for the article as a whole? Underline the section of the conclusion which relates back to the italicized paragraph and thus helps to unify the article.

Thinking and Writing

a. 1. Weiner states that "in the modern corporate world, where the ability to communicate effectively to large groups is a valuable commodity, an inability to do so can stunt the advancement of many otherwise promising executives." Conduct a survey of your program instructors and professionals in the career which you plan to enter to determine if this statement holds true for that career. Ask about the types of public speaking, the types of audience, the frequency and length of such presentations, and their importance to success in that career.

2. Write an essay in the form of a report on your findings.

Audience:

someone considering entering the program in which you are enrolled who may not be aware of all of the facets of this prospective field of employment.

b. Based upon your findings in section a, write an essay, aimed at the faculty member in charge of your program, in which you make recommendations concerning the incorporation of a course on public speaking into your program. Be certain to use specific data and logically developed arguments to support your thesis.

Audience:

as outlined in the topic.

Send a copy of your essay to your program supervisor.

Lotoland

by David Macfarlane

1. Little Debbie Gimbeau has never tasted avocado and shrimp. She does not own an Arabian pony and has never been to Martinique. Unlike her schoolmates, she has never known a home with a sauna, has never been chauffeured to fencing class, has never studied Fine Art in Siena. Life, for Debbie Gimbeau, is fraught with hardship, and she is not alone. There are thousands of Debbie Gimbeaus — children who wake each day to bowls of Shreddies and paper routes, children who wear orlon sweaters and who have no scuba tanks. They are the unlucky ones. They are children whose parents have never won a lottery.

2. Once they were referred to as the underprivileged. Now, in the wake of the economic revolution that has swept the country, unfortunates such as Debbie's parents are known as the New Losers, the people left behind by the laws of chance. Their existence might be traced to 1969 when an amendment to the Criminal Code exempted the government from antigambling laws. More accurately, their origins can be found in the landmark federal budget that a few years ago ushered in a new economic age, transforming Canada from a land of long shots into what Jimmy the Greek calls "just a society of lucky stiffs."

3. It was in the spring of 1981 that the federal government abolished the economy and launched the most elaborate lottery scheme the world has ever seen. Although a bold move, it was a decision that came as no surprise to anyone; for years it had been apparent that the only thing the government could do with any degree of efficiency was run lotteries. Singularly helpless at fighting inflation and unemployment, strangely unmoved by the disappearance of the dollar and Quebec, Ottawa nonetheless managed to persuade overtaxed citizens to spend $10 on lottery tickets that had a one in 800,000 chance of winning—people were twice as likely to be hit by a falling satellite—but which paid off at odds one-tenth of that. Clearly, with the chutzpah to con an entire population, the government was wasting its time on pedestrian concerns like inflation.

4. As economic revolutions go, this one was surprisingly simple. Federal taxes were raised a mere 10 percent, thereby giving Ottawa control of all the money in the country. This capital was then invested in high-risk, high-return commodities. With these monies the government inaugurated a massive series of million-dollar lotteries. Held every 15 seconds, the draws corresponded precisely to the number of Canadians in the most recent census. In theory, everyone could become a millionaire.

5. Has the gamble paid off? Preliminary indications are that it has. Department stores report that sales of ascots, blazers and white yachting caps have skyrocketed, while a French businessman, speaking from a Paris kennel, estimates that poodle exports to Canada have tripled. And a recent survey has shown that 80 percent of all Canadian households now subscribe to *Country Life* and *Gourmet* magazines.

6. The new economic system is not without its flaws, and inflation is certainly one of them.

7. But there is a bigger problem. While certain lucky lotophiles have won grand prizes three or four times, the sad fact remains that there are people, like the Gimbeaus, who do not win things, however favourable the odds. "Maybe I'm jinxed," says Clement Baddleboine, a Vancouver accountant and father of four, "but I've never won anything in my life—not a door prize, not a raffle, not even a coin toss. And now my children are paying for it."

8. The plight of the losing class is indeed a tragic one. While neighbors and friends give charity balls, take courses in Japanese flower-arranging and attend tennis camps, the habitual holders of unlucky numbers are forced to wear imitation Wallabies and count their change in restaurants. "Sometimes I don't think I can bear it," says Rhona Geffler, a petite blonde who wears seven rabbits' feet and who, after two years of empty hopes, is physically incapable of uncrossing her fingers. "When I think of the chintzy Laura Ashley prints, the crummy Nina Ricci perfume, the tacky Gucci

handbags, all the junk that the nouveau lucky squanders its millions on, it makes me sick. And I bet not one of them could answer a lousy skill-testing question."

9. Sad but true. As lotomania and its countless variants take the country by storm, reason, it seems, has given way to "the breaks." Whether passing fad or new reality, luck is now the cornerstone of Canadian society.

10. Students were the first to feel the effects of loto-consciousness. As high school literacy levels dip lower and lower, it had become increasingly difficult for universities to screen applicants—most students cannot read, much less write, an entrance exam. Selection of candidates by lottery has proven to be a happy solution. "It's a good system," says a Moncton high school principal, Hiram Needles. "It teaches these kids what life is all about."

11. Hospitals were the next to follow suit. In an effort to relieve overcrowded and understaffed emergency wards, accident victims are asked upon arrival to pick a number from an orderly's hat. Lucky winners are wheeled immediately to surgery. The less fortunate are thanked for expressing an interest in modern medicine and asked if they would care to donate their bodies to science.

12. In a precedent-setting case a Supreme Court judge asked defence and prosecuting attorneys to draw lots rather than waste time presenting their arguments. The decision has met with criticism, but its supporters are vocal. "Don't knock it," says Sammy Scarpelli, recently found not-guilty on 37 counts of murder. "You ain't gonna win if God don't love ya."

13. Odds are, the demands of the losing class will continue to fall on deaf ears. The insufferably lucky have, thus far, proven unsympathetic to the sad predicament of the Debbie Gimbeaus. It is hardly surprising; it is a common belief among winners that in order to win, somebody has to lose. For the luckless, there remains little hope. In a stormy confrontation with New Loser protesters, the new prime minister—his name was picked from a barrel last week—outlined his policy in a terse statement. "That's the way the cookie crumbles," he said. For Debbie Gimbeau and the other strangers to fortune, the future indeed looks bleak.

Style and Structure

1. Before you become aware that the article is a humorous one, how do you react to the "plight" of Debbie Gimbeau? At what point do you first get an idea that the writer is using humour to criticize the government and its treatment of certain social and economic problems?

2. Although a thesis is implied, it is never stated. State briefly the point that the writer is making.

3. What is the main humorous device employed by the writer? (Pay special attention to paragraphs 9 to 12.)
4. Is the writer seriously concerned about lotteries or is he just trying to make us laugh? What name do we give to this type of writing? What are some of the dangers and advantages of using humour to criticize people or institutions?
5. Great satirists sometimes drop their humorous pose and make their real feelings known. Can you locate any such passages in this article?

Thinking and Writing

a. Satire is a "genre" which brings creative writing and expository writing together. Thus the author is able to make his/her points without necessarily going into long, detailed, and factual arguments. "Lotoland" is a good illustration of such a "marriage of techniques."
Write an essay in which you use the straight expository form of writing to make the same points as the author does in this piece of satire. Use his main points as the starting point for your essay and try to add concrete evidence to support his stand.
Audience:
an "average" newspaper reader who occasionally buys lottery tickets.

b. Write an essay in which you support *or* reject the operation of lotteries by the government. Make certain that you use concrete evidence and well thought out arguments. Try to anticipate the objections of anyone opposing your stand.
Audience:
a person who knows something about the operation of lotteries but who holds an opinion which is the exact opposite of yours as to whether or not the government should allow or operate lotteries.
Send a copy of your essay to Gamblers Anonymous or any other group that opposes lotteries (if your essay defends lotteries), or your MPP (if your essay opposes lotteries).

38 watched stabbing

by Max Haines

1. The neighborhood was middle class; ordinary people leading ordi-

nary lives. The crime and violence often associated with New York City didn't apply to the Kew Gardens section of Queens. Tree lined streets, Tudor styled store fronts — Kew Gardens was a good place to live.

2. Catherine Genovese lived there. In the early hours of March 13, 1964, the twenty-eight year old bar manager cried out to her neighbors for help. Her plea went unheeded.

3. At precisely 3:20 a.m., Kitty, as she was known to everyone in the neighborhood, parked her red Fiat in the Long Island Railroad Station parking lot. She locked her car and, as usual, started walking toward the door leading to her apartment at 82-70 Austin Street. Shops along Autin Street occupy the first floor. Apartments are on the second. Because of this, the entrance to Kitty's apartment was at the rear of the building, about one hundred feet from where she parked her car.

4. Just as she was about to proceed to her apartment she noticed a man lurking at the far end of the parking lot. Otherwise, the streets were deserted. Apprehensive about the stranger, she decided to walk along Austin Street toward a police call box. Kitty could hear the footsteps of the man following her. He was gaining rapidly. Under a street light, in front of a bookstore, and directly across from a ten storey apartment building, the man grabbed the terrified woman.

5. Kitty screamed, "Oh my God, he stabbed me! Please help me! Please help me!"

6. Lights blinked on in the apartment building. Windows slid open. Someone shouted, "Let that girl alone."

7. The attacker shrugged and walked down Austin Street.

8. No one came to Kitty's assistance. No one called the police. The windows of the apartment building slid closed. One by one the lights went out.

9. Down on the street, Kitty Genovese got to her feet. Staggering slightly, she slowly retraced her steps, desperately trying to get to the safety of her apartment entrance. She made it to the side of her building. To her horror her assailant had returned. Again he grabbed her and stabbed her once more.

10. Kitty screamed, "I'm dying, I'm dying."

11. More windows opened, more lights went on. Kitty's attacker walked down Austin Street, got into his car and drove away. Behind closed windows, apprehensive eyes peered down at the scene below. Still no one came to Kitty's assistance. One by one, like snuffed out candles, the lights of the apartments blinked off.

12. Now bleeding profusely, Kitty rose once more to her feet. Staggering and falling, she made her way to the rear of her building. She managed to open the door to the building and half crawled to the foot of the stairs. Unbelievably, her assailant returned for the third

time and stabbed her once more, this time fatally. Then he disappeared into the night.

13. At 3:50 a.m. a neighbor of Kitty's called the police. They took only two minutes to arrive at the scene. The man who had made the call explained that he had consulted with a friend by phone in another section of the city before he placed the call. Why hadn't he called earlier? He told the police he didn't want to get involved.

14. The investigation into Miss Genovese's death was strange and frightening in many ways. Thirty two minutes had elapsed from the time she had parked her car in the station parking lot until the police arrived at the scene of the murder. On two occasions the killer had left and returned. Had anyone called the police, most certainly Miss Genovese would not have been killed. To summon the police by phone in that section of Queens, it is only necessary to dial zero.

15. Kitty's neighbors, many of whom knew her well, were interviewed by police and reporters. Incredibly, 38 individuals had witnessed the attacks and not one had called the police.

16. Hardened homicide detectives, who had thought they had witnessed every human emotion, were at a loss as to why all 38 citizens had chosen not to make a simple telephone call. They all recognized the reluctance of citizens to become involved when there is a risk of danger to themselves, but this was a different situation. An anonymous phone call from the safety of your own home cannot be considered a dangerous act.

17. Later the reluctant witnesses gave a variety of answers:
    "I put out the light and we were able to see better."
    "I don't know."
    "I didn't want my husband to get involved."
    "I was tired."
    "Frankly, we were afraid."
    "We thought it was a lovers' quarrel."
    "I just took a look and went back to bed."

• • •

18. Winston Moseley, a 29-year-old business machine operator was later charged with the Genovese murder. When questioned, he confessed to killing two other women, as well as raping and robbing scores of others. He was a married man with two children, and no previous record. He had returned to kill Miss Genovese for fear that she could identify him.

19. At Moseley's trial, when the jury brought in a verdict of guilty with a recommendation for the death penalty, the court spectators stood and cheered. Amongst those who cheered that day were several of the 38 witnesses who didn't dial zero to save Catherine Genovese's life.

Style and Structure

1. What does the author stress in paragraph 1? What techniques does he use? Why is he so concerned with creating this emphasis?

2. Underline the topic statements of the article. What effect is created by the sentence structure of this paragraph? What point about human nature is Haines implying?

3. The thesis that the writer implies could have been proved by presenting statistics about the number of murders and muggings in which witnesses did not try to aid a victim. Instead he chose to describe a specific case history involving public indifference. What type of audience would each approach appeal to?

4. Reread the narrative section (paragraphs 3 to 14) examining the relationship between the length of the sentences and the action being described. What effect does the writer create by varying the length of his sentences?

5. Up to paragraph 14 the writer simply gives us an account of the event. Beginning with paragraph 14, what technique does the writer use to condemn those who stood by and failed to help Ms. Genovese?

6. How does the emphasis on the characteristics of the murderer in paragraph 18 reinforce his thesis about ordinary people?

7. How does the irony of the final sentence drive home the implied thesis? Does this serve as an adequate conclusion to this essay?

Thinking and Writing

a. Write an essay in which you assume the role of one of the people who witnessed the murder of Catherine Genovese and try to explain and justify your behavior to the general public. Be careful not to construct fantastic scenarios or alibis: remember that each of these people probably has a very logical explanation that he/she feels justifies his/her behavior. Try to give the most rational and realistic justification possible (e.g., one that you yourself would believe if you heard it).
Audience:
as indicated in the assignment.

b. Write an essay in which you explain why "ordinary people" behave as the witnesses to the Genovese murder did (one interesting approach might be to explain why similar behavior could occur or has occurred in your community). Develop logical arguments and draw upon the types of explanations that you read in the article. In addition, you might want to turn to other magazines, newspapers and books in your library to examine the various explanations that psychologists, sociologists and the police give for such behavior; the card catalogue in the library, the *Reader's Guide to Periodical Literature*, the *Canadian Index*, and the index to a major newspaper will provide sources for you, but if you encounter any difficulty, contact the research librarian for assistance.

Audience:

the "average" member of the public who would have difficulty understanding why people would behave in such a manner and would certainly think that he/she would behave differently. Send a copy of your essay to a friend or member of your family. Before this person reads the essay, ask whether he/she would act as the witnesses did. Then see if your essay alters this person's opinion.

Help! There's sex in my soup. A small plea for an end to subliminal silliness

by Jerry Goodis

1. When I was a schoolkid in Toronto, there was a joke going around about a psychologist who was testing a subject by holding up ordinary geometric figures and asking what they made him think of. Each figure—square, oblong or rectangle—apparently made his subject think of only one thing: sex. Finally the psychologist could take no more. "Good God," he cried. "Does *everything* make you think of sex?" "You should talk," his subject retorted scornfully, "you're the one who keeps showing me all those dirty pictures!"

2. For years, every time I thought of that story, I believed it would take a very disturbed person or, conversely, some marvelously zany bunch like Monty Python's Flying Circus to see sex in such ordinary things. But, when I first read Wilson Bryan Key's book, *Subliminal Seduction*, subtitled "Ad Media's Manipulation of a Not So Innocent America," (New American Library paperback, $1.95) I realized that here was someone who *did* see sex, or at least *said* he did (in the understandable interest of selling more of his books), in virtually every picture, every illustration and every

advertisement in magazines, newspapers, films, TV shows and other entertainment and communication media.

3. And Key didn't mean only suggested or subtly-inferred sex. Key saw the actual word *sex* spelled out in bold letters on whisky glasses, on the faces and arms of infants, on Ritz crackers, in clouds, grass and trees, in every curve and indent of pneumatic *Playboy* cuties, and of course, even on his own portrait adorning the dust jacket of his book. But this astounding discovery was mild compared to the utter maelstroms of depravity and deception Key could readily find worked into your average, run-of-the-fridge *ice cube*, in some of the most prestigious and expensive advertisements for soft drinks and liquor.

4. *"The right side of the ice cube above the lime slice,"* Key points out on page 100 of the paperback edition of *Subliminal Seduction*, as part of his clinical dissection of a Sprite ad which appeared in *Esquire* magazine, *"forms the back of a large shaggy dog with a pointed nose, or quite possibly a polar bear. The animal's legs are extended outward to the left, parallel with the top of the lime. The animal's arms (or legs, as you will) appear to be holding another figure which is human with long, feminine hair. Her face is located just above the animal's head.*

5. *"The two figures, animal and human, are in what can only be described as a sexual intercourse position. The polar bear, dog, or whatever, is in sexual embrace with a nude woman.*

6. *"Bestiality may be illegal throughout most of the world, but, at the symbolic level, it appears to have sold a lot of Sprite. The Coca-Cola/ Sprite advertisement was designed to sell around a subliminal theme of highly taboo sex."*

7. This incredibly ludicrous excursion into the utterly absurd sent a chill up my spine. If it wasn't all so appallingly perverted, it might be mildly humorous.

8. My mind was still reeling when, a few pages later, Key claimed to have found, in a *fake* ice cube, something much more sinister:

9. *"The primary symbolic device, subliminally perceived in the Bacardi ad, appears at first to be an ice cube in the centre bottom of the glass. Look more carefully. The ice cube is a golden skull with a flattened nose, large eye sockets and jagged teeth....The thematic implication...implies that one might richly enjoy dying if well-fortified with Bacardi rum..."*

10. On page 115 Key declares, in the authoritative, straight-from-heaven style he employs throughout his book:

11. *"There is not even an outside chance, however, that major U.S. media embeds* [Key's own term for hidden messages] *inadvertently or without full knowledge of what they were doing."*

12. What malicious effrontery!

Although Key specifically refers to American advertising agencies in his convoluted indictment, he is damning all advertising agencies, Canadian as well, as he later confirmed. And since I've spent most of my life in advertising and am fiercely proud of the work my agencies have done, I consider Key's allegation a *personal* insult.

13. Also, I have another cogent reason for leaving the sidelines and jumping head-first into the controversy Key precipitated with his ridiculous, disturbed fantasies. For some years I have been travelling to Canadian universities and community colleges (at their invitations), talking to students about what I do for a living and how I sincerely believe advertising benefits society. And I've had some rip-snorting, knock-down, drag-out arguments in many a college bear-pit.

14. The connection between these collegiate confrontations and Wilson Bryan Key is that by the time I got around to perusing his first book—he's since done another one containing even more bizarre claims of alleged media malpractices and misdirections called *Media Sexploitation* (New American Library paperback, $1.95)—he was snugly ensconced as professor of journalism at the University of Western Ontario in London.

15. His inauspicious term at that institution lasted only one year, at the end of which its administrators undoubtedly heaved a collective sigh of intense relief as he headed back to California. But even in that relatively brief interval, Key's fantastic theories, and the bland certainty with which he spouted them, infected a good number of impressionable young people. He convinced them that there really was a deep, dark plot to poison people's subconscious minds with all sorts of unspeakable messages and suggestions, and that large advertising agencies like mine were only the evil front-men for "the merchandisers and the culture controlled by merchandisers."

16. I first found it incredible that anyone would swallow the Key brand of foolishness, except possibly as basic training for a career with the CIA. But I had to face the fact that hundreds of Canadian post-secondary students, bemused perhaps by Key's undeniable gift for high-flown rhetoric, had accepted his maniacal meanderings as valid research.

17. While Key was on staff at Western, he swore there was a secret room at the local daily paper, the highy-respected *London Free Press*. Here, Key claimed, unknown even to the publisher himself, expert retouching artists allegedly earned the tainted money supplied by big advertising agencies, by superimposing or cunningly inserting their sordid, hidden commands or scenes of debauchery, bestiality and other orgies on any photograph or illustration they could lay their filthy paws upon.

18. Further, on Key's own office wall, emphasized by its own special spotlight, was a *Time* magazine cover of Queen Elizabeth, on whose face and hair Key revealed he'd located the common, explicit word for fornication — not only once, but literally dozens of times.

19. But beyond these instances of Key's personal obsession as recorded by responsible people who knew him at Western, I think a statement of my own credo may help convince students and others that neither I nor my confrères could possibly be a party to such devilish plots against the public.

20. I am an advertising practitioner — a salesman, if you will — a man who does his damndest to persuade Canadians to buy the products people pay me to promote — Speedy Muffler, Hiram Walker, Alcan, London Life, The Permanent, Scotiabank and Molson's, to name only a few.

21. All the time I've been in advertising, we've tried to produce *tasteful* ads, whether they were slated for magazines, television, newspapers, radio, kids' balloons, shopping bags, mountainsides, fireworks displays, or to be towed behind low-flying aircraft. And if possible, not only tasteful ads, but often ads with a bit of humor added for good measure.

22. A lot of people who had read David Ogilvy's book. *Confessions of an Advertising Man*, published in 1963, firmly believed this last whim of ours would be the downfall of our little Toronto firm, because David, senior partner in a very successful American advertising agency, had decreed that though humor undoubtedly had its place in the cosmic scheme of things, that place was definitely not the advertising business. Wrong, David.

23. In every ad campaign we launch, we know what segment of the public we are aiming at, and how we should go about reaching them, usually because we've done exhaustive market research beforehand — or as much research as the client's budget will stand. Even so, we're sometimes wrong. But not too often. Every word in the copy block, every illustration, the precise positioning of the text in relation to the illustrations, the choice of colors, models and typefaces, the media to be employed, the amount of money to be allocated to each medium — these and a host of other details are all deliberately chosen to strike a balance between artistry and salesmanship. And always with good taste.

24. If anyone in my organization was "embedding" secret messages in our ads, I would certainly be aware of it. But what I must ask is this: what could possibly be the point of anyone inserting words like *sex*, death's-heads, earthy verbs, euphemisms for female fixtures or artfully concocted scenes of wanton bestiality into their

ads? What particular section of the consuming public would they be trying to reach with such messages? What possible financial gain could any sponsor hope to glean from the exhortation alleged by Key to be embedded in *Time*'s portrait of Queen Elizabeth, urging everyone to rush out and fornicate?

25. And who is paying for all this? As I read Key, the art of "embedding" is a very complicated one, requiring experts to do the job properly. Experts cost money — piles of it. We use them only in dire necessity. Just arranging for the word *sex* to be embedded randomly a dozen-odd times across each Christie Ritz cracker, as Key claims, would cost thousands of dollars for the molds used by the bakeries alone. And has Key's own market research proved conclusively that you can slip a Ritz under ham or a Ritz under jam much more easily and tastily if it happens to be slathered with the word *sex*?

26. Our ads, besides being in what we consider to be good taste, are usually subtle, requiring a little thought on the part of the viewer/reader to grasp their full significance, but often rewarding this cerebral exercise on our client's behalf with a chuckle. But however we do it, everything we want to get across to the public is right out there for them to see. Why? Because otherwise they might not get the message at all, even after thinking about it. And that would mean we've failed miserably at our job and should lose the account and our franchise to operate.

27. Unlike Key's ads, which, to detect their full significance, usually have to be held upside down or sideways, viewed through the paper onto the next page — or at the very least, examined under a magnifying glass (according to his directions) — we liberally estimate that we have about 10 seconds at the very outside to get our message across. If we have to instruct our audience how to hold the page or watch the screen, then we've lost before we've even begun.

28. It is noteworthy that Key is usually the only person able to see all these hidden messages. And even then, if I understand him, he is only able to do so by relaxing and letting his subconscious take command. The rest of us are obviously just too uptight and repressed, too brainwashed by the Machiavellian media and their lackeys, to see what to Key is exceedingly clear.

29. It astounds me that it has taken this long for someone to throw down the gauntlet to Wilson Bryan Key and expose his sick, perverted ideas.

30. What is even more disturbing than Key's infatuation with these ludicrous theories is that some misguided cynics actually believe them. And that *really* scares me.

Style and Structure

1. What devices does the writer use in the introduction to attract the reader's attention? For what types of writing would the above devices be appropriate/inappropriate?

2. Underline the thesis statement and draft a plan of the essay's organization.

3. Examine the writer's choice of words and determine if the tone of the essay is favorable, objective, slightly unfavorable etc. toward the topic. Give illustrations to substantiate your point of view.

4. What types of argument and supporting evidence does the writer bring to bear against Key's books? Use specific examples from the article to classify it as objective, or biased. Specify any points at which the writer allows his personal feelings to overcome his judgement.

5. (a) What effect does quoting Key's own writing out of context (paragraphs 4 to 11) have on the reader's perception of Key's theories?

   (b) In this part of his article does the writer actually disprove Key's statements? Give specific reasons for your answer.

6. The writer introduces quotations smoothly, employing the two standard methods: (a) the formal introduction using the colon (paragraphs 8 to 11) and (b) the technique of integrating quotations into his own commentary (paragraph 4). Rewrite the paragraphs listed above, reversing the writer's introduction (*i.e.*, use the colon to introduce the quotation in paragraph 4 and the integrated form of quotation in paragraphs 8 to 11).

7. In his conclusion does the writer actually confront Key's ideas? What propaganda techniques does Goodis employ to get the reader on his side?

Thinking and Writing

a. Go through a few popular national and international magazines, looking at the ads to see if you can find any of the "subliminals" which Key says should be there. Write an essay in which you take one side or the other of the "subliminal" debate and present concrete evidence to support your stance.
   Audience:
   an "average" reader who has not read Key's book or Goodis' article (*i.e.* knows little or nothing about subliminal advertising).

b. One of the reasons that advertisers have difficulty in convincing people that they are not using such unethical techniques as subliminals is that the popular image seems to have developed of advertisers going to any means to sell products, whether the products are good or not, and whether we need them or not. Write an essay in which you express your perception of the advertising industry and any changes that should be made to it. Use concrete examples and well thought out arguments to support your views.

Audience:

someone who is working in the advertising business. Make certain that you try to convince your reader, not to offend him/her.

Send a copy of your essay to the Advertising Standards Council, 1240 Bay St., Suite 302, Toronto, Ont., or to a local advertising agency or to the advertising department of one of the local media.

Test tube babies

by Tabitha M. Powledge

1. In a freezer somewhere in New York City there's a test tube whose contents may interest you. They interest me. And they certainly interest Columbia University and its affiliate, Columbia Presbyterian Hospital, because a jury told both of those estimable organizations last summer that the test tube was going to cost them fifty grand. Not bad, considering nobody even knows for sure what's in that test tube.

2. What's probably there is some semen from a middle-aged dentist and bits and pieces of the female reproductive apparatus, including, perhaps, one or more eggs. What's possibly there is a human zygote — a fertilized egg that had begun to divide, almost through with the first day of its nine-month journey toward the delivery room. What's definitely there is Doris and John Del Zio's hope for a test tube baby as a result of *in vitro* fertilization, down the drain or, rather, down the freezer.

3. Unless you vacationed underneath the North Pole, you are aware that last July we were treated to the most heralded birth in 2000 years, that of Louise Brown, the first human being acknowledged to have been conceived *in vitro* (that is, in a laboratory dish). Louise was the culmination of many years of effort to overcome a particular kind of infertility in which there is blockage of the fallopian tubes, the passage that monthly guides an egg from the

ovary to its final destination in the womb. If these tubes are blocked, sperm can't get to the egg to fertilize it. *In vitro* fertilization involves an attempt to bypass that blockage by operating on a woman to remove some eggs from her ovaries and fertilizing them (in a Petri dish, actually, not a test tube) with her husband's sperm, "obtained manually", as the doctors delicately put it. The resulting embryo is grown in the lab for a few days and then implanted, via the vagina and cervix, into the woman's uterus. From that point, the pregnancy proceeds in the usual way.

4. Louise was born in Britain but it could have been an American first. It should have happened in New York, in the spring of 1974, or so say the Del Zios, who successfully sued the university, the hospital, and Raymond Vande Wiele, head of obstetrics and gynecology there, for bringing to a halt (by placing the test tube in the freezer) a similar attempt being made on their behalf by one of Columbia's researchers.

5. In his defense, Vande Wiele listed several reasons for his action. One of them was that as a member of a special committee set up by the federal government to examine the matter, he knew that there were a lot of unanswered questions about the moral and legal propriety of *in vitro* fertilization and that the government was holding off underwriting any of it (a decision tantamount to an unofficial moratorium), pending further public discussion.

6. A lot of people, it appears, are worried about the test tube babies: the Archdiocese of New York, Ann Landers, and the editorial board of *The New York Times*, as well as the right-to-lifers and proponents of zero population growth, feminists, anti-feminists, possibly even you. Do you fear test tube babies? Should you? Perhaps, but maybe not for the reasons they've told you. I list here several worries and a few reassurances.

7. *Worry #1:* Test tube babies might have birth defects. This is a reasonable fear on the face of it. *In vitro* fertilization certainly *sounds* scary. Recovering eggs via surgery, fertilizing them outside the body, letting them grow and develop for a few days and then implanting them in a uterus – a lot of things could go wrong in all that fiddling around. And in fact a lot of things probably do, which is why it took us so long to get to Louise Brown despite the fact that we've been doing all this with rabbits since 1890. Louise herself seems, blessedly, to be alright, though it's too early to be absolutely sure.

8. But lots of things go wrong, even in a pregnancy achieved in the usual way. It is estimated that at least 20 percent of conventional conceptions never make it to labor and about five percent of those that do suffer some kind of birth defect. So Nature is not altogether perfect either. Furthermore, much of the animal work on *in vitro*

fertilization is rather soothing on this point; animal embryos appear to be astonishingly resistant to damage during transfer, and the damaged ones don't survive. On that score, we're not likely to differ much from mice.

9. *Worry #2:* Test tube babies will suffer psychological damage because of all the publicity. In other words, out of the test tube, into the goldfish bowl. Remember the Dionne quintuplets? Poor Louise, it *is* too bad her parents couldn't resist the media madness, but how many people can resist their only chance for limelight, glamour, and money? Maybe, with the precedent of the Dionnes before them they will manage it all more sensibly. And maybe if she knows she was one of the most wanted babies in human history, that will compensate. Of course the publicity problem will apply almost exclusively to Louise; subsequent babies born of *in vitro* fertilization will be greeted first with a few polite handclaps, then with yawns, and then, alas, with an ear-piercing silence. We will all be paying attention to some different nine-day wonder.

10. *Worry #3:* Laboratory manipulation of a fertilized human egg denies to a human being its basic rights. This is a complicated worry with a number of sub-worries:
    (*a*) It is experimentation on a human subject, the zygote, without that subject's voluntary informed consent. Since, of course, such consent can never be given, this work will always be unethical.
    (*b*) Since a number of eggs are often fertilized but only one selected for implant, discarding the others is a form of abortion.
    (*c*) Researchers who pursue *in vitro* fertilization because they are interested in very early human development and who have no plans to implant the results are, when they discard those results, indulging in the wanton destruction of human life.

11. All of these worries rest on the belief that human life begins at the moment of conception. The abortion melee has shown us that there are those who believe this and those who don't. Such opinions are, for the moment at least, articles of faith rather than rationality. It does not, however, make much sense to adopt the policy of protection of each fertilized egg in the laboratory when we have made the political decision that women should have the choice to abort or not for up to two-thirds of a conventional pregnancy.

12. But even people who think women ought to have that freedom are sometimes troubled at the idea of the wholesale dispatch of human embryos, no matter how laudable the purpose, because of what those embryos might have been. We might, therefore, want to set limits on the kind of things a researcher can do with the products of *in vitro* fertilization and also require that those products be treated with dignity and disposed of with decorum (as is the rule with cadavers in anatomy labs). Such steps will not, of course, satisfy

the absolutists on either side, but no other compromise would either, so we might as well try to soothe those many of us who waffle around somewhere in the middle.

13. *Worry #4:* Isn't it crazy to spend money, time, and brainpower solving people's infertility problems in an overpopulated world? The answer is yes, it is. Infertility research of all kinds (not just *in vitro* fertilization) should be a low-priority item on our national agenda. That's a position I've always found good for a few angry letters to the editor, accusing me of being inhumane and unfeeling and insisting that people have a right to children of their own. Do they? No matter what? That's a proposition we need to examine closely in an era of scarce resources. Infertility is a great sorrow, but it is only one of many plaguing humanity and nowhere near the most important one, either. For one thing, this planet is awash with children abused, starving for both food and love. It's not a question of supply, it's a question of distribution, and the sad fact is we don't seem to be directing resources to improving that distribution. Let's take care of the kids we've got.

14. *Worry #5: In vitro* fertilization divorces procreation from sex, and that is a Bad Thing. This is one of the chief worries expressed by organized religion. It is certainly true that *in vitro* fertilization bypasses a good deal of fun as it bypasses the fallopian tubes, and while that's a pity, it's not quite fair to say it's a Bad Thing in the cosmic sense. Nor is it the first technique to do so. We've been trying hard to find an effective way of divorcing sex from procreation ever since we made the connection between a night of love and the day of reckoning nine months later. It's called birth control. In comparison with the Pill, *in vitro* fertilization is an inconsequential toy.

15. *Worry #6:* "My God, Professor, this time you've gone too far in probing the secrets of the universe."

16. Will you believe me if I tell you that all the preceding worries are rationalizations constructed by inventive human minds to cover up the fact that *this* is the real reason *in vitro* fertilization makes us nervous? This worry takes two general forms, both of them literary in inspiration.

17. (*a*) My colleague Willard Gaylin calls the first the *Frankenstein* Factor, the terror of human intervention into natural processes, particularly by means of elaborate technology. A portion of that terror is, of course, perfectly rational. Look at the record. It is spotty. The rest is geared to something like religious awe, a dread of human hubris in the assumption of such God-like powers.

18. It's good to try to improve our ability to predict the consequences of technology, and we ought surely to have learned by now that caution and conservatism in applying it is wise. But we are kidding

ourselves if we don't face the fact that we are nature's experiment in an interventionist animal. We humans, or rather something very much like us, only smaller and not quite so bright, made and used tools millions of years ago. Attempting to call a halt now is about as effective as trying to make a well-fed housecat stop chasing birds. Of course, that doesn't mean the fat tabby won't fall out of a tree and get killed, and we may blow it too. But our chance to succeed depends on learning to cope with our powers.

19. (b) The Brave New World Brood. A pity Aldous Huxley hasn't been around to hear himself so often hailed as a prophet in past months. It was he who predicted totally artificial reproduction and genetic manipulation in his novel almost half a century ago, and now many others are looking into the Petri dish that gave rise to Louise Brown and seeing it too.

20. Reproduction totally *in vitro* – from conception to decanting an infant nine months later – is, for technical reasons, so far away it's hardly worth listing as a worry. Some people think we may never be able to manage more than a shabby and inadequate approximation of the miraculous apparatus half of us come equipped with. Work will go forward on the artificial placenta because of its medical applications in saving very premature babies, but it will go slowly because it makes more sense to try to prevent premature birth by finding ways of mantiaining pregnancy for the proper length of time.

21. Surrogate mothers — women who lend their womb for the duration of pregnancy – are certainly a technical possibility before too long, and there may even be an occasional reason why such an arrangement would be desirable. Some have wondered what would happen if either party changed her mind, and other such ingenious scenarios. But why couldn't a contract drawn up beforehand take care of such issues and also specify that, for instance, the surrogate mother agrees to avoid substances known to be harmful to a fetus, such as tobacco and alcohol?

22. People who worry about surrogate mothers, however, are usually worried that they will be used to relieve other women (usually pictured as those vicious, narcissistic, hard-driving career women) of the inconvenience of pregnancy. Well, maybe. But consider these factors against it:

23. (a) To obtain the eggs requires abdominal surgery, beside which the inconveniences of pregnancy seem minor.

24. (b) The uterine environment is so influential that a child carried by one woman will differ from one carried by another, even though the eggs and sperm they come from are identical. Thus a woman who wants "a child of her own" will be losing something if she limits her role to egg donation.

25. (c) She will probably be missing some pleasure too. Pregnancy is not a pathological condition; it's a normal female state. It often feels good, and so it should. There are very few jobs it interferes with. Pregnancy, in fact, is the simple part of being a parent. Ask any mother which is harder, the first nine months or the next 20 years. That's the point at which a woman who wants to avoid inconveniences needs a surrogate mother.

26. But the big argument against worrying about artificial reproduc-tion–assuming it were technically possible—is that there is no sense whatsoever in going to all that trouble and expense. Tell me a clear economic reason to reproduce this way and I'll join you in worrying, but until you think of one, ponder the following:

27. (a) making babies the usual way is so easy that we have to go to some lengths (sometimes even life-threatening ones) to avoid it; (b) it's also more amusing.

28. There may, of course, be economic benefits arising from the use of these techniques in domestic animals. A large cow could mother many calves simultaneously, just as a prize bull fathers many now, if her fertilized eggs were implanted in less valuable surrogates. Or the embryos could be frozen and implanted in a surrogate many years later after her death. Which brings us to genetic manipula-tion, a subject so complex and touchy that I can give it only the sketchiest attention here. But, to allay anxiety on this score a bit: (a) Precise manipulation of individual genes is a long way off–not as long as the artificial uterus, but long enough so that you can probably safely leave this worry to your grandchildren in your will. Manipulation of characteristics controlled by several genes (height, I.Q., and most other things we find interesting about ourselves) is a worry they can probably leave to their grand-children.

29. (b) We are not without experience in these matters. Genetics, in fact, is our second oldest science (astronomy is our oldest), and civilization as we know it is built on the purposeful breeding of animals (for at least 20,000 years) and plants (for at least 10,000). Do you like roses? Corn? Your dog? You invented them all.

30. (c) Any society tightly controlled enough to make possible planned breeding of people for specific purposes would be in such trouble in so many areas that its reproductive methods would be the least of it.

31. *In vitro* fertilization is a breakthrough more psychological than real, but it is glamorous and full of human interest and therefore captures an inordinate amount of our attention. In the process, unfortunately, it distracts us from our genuine and pressing tech-nological problems, such as the disposal of nuclear waste, the decreasing quality of our water, and the proliferation of carcino-gens. And those, friends, are worries worthy of the name.

Style and Structure

1. How does the opening paragraph affect the reader? What is the writer's aim in opening with an air of mystery?
2. Note the writer's choice of words in this article:
   (i) "fifty grand" (paragraph 1); (ii) "...some semen from a middle-aged dentist and bits and pieces of the female reproductive apparatus, including, perhaps one or more eggs" (paragraph 2); (iii) "Unless you vacationed underneath the North Pole" (paragraph 3).
   (a) What tone (attitude toward her subject and her reader) does such choice of words imply?
   (b) Locate other examples in this article with a similar tone and rewrite them in a more serious tone. Do these revisions improve the article?
3. What basic essay organization does the writer use in paragraphs 7 to 30?
4. (a) Why does the writer begin the body of her article by appearing to give a fair, unbiased, and detached consideration to both sides of the argument (paragraphs 7 and 8)?
   (b) At what point does the writer diverge from this format?
   (c) Does the change in format strengthen or weaken the credibility of the article?
5. Select examples of choice of words and ways of presenting evidence which indicate which side of the debate the writer supports.
6. For what purpose does the writer use the concluding paragraph?

Thinking and Writing

a. Write two short essays which would be suitable for publication in the "letters to the editor" section of your local newspaper. In one make a plea for continued research into "test tube birth"; in the other, argue for its immediate cessation.
   Audience:
   an "average", non-scientific reader whose only knowledge of the subject comes from highly sensationalized newspaper accounts, but who, nevertheless, takes a position opposed to yours.

b. Write an essay in which you support *or* refute the opinions stated by the author in her concluding paragraph (paragraph 31). Try to anticipate and counter the arguments that might be raised by someone opposing your point of view.

Audience:
the same reader as outlined for section a.
Send a copy of your paper to the editor of a newspaper in your area.

How to be a leader

by Andrew Weiner

1. Where have all the leaders gone? We used to have strong men —a Churchill, a de Gaulle, a John F. Kennedy —men who knew what they wanted, and who could inspire us to follow them. Today, such men seem to be gone —and the same is often true at the more mundane level of corporate life. Bosses, it seems, aren't what they used to be.

2. What makes a leader? And how does an individual become one? All of us have fantasized about being leaders of men. Some of us are; others of us aren't —don't want to be and never will be. And some of us try to be leaders —and fail.

3. Behind the idea of leadership is the traditional assumption that leaders are somehow a breed apart, rare and superior beings who descend upon us from on high only irregularly. Most of us tend to believe that leaders are special people. Yet most of us, at one time or another, have thought that we could do a much better job than the people currently at the top (and indeed in some instances such as, for example, the Canadian Post Office, it is very hard to imagine doing a *worse* job).

4. All of which comes down to a very old debate. Are leaders born, or are they made? Can anyone be a leader, given the appropriate circumstances, or must leaders have some quasimystical, charismatic quality? And in that case, just what qualities should a leader possess?

5. Historians have often speculated as to whether a Lenin or a Napoleon would have risen to the top regardless of the time or place in which they were born; or whether they were just the right men in the right place, helpless instruments of historical inevitability. In J. M. Barrie's play *The Admirable Crichton*, we can see the dramatization of the right-man-in-the-right-place hypothesis: an upper-class family is shipwrecked on a desert island, and their butler, who has the best survival skills, almost immediately assumes leadership. When the family is rescued and returned to

civilization, the butler returns to his previous place in the order of things.

6. In recent times, psychologists have tried to resolve this old debate through a myriad of studies designed to track down that elusive quality — or qualities — of leadership. If leaders need some unique quality in order to lead, then they should be substantially different from their followers in some consistent way, and leaders in all situations should share these qualities.

7. In their attempts to identify such consistent differences, psychologists have looked at traits ranging from physical factors such as height and weight and general health, to psychological factors such as self-confidence and dominance; and in settings ranging from nursery schools to prison yards to the upper echelons of industry. These studies, in fact, have identified some differences between those who lead and those who do not: leaders do tend to be bigger and taller than their followers; to have better health, greater intelligence and energy, and to be more self-confident, extroverted, better-adjusted, and more sensitive in dealing with other people. But — and it's a big but — not one of these traits held true for *all* leaders across the whole range of leadership situations. And the more diverse the comparative situations, the more different the kinds of leaders they produced.

8. "If you look at these personality studies," says York University social psychologist Dr. Norman Endler, "there's very little consistency from one situation to another. I may be a very good chairman of this department, but make a terrible captain of a baseball team."

9. Such findings are in direct contradiction to the popular notion that a leader in one situation will be a leader in all situations — that a highly successful general such as Eisenhower will make a good president of the United States, that the leader of a boy scout troop will naturally make good executive material. Dr. Alan Marcus, a Toronto industrial psychologist and management consultant, is concerned with the amount of emphasis placed by many companies on such biographical evidence of "natural" leadership ability.

10. Dr. Marcus recalls a case in which a company was highly impressed by a candidate who had captained his high-school football team, and was now a leading organizer in his local service club. "Basically this was a person who liked to be at centre stage. And so he gravitated to leadership positions in informal groups. He did this by taking on all the joe-jobs, the tasks that no one else wanted to do. But these qualities didn't make him suitable as an executive."

11. Moreover, as Dr. Endler points out, "you can't have leaders without followers. It's an interactive thing; the fit between the person and the group." In one classic study, a researcher formed play groups of

passive, "follower"-type children, and allowed them time to develop their own way of doing things, their own values and rules. He then introduced a dominant, "leader"-type child into each of these groups. These leader children immediately attempted to take control of their groups, issuing orders left and right. But their orders were completely ignored when they conflicted with the way the original group had grown accustomed to doing things. Finally, these "leaders" got the message. They began ordering the other group members to do things they already wanted to do. Only by conforming to the rules laid down by their followers could these dominant children assume command.

12. Dr. Edwin Hollander, of New York State University at Buffalo, has observed much the same dynamic at work in groups of adults. Before a leader can attempt to lead his group in new directions, he must first of all build up "idiosyncracy credit" — that is, he must conform to the established way of doing things even more fervently than any other group member before he can try to lead them into noncomformity. Leadership of any kind requires the consent of the led, and often that consent must be worked for. Hollander's findings may explain why sometime "radical" politicians, ranging from California's Tom Hayden to Toronto's John Sewell, must don the traditional three-piece suit when seeking electoral office.

13. Studies like these would seem to conflict with another widely held popular notion of leadership — that the leader is the most independent member of a group, able to give orders at will and count on the unquestioning obedience of his followers. This kind of autocratic, highly directive leadership style — in which the leader concentrates exclusively on getting on with the job at hand — may have been effective in the past, but it is rarely acceptable in today's more egalitarian society. Except under conditions of extreme stress, such as war or economic emergency, leaders in our society must adopt a much more democratic, participative style, paying close attention to the needs of their followers and involving them in the work at hand.

14. This participative style is quite obviously a necessity in the sphere of political leadership, where leaders who fail to attend to the needs of their followers can simply be voted out of office. But it is almost equally a necessity even in business settings where the leader — the manager — gains his authority not by election, but by appointment from above.

15. According to Brian Smith, of the Toronto consulting firm of Jackson, Smith & Associates Ltd., "one of the strategic aims of a leader is to be accepted by the group." If a manager pulls rank all the time, he "depletes his assets. You have to build up more bases of leadership than you begin with."

16. An effective manager must be technically competent and task-oriented, able to get on with the work at hand. But he must also be people-oriented. And, Smith says, in today's business world, this is more critical than ever. Society as a whole is much better educated and less authoritarian than it used to be, and as a result, the average employee is much less willing to be ordered around.

17. The people-oriented manager became something of a cliché in the '60s, as many industries climbed on the human-potentialist bandwagon, and began offering T-groups and sensitivity training to their employees. Suddenly, many managers found themselves in a position where their subordinates could tell them exactly what they thought about them. And the effect of this, Smith says, was not necessarily beneficial to the companies concerned: "There was an overreaction on the part of a lot of managers. It made them very confused about their roles. They became so concerned about how people would feel about them, they couldn't lead anymore."

18. A manager must be people-oriented, but not to the extent that it makes it impossible for him to manage at all. Today, sensitivity training in industry has largely given way to training programs focused on much more specific skills and objectives involved in a participative leadership style: assertiveness, empathy, and so on.

19. But, for all the new rhetoric about human skills, Dr. Marcus doubts that things have changed all that much. "The problem with a lot of young managers is that they just want to get the job done. They don't see the necessity of team-building, of making your co-workers comfortable and being accessible to them. There's a tendency in all of us to be autocratic. It's so much easier to give orders than to hold a dialogue with people. You almost have to force yourself to communicate."

20. And he warns that the consequences of not communicating can be very dire. "You may know what your subordinates are doing. But what about their subordinates? Getting cut off from information coming up within the organization can be the kiss of death." He cites the case of a company vice president who was always the last to know when someone quit, even though they were quitting as a direct result of his own leadership style. When, for example, the field sales manager came to him for advice, he told him, in effect, "You're the field sales manager," instead of providing advice and support. The man subsequently quit. Poor executives, Dr. Marcus says, "don't see their subordinates as human beings but as people filling slots."

21. And again, in his studies of the U.S. State Department, the American sociologist Warren Bennis found that junior foreign service officers often didn't tell their bosses the truth about field situations, for fear that they would not accept it. Later they learned that

their bosses could accept it, but that they were afraid to tell *their* bosses... and so on, all the way up the chain of command. It was at least partly through such a series of miscommunications that the United States became entangled in Vietnam.

22. Dr. Marcus believes that "an incredible amount is demanded of managers these days. You can't just be a good engineer, or even a good administrator. You're expected to be a psychologist as well." Today, many companies will no longer promote only on the basis of past experience, but also rely on the results of psychological tests designed to uncover leadership potential. Potential leaders are then bombarded with the full range of management training courses. And meanwhile the MBA diploma, which is presumed to represent a grounding in human resources management, has become the new ticket to the upper echelons of industry.

23. "In assessing people to be hired or promoted," says Dr. Michael Godkewitsch, a senior employee relations adviser at Imperial Oil's executive offices in Toronto, "the dimension of leadership almost inevitably comes up. It is in the interests of any business to hire people of some leadership potential, because you hire not just for the ability to fill an existing job, but also to meet leadership requirements in the future."

24. By comparing successful and unsuccessful managers within the organization, Dr. Godkewitsch has built up a profile of the potential leadership candidate:

25. *Intelligence.* A successful manager will usually have above-average intelligence, although it is by no means necessary for him to be a genius. In fact, Dr. Godkewitsch points out, "the very brightest people are more likely to prefer to work in specialized staff positions—for example, in research labs. They're not interested in leading. They don't have the personal need."

26. *The need to lead.* "If you don't have a need to be a captain of industry, you're not going to be one." But this doesn't mean simply the desire to dominate others. "You have to see yourself as a strong leader, yet also be restrained, in control of yourself. To have a high level of energy but be capable of focusing it in a controlled way."

27. *Dealing with stress.* "The leader must be able to deal with stress, yet he must also be sensitive to it." If a middle manager makes a mistake and his supervisor criticizes him in great detail, that manager must be able to listen and learn where he went wrong, and then disregard everything else. If he is totally insensitive to criticism, he will learn nothing at all. But he must not take that criticism personally, even when it's *intended* personally. "To be too touchy and defensive is suicidal for a good leader."

28. *Seeing beyond the nuts and bolts.* "Good leaders are reflective people, capable of using their brains on a theoretical level, of

seeing beyond the nuts and bolts. At the higher levels, they must be able to smell what is going on in society and be prepared to look at it." As an example, Dr. Godkewitsch points to the new problems surrounding executive transfers. In the past, large companies could move their employees around almost at will; but today, they are finding that for family and personal reasons, many employees are much less willing to be relocated. Asking the wrong person to move creates difficulties and unhappiness all around. "Rather than have to fight fires all the time, the effective leader looks at the overall picture — to try to assess the impact that a move will have on their lives."

29. *Knowing your limitations.* The effective leader must acknowledge that he isn't the ultimate expert on every subject, and be prepared to "seek consultation within or outside the company."

30. *Dealing with people.* Dr. Godkewitsch considers the ability to deal with people to be among the most important of all leadership qualities. First of all, the leader must be capable simply of being with other people. He should be gregarious, yet not too gregarious, "because then your personal needs to be with other people may take precedence over the other things a leader must do to be effective." At the other extreme, the leader who is too much of a loner finds it hard to maintain good working relations with his subordinates.

31. Striking the right note requires considerable social skill. "If you are too friendly, people will inevitably accuse you of having an angle, whether you do or not." Research has shown that successful managers are not the most friendly people. They have a full range of social skills which they use to get along with their superiors, equals and subordinates. But they don't go out of their way to please everyone all the time.

32. Above all, Dr. Godkewitsch says, "good leaders need to be compassionate people. To have a basic tolerance and respect for others, to be able to accept them for what they are, and to recognize their needs and their contributions." The leader who does not have this quality, who attends only to the bottom line, will ultimately fail, because "production will suffer if the human needs of the followers are not met." Dr. Godkewitsch points to the Post Office as a "classic of mismanagement of human and non-human resources."

33. Through tests designed to tap all these qualities, Dr. Godkewitsch has been able to successfully predict which new employees at Imperial Oil will become the most successful managers. The tests themselves have no influence in determining promotion within the company — that is decided upon on the basis of a yearly assessment of performance. Their main function is in career counselling.

Employees taking the tests can get full feedback as to their results, and advice as to their strengths and weaknesses.

34. If leadership in business requires a complex mix of qualities, what happens to the management contender who is lacking one or more of them? Can effective leadership be learned? John Malowaniec, another senior employee relations adviser with Imperial, believes that it can be.

35. Malowaniec is involved in interpreting the company's yearly assessments of performance, in order to design new management training programs. He points out that these assessments do not simply focus on the bottom line. An autocratic manager may achieve the same production results as a participative leader in the short run. But when he moves on, he will leave an atmosphere of frustration and dissatisfaction behind him, and his successor will have to "pick up the psychological pieces." The participative leader, meanwhile, will have achieve results not measurable on the bottom line, such as a "growth in his human resources," which will ultimately benefit the company as a whole.

36. In management training workshops, the need for participative leadership is stressed through a case study approach, comparing the results of participative and non-participative management methods. Through videotaped group exercises, the management candidates then learn "how their style impacts on others." They learn that autocratic and controlling behavior is seen as unacceptable by their co-workers. And they learn to function effectively as members of a team.

37. In these workshops, potential managers also learn two related techniques derived from behavior modification that can be used to foster participation: psychological contracting, and the use of positive reinforcement. Psychological contracting involves discussing with subordinates not only the activities at hand, but also the expected standards of performance, and how that performance will be assessed. Fulfillment of a contract leads to built-in social rewards such as recognition and approval — what behavioral psychologists call "positive reinforcement." Such reinforcements should be a part of the everyday work routine. They make for a far more effective management style than "management by exception" — where the supervisor says nothing about his subordinates' work until things go wrong.

38. Through such techniques, Malowaniec believes, a management candidate who is initially weak in people-handling skills can correct this deficiency. "You can behave in an appropriate manner, despite the fact that it doesn't feel right. And if you persist, it becomes more natural to you."

39. Other management experts are more cautious on the question of

training for leadership. Dr. Marcus believes that you can do so "only if you already have the raw attributes. You have to be able to get along easily with people. You have to have some insight and sensitivity into what they do. You can't learn these qualities, although you can improve on what you have. And you can compensate for your weaknesses to a certain extent. If you realize that you're not as sensitive as some people, you can compensate by asking more questions."

40. In the future, Dr. Marcus suggests, training programs may be phased out in favor of a process called "developmental counselling," already used by several large American companies. Here, older managers meet regularly over a period of years with raw but promising young executives. Such counselling is extremely expensive in terms of man-hours. But it may yield the biggest payoff in terms of developing future managers.

41. The qualities required for leaderhip in industry are obviously different in some degree from the qualities required to head a government, a church, or an army. In fact, different industries, and even different sections of the same industry, may require different kinds of leaders as well. Even so, certain things would seem to remain true across nearly all leadership situations.

42. Given the sheer size and complexity of contemporary institutions, and the proliferation of vast, bureaucratic hierarchies, there can no longer be any such thing as absolute power. The old, autocratic style of leadership no longer works. Leaders today must lead, if they are able to lead at all, by relying on the information provided them by their advisers. And those advisers must in turn be able to maintain good relations with their own subordinates. At all levels, in fact, people-handling skills become critical.

43. In certain spheres, particularly the political, there may be good reason to doubt whether anyone can be an effective leader. Warren Bennis, in his book titled *The Unconscious Conspiracy: Why Leaders Can't Lead* (American Management Associations Inc., 1976), suggests that "true leaders today are an endangered species... because of the whirl of events and circumstances beyond rational control."

44. And then again, it may be that we expect too much of our leaders: that we persist in seeing them (or at least, in wanting to see them) as superhuman beings capable of working miracles on our behalf, rather than as ordinary human beings with a few specialized skills. And as long as we continue to seek such leaders, we are certain to be disappointed.

Style and Structure

1. Instead of employing a thesis statement, the writer chooses to

ask a series of questions in the introduction. Why is this an effective technique?

After reading the article, write out a series of thesis statements to replace the various questions, and comment on which approach (questions or thesis statements) is more effective.

2. Does the writer attempt to answer all the questions he raises in the introduction?

3. Draft a detailed plan of the article. Does the article proceed in logical order? Explain your decision.

4. What different types of proof does the writer bring forward to substantiate his opinions? What is your opinion of the quality of the writer's proof?

5. Examine the conclusion (paragraphs 41 to 44) and determine what function it serves in the essay.

Thinking and Writing

a. All of us participate in many groups, each of which has a leader, whether this leadership is formally recognized or not. (The president is the formal leader of the college; whereas, in any group of friends there is usually one member who stands out as the informal leader.)

Examine the personality and leadership style of the leader of one group of which you are a member. If the individual is leading effectively, determine what techniques he/she is using. If the individual is a weak or ineffective leader, suggest how the person's leadership style could be improved.

Write an essay on your analysis.

Audience:

the particular leader concerned (discretion may dictate that you do not actually give a copy of this paper to the individual analysed).

b. An effective teacher has to be a good leader. Based on your own experiences with teachers throughout your school years, write an essay in which you outline the qualities of leadership you most admire in a teacher. Remember to illustrate your observations with examples of effective leadership taken from your own experiences as a student.

Audience:

your English instructor.

The second sex

by Susan Cheever Crowley and Betsy Carter

1. For years they were not taken seriously: they were denied equal pay for equal work, discriminated against on the job, and stereotyped as beautiful but dumb. But baby, male models have come a long way. The phenomenal growth of the men's fashion, cosmetics and accessories industries has more than doubled the market for male models in the last five years, and men's rates — as much as $75 to $100 an hour — now equal all but the top female fees. Top agencies like Ford, Wilhelmina, Zoli and Elite have all beefed up their male divisions; at Ford, for example, male bookings have soared from 10 per cent of the business to 30. "As male modeling has grown, it has become more professional," says Jerry Ford, Eileen Ford's husband and the president of Ford Models, Inc. "The men are finally challenging the women in importance."

2. Although these men still can't expect celebrity or six-figure contracts from cosmetics firms, the world of male modelling does have its top-priced Cheryls, Laurens and Margauxs. Such supermodels as the sultry, sunken-cheeked Matt Collins (Head & Shoulders, Budweiser), the tweedy, middle-aged Ted Dawson (Ralph Lauren, Winston cigarettes), the all-American Scott Mackenzie (Gant shirts, Jovan cologne) and the baldish, clean-cut Peter Keating (Cuervo Tequila) often make more than $100,000 a year.

3. Traditionally, the male model has been used simply as a static prop in advertisements and mail-order catalogs. But as men's fashions have become increasingly important, models have been doing more of the glamorous runway and editorial work (this month's Vogue even features a pilot issue of Vogue for Men). And as their market has expanded, the male-model look has also evolved. Fifteen years ago, the most successful male models were blond and broad-shouldered types with boy-next-door grins. Then, the European influence on men's styles in the late 1960s ushered in the Latin look, and more recently he-men like model Steve Runnalls have been in demand.

4. *Sneer for Sale:* The current "in" expression is the surly, sometimes unshaven scowl. Collins, 28, one of the first models to put on the cool, cruel look, recalls that he looked grim when he started to work as a model primarily because he was nervous. "Then I found out the sneer was marketable," he says, "so when I relaxed I kept the look anyway."

5. In modeling, however, men are still the second sex. In spite of the recent changes, the work of the male model is still more boring and matter-of-fact than the female's. While women dance and whirl through the glossy pages of fashion magazines, men must pose stiffly. Many photographers are less interested in them and the bulk of their work is still for mail-order catalogs. "You get treated like you're a hanger," says dark-haired Rob Yoh, 25, who came to the job from the University of Pennsylvania. "You're there for advertisers to hang their clothes on."

6. *Longevity:* Men are also expected to work faster, spend a minimum of time doing their hair and makeup, and bring their own accessories. But the male model still has one important advantage over the opposite sex: his career lasts a lot longer. While most female models are over the hill at 30, many successful males are in their 40s and a few, like 58-year-old William Loock, have been working for more than 30 years.

7. But even with this advantage, only a small percentage of male models make more than $30,000 or $40,000 a year. Of the 500 male models working in New York City, about 50 make a living at it, according to Uva Harden, head of the men's division of the Elite Agency. And even for the most successful male models, survival is a discouraging business. Along with the grueling schedules, uncertain job security and stultifying boredom of the job, male models have to face a public image of dubious masculinity. Male modeling does attract homosexuals, and some models estimate that as many as 80 per cent of New York's male models are gay.

8. But higher rates are bringing more heterosexuals into the business at the same time that the public has become more tolerant of sexual preferences. "I use to think of male modeling as, you know, yeccchhh!" says Keating, 36, who went from being a McCann-Erickson account executive to posing for American Express ads. "When I started, my parents were horrified. Now they get a kick out of it."

9. Still, few men ever start out intending to be male models—and those who do often hedge their bets with other jobs or careful investments. Pat Andersen, who is featured nude in this month's Vogue, turned to modeling after a hand injury ended his career as a pitcher for the Baltimore Orioles. Tim Saunders was a vocalist in a failing British rock group when a Cadbury chocolate representative offered him a modeling job; now he is the chagrined smoker with the broken cigarette in the Benson & Hedges 100s ads. Runnalls, 34, was a carpenter in Malibu, Calif., before he started modeling and now owns real estate in California and Aspen, Colo. Loock has kept his job as an insurance broker to supplement his modeling income. And Collins, who was discovered by Wilhelmina

while he was riding show horses in Madison Square Garden, recently appeared briefly as Valentino in the film "The World's Greatest Lover."

10. *Impact:* Like their female counterparts, many of the younger male models have aspirations to be movie actors, but so far none have managed to parlay their physical perfections into full-fledged screen personalities. And despite their new-found respectability and highly paid glamour, male models still don't have the psychic impact of the best and most beautiful female models. Even with their new equality, there's still a long way to go before the male model becomes a male role model.

Style and Structure

1. Which sex do you think of when first reading the title? In view of the topic is this a good title for the article? Why?
2. Examine the *first* sentence closely:
   (a) Who do we think the writer is referring to?
   (b) Where have you heard sentence two or a variation of it before? What effect does its use in this situation have on the reader?
   (c) What rule of grammar does sentence one break? Would the introduction be more effective if the grammar error were corrected?
   (d) Why are the above devices effective as an opening for an essay on this particular topic?
3. Isolate all instances in this article where the writer opens a sentence with "and" or "but". What is the normal function of these words and where are they normally used in a sentence? In this situation is the writer's positioning of these words effective? Would the technique be appropriate to more formal writing situations?
4. Underline the topic statement and draft a plan of the article's organization. How does the contrast in the introduction prepare the reader for the writer's organization of his material in the body?
5. If the author had left out the word "however" in the first sentence of paragraph 5, the basic meaning of the sentence would not change. What function does the word "however" serve? What other words and phrases can you find in this essay that serve the same function?
6. What central problem facing the male model does the conclusion deal with? Why is this an appropriate conclusion for the article? How does the pun in the last sentence function in the conclusion?

Thinking and Writing

a. Conduct an informal survey amongst your friends and relatives designed to determine their attitudes toward male and female models. You could ask a man, for example, if he would consider being a model. Be sure to note such characteristics as the age, sex, educational background, type of employment, etc. of your respondents to determine if these things influence their attitudes.

Write a report on the results of your survey and draw conclusions, based on these results, about whether or not society applies sexual stereotyping (images of specific sexual roles appropriate to men or women) as rigorously to men as it does to women.

Audience:

a member of the general public who is unaware of any sexual stereotyping in the society around him/her.

b. Write an essay in which you discuss the usefulness of modern male and female roles in helping society to function harmoniously.

Audience:

someone who has seriously thought about "sexual roles" but has come to a conclusion that is the opposite of yours.

Send a copy of your essay to anyone that is actively involved in the "Women's Movement."

Who's going to read this anyway?

Many hours of research, writing and rewriting are frequently wasted simply because the writer has forgotten one cardinal rule of good writing: *Research into your topic must be accompanied by research into your reader.* Put another way, with the possible exception of creative writing, we do not write to communicate with ourselves; we write to communicate with others. Consequently, any insight we can get into the strengths, weaknesses, and prejudices of our readers may well improve the effectiveness of our writing.

The very worst thing a writer can do is to follow the misleading advice, frequently heard in colleges and universities, that it is somehow dishonest to employ a certain style, vocabulary, and format that you know is preferred by an instructor on the grounds that it does not reflect your 'normal style' – whatever that is. Surely our conversations reflect our *attention to audience* every day. Imagine some of the problems that would arise if we employed the same vocabulary, jokes and tone of familiarity in conversation with our teachers and employers that we use with our friends. By all means write what you think you should write, but do not forget that the reader's knowledge of the topic, his preference for certain styles, format and vocabulary, and in some cases his attitudes must be judged and the style varied accordingly.

"But how," you may ask, "can I hope to research my reader?" Obviously in some cases you cannot, and in those situations you would be best to adopt the middle road (employ generally accepted styles, formats and vocabulary). On the other hand, most of your writing, both in school and at work, will be going to the same few people, so you should have little trouble following these three guidelines.

A. Pay careful attention to the instructions which precede the writing assignment.

Even in the workplace supervisors usually have time to explain to new employees how they want reports, time sheets, correspondence, etc., written. If you ask, some supervisors will provide you with examples of formats and styles peculiar to their company. They may even be willing to comment on the appropriate technical level of writing for various situations. Certainly college instructors are willing to give students detailed information concerning format, documentation, style and vocabulary requirements. Remember, if you are unclear on any of the above points —ask.

B. Seek the advice of more experienced employees or students.

If your supervisor is not available to discuss your writing with you, you can always seek out a more experienced employee for advice. Most of us are genuinely flattered when someone approaches us for advice and we are frequently more than willing to help.

C. Request an evaluation of your writing.

In school, we get used to instructors evaluating our written work, but even here the keen student can improve his chances for success. Ask the instructor if he will take ten minutes to go over your work in detail. Go prepared with a set of intelligent questions, not just complaints or pleas for a higher grade. Ask your instructor how the paper could be improved and if there are any elements missing. Supervisors in the workplace are not in the habit of evaluating your written work unless there is an obvious problem such as poor spelling or incomprehensible sentences, etc. In any case, it is a good idea for junior employees to request a few minutes of a supervisor's time to discuss his first few reports. Again, most people are pleasantly surprised to be asked for advice and will generally comply with any reasonable request.

If you are tempted to sit down and write before carefully considering your audience, please remember the 'Edsel'. The Ford Motor Company spent millions to design, build and market this luxury automobile only to see it fail miserably in the marketplace. Eventually, it cost Ford Motor Company several hundred million dollars to learn that they had produced a well-engineered and constructed automobile for which no appreciable market existed. You can avoid the same mistake for nothing.

Planning your written communication

Whenever you talk to people, you use all kinds of "non-verbal" devices to clear up any ambiguities for your listener that may arise from the imprecise communication of your oral presentation. You make gestures with your hands, face and body, you alter the tone of your voice, you watch for puzzled looks, and so on. If you want proof of just how much we all depend upon such devices to help to convey our verbal messages, watch people talking on the telephone: everyone using the phone will still gesture, smile and use body language as if the person being spoken to were present in the room.

When you turn to written communication, on the other hand, your habitual reliance on such non-verbal devices may all too easily lull you into relying upon the spontaneous and vague language that you are able to "get away with" in oral presentations. The precise communication of a written message, therefore, requires very careful consideration of how the material is to be presented to your reader.

Many people make the mistake of just sitting down and beginning to write. Yet charging ahead in this way is actually the hardest way to write effectively. The writer has to keep too many things in mind at one time: he has to try to think ahead to what will come next, think back to what has gone before, try to find just the right wording for the idea that is being dealt with right now, and make certain that the relationship of all of these words is complete and clear to a reader. In short, the "sit down and write" technique almost guarantees failure. Once you have tried another approach to the task of writing, you will understand why most people who say that they "can't write" are actually saying that they cannot communicate effectively by using the "sit down and write" technique. Unfortunately, since these people are not aware of any other technique for writing, they make the mistake of giving up all hope of ever writing well.

As a matter of fact, there are a few easy steps that you can take before you begin to write that will greatly improve the effectiveness of your expository writing. At first they will take a little extra time, but after you have used them a few times, they will actually speed up the process of writing for you. Think, for example, of how often you have had to waste time going back over what you have written to add some point that you left out when you used the "sit down and write" approach. How often have you later discovered that you wandered away from the main point into some alluring but relatively unimportant side issue? How often have you wasted time putting down far more information than the situation called for? How often have you found that you have ended up putting ideas down in a piecemeal way that actually confused your reader? Thus, although many people who have never used a preliminary planning stage think that they are going to "waste too much time", the steps outlined below will really save a great deal of time, worry, and confusion while going a long way toward guaranteeing that your reader will understand your point exactly as you intended it.

Step 1: Decide on your topic and the approach that you will take to it

In school you are usually either assigned a specific topic or given a choice of predetermined topics upon which you are asked to write. This procedure corresponds far more closely to what will happen to you in the working world than you may think. Your employer may assign a report on a specific topic; a customer may present you with a specific problem to be solved; or your job itself may present a difficulty that can only be overcome by a written explanation to a superior; all these situations contain "topics".

Whatever the source of your "topic", the best way to proceed is first to *define* the "topic" as precisely as possible, and then to decide what *approach* to the "topic" is called for. Jot them down at the top of a piece of paper, e.g.

> Topic: office efficiency
> Approach: morale of the employees
> *or*
> Topic: Excavating equipment
> Approach: To find the best equipment with the best price and servicing.

Remember that at this stage of your planning you may not know all of the implications of the problem or all of the details of a process, so you may have to modify the topic or the approach as your research proceeds. Still, you now have a solid starting point.

Be careful not to choose an approach that is too broad or too narrow for the situation or for the length of the report. Ask yourself: What approach will achieve the needs of your reader? What approach fits the context of the problem? If your employer asks for a report on how to improve office efficiency, an approach such as "The History of Employment Practices and Their Effect Upon the Morale of the New Employee" will be far too general to suit the context—your employer wants a solution, not a history lesson.

In short: (i) determine the *appropriate* topic
(ii) determine the *appropriate* approach

Step 2: Explore the topic and the approach

a. If you are not certain of all of the details involved in the "topic", do research. Read about your subject, and make notes on what you read (remember to write down titles and page numbers for your sources. You may need to use them later to give credit to your sources or to give authority to your opinion).

b. Think about your topic and your approach. Consider how the information that your research has turned up relates to them. Are you going to have to modify your original statements? Are you going off on a tangent with your present line of research?

c. Discuss your topic, your approach, and your research materials with someone else. In the process of defining the material for this person, you will gain clearer insight into it yourself.

d. Complete your research.

These steps may at first sound as if they are only meant to be used for a major project on a subject that you do not know well. Nevertheless, they hold just as well for the situation in which you are writing about something with which you are very familiar. Perhaps rewording the above process to fit this situation will clarify the point:

a. If you know the topic thoroughly, you will probably not have to do outside research.

b. Take a moment or two and think over the process, the situation, or whatever it is that you are going to explain. What details are really involved? Are there any underlying factors that may not at first be visible? Is your approach too one sided?

c. Discuss the ideas with someone else, if you can. By talking something over with another person, you will get a clearer concept of what the idea really entails and of how you will have to deal with the idea in order to get someone else to understand it.

d. Jot down your ideas as they come to you, in point form and at random. Put down everything that comes into your head that has any relationship at all) to your topic and approach. Often such a "brain storming session" will bring to light all kinds of interesting insights.

Step 3: Select material from your collected data that is appropriate to your topic and approach

When your research has been completed, whether it is a list of random thoughts or a pile of extensive notes taken from outside reading, review the material that you have collected.

For each item or point, ask yourself whether it really does relate to your topic and approach. If it does not, throw it away or scratch it out of your list. If it does, jot down beside it in a word or two exactly how it relates to them (explains, illustrates, etc.).

What you are doing in going through this step is ensuring that your finished product has UNITY.

Step 4: Group points that are related to each other into "clusters"

Go through the items that still remain in your "research material" and look for points that relate to the general topic and approach in the same way. This should be a relatively simple process because you have already noted in a word or two how each point relates to the main idea.

If you are working from a modified list that we suggested for a topic that you know well, you may find it easier when you first try this stage of planning to rewrite your list completely so that the "clusters" of related ideas are physically near to each other.

With a little practice you will soon find that simply writing the same number or letter beside related points will be adequate at this stage for such material.

If you are working with extensive research notes, now is the time to get out the scissors and cut out the various points that you have collected: you can then deal them in to piles of related points in the same way that you would sort out the suits of a deck of cards. Remember, however, to note on each scrap of paper where the material came from or you may find yourself doing a great deal of rereading so that you can give credit to your sources.

Whichever method you use for grouping your points into "clusters", make certain that the points in any one "cluster" do not cover too wide a range of ideas. These "clusters" are going to form the basis for your paragraphs, and if a paragraph tries to cover too many points, the importance of each one will be "lost in the crowd". If you find that a "cluster" is becoming too broad in its range, divide it into two or three separate "clusters".

Write a point form summary of the concept that binds each "cluster" of points together in their relationship to your topic and approach.

Step 5: Arrange your "clusters" into an order that gives them their most effective impact

At this stage you must decide upon the order in which you are going to present your "clusters" or paragraphs to your reader. Usually your material/topic itself will suggest the most logical organizational method. A report concerned with declining office morale might well suggest the chronological or time sequenced organization; on the other hand, a report on the best available excavating equipment might require a compare/contrast organization; an attempt to convince someone to follow a plan of action proposed by you might call for an organizational structure in which you present your second weakest argument first, followed by your weakest, and conclude with your strongest point. Your purpose in writing on the topic will invariably determine the best approach for you to use.

The important thing to remember at this point in planning your written work is that this is the stage that is going to "make or break" the impact of your final product. A well organized work will impress your points upon the reader. A work that lacks organization, logical development, and, hence, coherence will at best cause the reader to question your competence to tell him anything worthwhile; at worst, he will simply stop reading (an unfortunate event in the case of an employer, as he may stop reading your work *permanently*).

Step 6: Within each "cluster", arrange the points into an order that gives them their most effective impact

Taking each "cluster" separately, examine each of the points that you have included in that cluster. Make certain, once again, that they do indeed have a direct relationship to the central "binding idea" that you jotted down for that cluster.

In deciding in what order these points should be arranged, always place your "binding idea" first. Then ask yourself the same questions that you asked when deciding upon the arrangement of the "clusters" themselves within the overall organization. The arrangement that gives the points a logical, coherent impact is the one to choose.

Step 7: Begin to write

By going through these stages or "steps" of planning, you will have saved yourself a great deal of anxiety, turmoil and wasted time. You will have ensured that you will stay on the topic when you come to the writing stage and that you will present your material in an orderly fashion. You have also helped to ensure that the rest of your task will be easier because now all that you have to worry about is the actual wording of the paper and the creation of an appropriate concluding paragraph when the time comes.

The writing stage

Step 1: The introductory paragraph

A good opening or "introductory" paragraph serves three purposes in getting your message across to your reader: (i) it must focus the reader's attention on your topic, (ii) it must provide the reader with a general idea of the approach that you are going to take to this topic, and (iii) it must impress upon the reader the importance of your topic and approach by capturing his interest.

(i) Focusing the reader's attention

Many inexperienced writers make the mistake of beginning their written work simply by presenting the data that they have gathered without first focusing their reader's attention on the general topic that this data is supposed to present or explore. The result is inevitably disastrous, for the writer has forgotten that although he may know the topic well enough to understand the significance of the data, the reader is probably coming to the topic for the first time. Attempting to read an essay that lacks a topic statement is like setting out on a journey without any clear idea of your destination: it is a frustrating experience that is more likely to arouse anger than provide knowledge.

The most common method of introducing your topic to the reader is the use of a topic or thesis sentence which succinctly states the purpose of your essay. Usually it is best to place this sentence right at the beginning of your introductory paragraph, e.g.

The Massey-Fergusson XL2000 Earthmover would be the best purchase for our company.
or
Child beating is far more widespread in our society than commonly imagined.

If you have been following our steps of preliminary planning for your work, the construction of this topic sentence should be relatively easy, for all you really have to do is expand the idea that you jotted down as your topic at the beginning of the planning process into a complete sentence.

(ii) Providing the reader with a general idea of your approach

If, to go on with our comparison of reading an essay to taking a journey, the topic sentence provides the reader with a "map", the next few sentences of the introductory paragraph provide him with an idea of the roads that he will be taking as he crosses the map. This information, especially if it reveals the order in which the body of the essay will proceed, enables the reader to grasp some idea of the scope of your essay before he reads it.

An example may clarify the point. Let us assume that you opened your introductory paragraph by stating that your firm should purchase the Massey-Fergusson XL2000. In order to reveal your approach to your reader you might add a sentence or two which indicate in general terms why that piece of equipment is appropriate for your firm at the present time, e.g.

"Compared to the other machines available to us, the XL2000 will provide us with the highest efficiency at the lowest initial cost and the lowest operating costs. The capacity of the machine is slightly larger than called for by our present requirements, but with our proposed future expansion this attribute would be a bonus for us. Moreover, the service policy of the company, though it would require a slightly longer 'shut down time', would in the long run be far cheaper and more efficient."

In this way you have outlined the basis for your judgement and shown the reader the direction that the rest of the paper will take.

As with the construction of your topic sentence, the construction of this section of your introductory paragraph should be relatively easy if you have been following our steps of preliminary planning: all that will be involved now will be the expansion of the idea that you developed in your plan as "Approach" and adding to it the main points of your paper (when this addition is appropriate). Be sure, however, that the sentences that present your approach to your reader have a logical order to them, preferably an order that reflects in a general way the order in which you are going to present your data in the body of your essay.

(iii) Capturing the reader's interest

Whenever you are writing in the working world, your topic is most likely to be one that is of importance to you for one reason or another. If you are going to impress the importance of your topic upon your reader, you are going to have to make certain that your introductory paragraph arouses his interest. This may not seem to be an easy or appropriate task in vocational writing, but it can be done with relative simplicity by the careful wording of the paragraph. Nothing is more boring, for example, than an introductory paragraph that begins "The topic that I am going to write about in this paper is" Although such a sentence may present your idea to the reader, the dryness of the presentation does nothing to cause the reader to become involved with your ideas on any more than a very superficial level. Simply by providing a more stimulating wording, you can change your reader's attitude from bored perusal to interested exploration of an idea, e.g. compare

The subject of this report is the appropriateness of the Massey-Fergusson XL2000 for our firm's needs.

with

The Massey-Fergusson XL2000 seems to fit every need of our company not only at our present stage of development, but also in our projected expansion.

The sense of discovery conveyed by the second opening sentence will catch the reader's attention.

There are of course even more dramatic techniques that you can use, but you must be careful that they are appropriate for the situation for which you are writing. There is nothing wrong, for example, with starting off your introductory paragraph with a provocative quotation, question, statement or other dramatic device to stimulate your reader's interest. The effectiveness of this technique can be appreciated by an examination of the following opening sentences:

"This essay is going to deal with the topic of child beating."

"Would you turn your head the other way and try to ignore a neighbour who was beating his child into insensibility? Of course you wouldn't. Yet with the present attitude of our society toward child beating in the community that is precisely what we are all doing."

The personal involvement called for by such a presentation as that made in the second quotation is going to arouse far more interest and, hopefully, action than that of the first.

On the other hand you must always be very careful that your attempt to capture interest does not distort the message that you want to convey. You must still make certain that the introductory paragraph says precisely what you mean. Too often inexperienced writers fall into the trap of melodrama or exaggeration and render their topic ridiculous rather than important. An opening statement such as "The beauty and symmetry of the Massey-Fergusson XL2000 puts it in the ranks of Taj Mahal" would make your report more appropriate for a comedian than for an employer searching for machinery.

Step 2: The "body" or development section

The "body" of your written communication is the section that carries the burden of your exploration of your topic. By organizing your material into a series of paragraphs that lead logically from your introduction to your conclusion, you are providing verification for your observations in the introductory paragraph and expanding upon them.

The writing of this section of your paper should be just as simple as the writing of your introductory paragraph was if you have been following our preliminary planning process. You will have already collected the information that you want to convey and have arranged it in clusters that are going to form the basis of the paragraphs of this section. Indeed, if you have followed Step 6 of our planning stages, you have even guaranteed that the writing of each paragraph is reduced to the problem of worrying about using just the right words to capture your exact meaning. Make certain that these words are grouped together in such a way as to make your reader hear your voice in his/her head, with all of the proper pauses and inflections. *i.e.*, to make certain that you have used complete sentences and proper punctuation. See the two sections of this book that deal with these topics if you have any doubt at all about your abilities to do either.

Step 3: The parts of the body: the paragraph

Every paragraph in the body or development section of your paper forms a complete unit of "points" that develops, explains, illustrates, or contrasts with one aspect of the topic and approach that you are presenting. In order to be "complete", each paragraph needs a "topic sentence" which focuses your reader's attention on the aspect of the topic to be dealt with in this paragraph; since you have already noted the "binding idea" of each cluster of points as you went through the planning process and each of these clusters is going to form the basis of a paragraph in the body of your paper, you simply have to expand this "binding idea" into a complete sentence to create the topic sentence for each paragraph. In other words, the topic sentence presents a generalized outline of the material to be dealt with in the paragraph.

The sentences that follow the topic sentence simply develop the aspect of the topic and approach introduced by that sentence. If you have been following our plan, you have already ensured that these sentences will have a unified and logically developed impact upon your reader because you have already eliminated unrelated points and arranged the remaining ones in Step 6 of that process. All that really remains to be done is the expansion and/or combination of these points into complete sentences. As you write, of course, you can double check to make certain that the arrangement of the points that you have chosen earlier is in fact the most effective. Ask yourself, "Do the sentences in this paragraph present the reader with a clear, logical sequence that will allow him to under-stand and feel the real importance of my ideas?"

The last sentence of each paragraph "rounds the paragraph off", by refocusing the reader's attention on the main idea that the other sentences of the paragraph were explaining, illustrating, etc. Without this "concluding sentence" you will leave your reader "hanging in mid air". He will either have to try to draw his own conclusions about these points or else go on to the next paragraph without really thinking about the importance of the points that you have made. In either case, by omitting a concluding sentence you have undermined the impact of your idea.

Examine the structure of the preceding paragraph if you want an illustration of how a topic sentence introduces the subject of a paragraph and a concluding sentence summarizes and drives home your point.

Only when all three components, the introductory sentence, the body, and the concluding sentence, are present in your paragraph will your idea appear "complete" to your reader.

Step 4: The concluding paragraph

Just as a paragraph will lose its impact upon the reader if you omit a concluding sentence, so too will the entire work lose much of its impact if you forget to end it with a concluding paragraph.

A concluding paragraph serves to refocus your reader's atten-tion on the topic as a whole and the point that you want to make about it. Thus the concluding paragraph summarizes or makes a comment on what you have said in the body of the paper. It should leave your reader, if not agreeing with you, at least with a clear understanding of your point of view and the need to think about it seriously.

The stages of planning and writing that we have outlined in the preceding pages may at first reading seem intimidating if you have never tried to plan an essay before you sat down to write. With a little practice, however, you will find that these procedures will become a natural part of your writing and actually speed up the process for you (to say nothing of simplifying the process by break-ing it into smaller more easily manageable units). They become natural so easily because they really only reflect what your mind is trying to do with any idea when presenting it to a reader: they break the overall topic into its component parts, give these parts a logical order, and then put the parts back together again in a unified whole that is easily understood by your reader.

Make certain that the first few times that you try to plan your writing according to our suggested planning stages that you do not take on large topics. Narrower topics will be easier to manage at first and will give you the opportunity of going through the process more often.

Always remember that just going through the motions of planning will not accomplish anything: think the problems through as you go. Nor should you expect planning to remove all of your difficulties the first time that you use it. It will remove many of the difficulties that you have experienced when using the "sit down and start to write" technique, but only practice makes perfect.

Finally, you will have noticed as you read through the articles in this book that the authors of those articles use a variety of approaches to constructing their introductory paragraphs, development paragraphs, concluding paragraphs, etc. These examples may give you the impression that the formats that we have suggested for these components will be too formal and restrictive for you. Nevertheless, what we are trying to do here is to give you a solid foundation in explanatory writing. Once you have this format firmly under control, you will begin to explore other formats almost naturally.

Proofreading your composition

I. Sentence errors

People usually define the sentence by saying that it expresses a complete thought. However, don't "Wow", "Beautiful, man" and "Dumb" express "complete" thoughts? In one way, of course, such expressions are complete in themselves; indeed they are often used in creative writing where their context gives them appropriate significance. Nonetheless, for the more formal situations which call for the clear, precise and complete explanation of an idea to a reader, such expressions are not normally adequate. In short, good expository writing calls for the use of complete sentences, for the structure of sentences demands a clearer definition of the ideas being presented to the reader: they require that something (a *subject*) be carefully defined as *being* whatever it is, or as *doing* whatever it is doing. A complete sentence, that is, demands a subject and a predicate.

Thus, if you read "The growling dog" you find yourself waiting for more information: Did the growling dog bite the writer? Did it turn tail and run? The fragment lacks an action (i.e. a verb or predicate) that would give you a complete idea of what actually happened.

If, on the other hand, you read

The growling dog stood across the body of his fallen master.

you have a complete idea of the situation; you have read a sentence.

Since most people use complete sentences when they find themselves *talking* in "formal" situations such as job interviews or visits from the minister, it is usually easy to write using complete sentences. Occasionally, however, you will find that in the heat of the battle to get words down on paper, you use incomplete sentences or run several sentences together into one: you must reread everything that you write carefully to make certain that in your haste you have not actually obscured your meaning by presenting the reader with incomplete ideas, or with ideas that have been run together with others.

1. The sentence fragment

I came home late one night to find garbage strewn all over my front lawn. An awful mess.

Read the second "sentence" of the above statement again, without rereading the first sentence. Obviously this "sentence" does not really tell the reader anything by itself, for it depends on the first sentence for its meaning. Such "partial" sentences are called SENTENCE FRAGMENTS.

Sentence fragments are usually created in only 3 situations:

a. When you isolate "words in apposition" to the last words in the previous sentence.

> Children love plants such as venus flytraps, pitcher plants, egg plants, or sensitivity plants. *Any plant that is odd or unique.*

The writer of this fragment tried to stress the concept that children love unique plants, but instead created a sentence fragment. He should have used the dash, as its purpose is to give dramatic impact (see The Dash, p. 284).

b. When you isolate a "subordinate clause" (used to expand upon the idea of the previous or following sentence).

> He could always find an excuse to go out after dinner. *Especially when he did not want to help with the dishes.*

Such words as "when", "if", "since", "as", "because", etc. alter the meanings of the sections of a sentence that they introduce by making them "subordinate", or secondary, in meaning to the main idea of a sentence:

> I was late (main idea) because I took time for a cup of coffee (secondary or subordinate idea that simply adds further information to the main idea).

But a subordinate idea always needs a main idea to expand upon: by itself it is meaningless:

> Because I took time for a cup of coffee

means nothing by itself. How often might we mistakenly write, however,

> I was late for work again. *All because I took time for a cup of coffee.*

c. When you isolate verbal phrases containing a verb ending in "ing". Consider, for a moment, the following:

> having been there already
> being an example of ingratitude
> doing what should have been done
> after having arrived in Hong Kong

Obviously none of these statements makes any sense; "ing" verbs depend upon other words for their meaning: used alone, as they are in these examples, they are meaningless. Yet how often in our rough drafts do we write such things as the following:

> We must never use verbs ending in "ing" as independent verbs. *The reason being that they depend on other words for their meaning.*

(If you didn't catch the problem with the second "sentence" the first time you read the example, reread that second "sentence" through again without looking at the first sentence.)

How to recognize sentence fragments

As you have seen in examining the examples given above, you subconsciously know already how to recognize a sentence fragment when you view it in isolation. The way to recognize them in your own rough drafts, then, is to isolate them from the rest of the essay.

Put the paper or article away for a day or two; rereading a paper some time after you originally wrote it makes you more objective, i.e. tends to place you in the situation of a reader coming upon a work for the first time; you will more easily recognize fragments. Reread your paper one sentence at a time. Reread your work aloud, making certain that you read what you have actually written (keep in mind that all too often we "see" with our minds; that is, we know what we meant to write and this knowledge causes us to think that we "see" things like complete sentences when indeed we have written only sentence fragments).

How to correct sentence fragments

Since the sentence fragment is not "independent" because it usually depends upon the sentence that precedes or follows it for its meaning, there are two methods for correcting sentence fragments:

(i) Make the fragment independent by adding a subject or a verb, e.g. change

> From that time on he was a perfect citizen. *Doing what should have been done from the beginning.*
>
> $$to$$
>
> From that time on he was a perfect citizen. He did what should have been done from the beginning.

(ii) Incorporate the fragment into the preceding or following sentence, e.g. change

From that time on he was a perfect citizen. *Doing what should have been done from the beginning.*

to

From that time on he was a perfect citizen, doing what should have been done from the beginning.

2. The comma splice

The comma splice is an error that occurs when a writer uses a comma to replace the period at the end of a sentence. In almost every instance in which such an error occurs, you will find the comma has been used to replace a period between two sentences that are very closely related in their meanings (the second sentence may illustrate the point made in the first one; it may add additional information about the point made in the first sentence; or it may give the effect of a cause that was outlined in the preceding sentence). Example:

We are robots, our ideas and opinions are often not our own.

The writer of this comma splice was trying to create a certain effect in his reader's mind, but unfortunately fell into a trap. He wanted to drive home to the reader just how people are like robots. Subconsciously he realized that if he used a period he would bring the reader to a full stop and that such a full stop would destroy the dramatic impact of his second point. Therefore he mistakenly resorted to the comma (he should have used the semicolon; see the section on the use of the semicolon).

How to recognize comma splices

The easiest way to spot comma splices is to listen to yourself carefully as you read your written work over *aloud*. Make certain that you read exactly what is written on the page (the mind has a strange way of fooling the eye into thinking that it has seen something that it knows should be there but is not, in actual fact). Most people, when they try to explain something with precision to someone else, think in sentences; thus you will find that when you encounter a comma splice and read it aloud as it is punctuated (i.e. given only the short pause that is symbolized by the comma), the passage will not "sound right"; your mind recognizes the confusion that the use of the comma can create. You will see the point being made if you read the following "sentences" aloud:

I knew that I had made a mistake, when she slapped my face, it was all too obvious.

Whenever I came to call, no one seemed to be at home, maybe they were giving me a hint.

Many recent films have tried to imitate *Star Wars*, not one has succeeded.

In many cases the identification of comma splices is made much easier by the fact that they very often occur just before "adverbial connectives":

> I had no warning about the test, *therefore,* I was not prepared.
>
> A person who owns a small piece of land can save money, *for instance,* one might grow vegetables.

Some other "adverbial connectives" are: so, yet, thus, hence, however, moreover, consequently, henceforth, furthermore, nevertheless, otherwise, therefore, on the other hand, namely, for instance, that is, for example.

N.B. Do not confuse "adverbial connectives" with "co-ordinate conjunctions" (and, or, but, for, nor) which take commas.

> I was late for work; *however,* I wasn't put on report. I was late for work, *but* I was not put on report.

How to correct comma splices

You can correct the comma splice by using any one of the following three methods.

(i) Use a semicolon between the two sentences. It is designed specifically to draw the reader's attention to the close connection of the ideas that precede and follow it, and thus gives the impact to the second idea that you mistakenly strove for when using the comma, e.g. change:

> My English class was cancelled today, my instructor was sick.
>
> *to*
>
> My English class was cancelled today; my instructor was sick.

(ii) Subordinate one of the ideas to the other *i.e.* one of the sentences to the other, by introducing a subordinate conjunction), e.g. change:

> My English class was cancelled today, my instructor was sick.
>
> *to*
>
> My English class was cancelled today because my instructor was sick.

Be careful to subordinate the appropriate idea: "Because my English class was cancelled today, my instructor was sick" completely changes your meaning by changing the emphasis given by the subordination.

(iii) Join the two sentences with a coordinating conjunction (and, but, for, or, nor); e.g. change:

> My English class was cancelled today, my instructor was sick.
>
> *to*
>
> My English class was cancelled today, for my instructor was sick.

Pay careful attention to make certain that the meaning that you are striving for stays the same when you add a coordinating conjunction: "My English class was cancelled today, and my instructor was sick" has a completely different meaning than the one you had in the original comma splice.

3. The run-on sentence

The run-on sentence occurs when a writer uses no punctuation at all at the end of a sentence; e.g.

> My English class was cancelled today my instructor was sick.

Actually, the run-on sentence is exactly the same error as the comma splice, except that here even the comma has been left out. The writer is trying to achieve the same effect as the writer of the comma splice (i.e. the writer is trying to point out the connection between the ideas of two sentences by speeding the reader through to the second idea) and you should be able to use exactly the same methods outlined in the section on the comma splice to identify and correct the run-on sentence.

II. Agreement

1. Subject and verb agreement (number)

The subject and the verb of any sentence must always have the same number (i.e. singular or plural).

Most of the time we have no difficulty with subject/verb agreement because our use of the language has so accustomed us to using correct agreement that errors immediately strike us as "not sounding right". None of us would have difficulty in recognizing the problem in such sentences as "He go to the store", or "They goes to the store".

Occasionally in more complex sentences or in constructions that we do not use frequently, we become confused or "forget" just what word is the subject of the verb, or what the number of the subject really is. The following section outlines the most common instances in which writers make errors in subject/verb agreement and suggests how they can be corrected and avoided.

Common problems of subject/verb agreement in number

SITUATION	EXAMPLE OF ERROR	CORRECT FORM
(i) A group of words comes between the subject and the verb, one of which is a noun of a different number than the subject.	One of the eggs are rotten.	*One* of the eggs *is* rotten.
	Life with all its trials and tribulations are hard to bear.	*Life* with all its trials and tribulations *is* sometimes hard to bear.
(ii) When the word 'there' begins a sentence. In such expressions as 'there is', 'there are', 'there was', and 'there were', the number of the verb (e.g. 'is' or 'are') is determined by the number of the noun that *follows* the verb (the real subject).	There is many cases of unnecessary surgery.	There *are* many *cases* of unnecessary surgery.
	There was times when I almost gave up.	There *were times* when I almost gave up.
	There is a man and his wife at the door.	There *are* a *man* and his *wife* at the door.
(iii) When a 'collective' noun is the subject of the sentence. 'Collective' nouns are nouns that represent groups of people or things: e.g. group, herd, crowd, jury, audience, class.	The class are late for the examination.	The *class* is late for the examination.
If the group is acting as a unified whole, a *singular* verb is used.	The jury agree on the verdict.	The *jury agrees* on the verdict.
If the members of the group that comprises the collective noun are not acting as a unified whole, use a *plural* verb.	The crowd disagrees on what to do.	The *crowd disagree* on what to do.

Actually you can avoid the entire problem of awkward sounding plural verbs in these circumstances by rewording the subject of the sentence.

REMEMBER: (i) When the members of the group agree, use the singular verb.
(ii) When the members of the group are not unified, *change the subject* to a noun that represents the members of the group, e.g. change:

The herd are going off in all directions.
to
The *cows* are going off in all directions.
or
The *members* of the herd are going off in all directions.

SITUATION	EXAMPLE OF ERROR	CORRECT FORM
(iv) When the usual order of the sentence is reversed, so that the subject follows the verb, make certain that you have the same number for the subject and the verb.	In the doorway was standing two gigantic policemen. What was I to do?	In the doorway were standing two gigantic policemen. What was I to do?
(v) Indefinite pronouns such as the following are *always singular* and therefore always have *singular* verbs: one, each, everybody, no one, nobody, someone, somebody, either, neither, anyone, everyone.		*Neither* of the men *is* able to do the job. *Someone* representing the colleges *is* to blame. *Nobody is* interested. *Each has* its proper place. *One* of the men who was imprisoned *is* my uncle.
(vi) Two separate subjects of the same verb, joined by "and", form a *plural* subject; they require a plural verb.		*My brother and I are* going to travel this summer. *Halifax and Quebec City have* citadels.

SITUATION	EXAMPLE OF ERROR	CORRECT FORM
(vii) Two subjects of the same verb, joined by "both...and" constructions always form a plural subject; they require a plural verb.		Both my father and I are going.
(viii) Two subjects of the same verb, joined by "either...or", "neither...nor", "not only...but also" may take either a singular or a plural verb: if the subject *closer* to the verb is singular, use a singular verb.		Neither mother nor *Aunt Helen is* able to go. Neither the children nor *Aunt Helen is* able to go. (NOTE THAT EVEN THOUGH "children" IS PLURAL, "Aunt Helen", WHICH IS SINGULAR, IS CLOSER TO THE VERB; THEREFORE, THE VERB IS SINGULAR).
If the subject closer to the verb is plural, use a plural verb.		Either the instructor or the answers in the book are wrong. (NOTE THAT EVEN THOUGH "the instructor" IS SINGULAR, "answers", WHICH IS A PLURAL SUBJECT, IS CLOSER TO THE VERB; THEREFORE, THE VERB IS PLURAL.

REMEMBER: When in doubt, or when you get caught up in an awkward, confusing situation, take the easy way out: reword the sentence so that "either" comes before one subject *and* its verb and "or" comes before the second subject *and* another verb. e.g. "Either *the textbooks are wrong* or *the instructor is*."

SITUATION	EXAMPLE OF ERROR	CORRECT FORM
(ix) Who, Which, That (relative pronouns). When these words introduce a subordinate clause *and* act as the subject of the		The stor*ies* that *are* told about him are all lies. The stor*y* that *is* being told about him is a lie.

SITUATION	EXAMPLE OF ERROR	CORRECT FORM
verb in that clause (e.g. "the man who was coming to dinner"), they always refer to a specific word used earlier in the sentence (e.g., in our example, to "man") [See "Pronoun Reference", p. 274], and take their number from that word. Thus, if the word referred to is singular, use a singular verb after "who", "which", or "that"; if the word referred to is plural, use a plural verb.		The *girl* who *is* telling the story is a liar. The girls who *are* telling the story are liars.

2. Agreement: Pronouns and Antecedent

A pronoun always agrees in number (*i.e.* singular, or plural) with the noun to which it refers.

The *men* said *they* were tired.

Most of the time you will have no difficulty with pronoun/antecedent agreement, but there are four situations which might cause you confusion:

SITUATION	EXAMPLE OF ERROR	CORRECT FORM
(i) collective nouns (crowd, jury, pack, group, etc.) are considered singular if all the members of the collection are acting as a unified whole.	After the *jury* deliberated for 6 weeks *they* reached a verdict.	After the *jury* deliberated for 6 weeks, *it* reached a verdict.
(ii) collective nouns are considered *plural* if the members of the collection are *not* acting as a unified whole.	The *jury* still disagreed on whether *it* should ask for advice.	The *jury* still disagreed on whether *they* should ask for advice.

SITUATION	EXAMPLE OF ERROR	CORRECT FORM
(iii) indefinite pronouns (one, each, everyone, either, neither, etc.) are *always* singular.	*Everyone* did as *they* were told.	*Everyone* did as *he* was told.
(iv) make certain that you know which word the pronoun refers to.	Neither of the boys knew what they wanted to do (the word which the pronoun refers to is not "boys" but "neither").	Neither of the boys knew what he wanted to do.

3. Agreement: possessive pronouns (my, your, his, her, its, our, their)

Just as a pronoun takes its number from the noun that it replaces, so too does the possessive pronoun.

Usually a writer has little difficulty in recognizing the appropriate number of the pronoun to use; we do it almost every time we speak:

Where is Hilda's hat? *It's* with *her* coat.
Here come the kids. Do they have *their* coats on?

A problem normally occurs only in the same four situations that we encountered when discussing pronoun agreement:

SITUATION	EXAMPLE OF ERROR	CORRECT FORM
(i) collective nouns (crowd, group, jury, etc.) are considered singular if all the members of the collection are acting in a unified way.	The *flock* was sleeping quietly in *their* fold as the wolf crept closer.	The *flock* was sleeping quietly in *its* fold as the wolf crept closer.
(ii) collective nouns are considered *plural* when the members of the collection are *not* acting in a unified manner.	The *flock* ran off in all directions as the wolf attacked *its* fold.	The *flock* ran off in all directions as the wolf attacked *their* fold.

SITUATION	EXAMPLE OF ERROR	CORRECT FORM
(iii) indefinite pronouns (one, someone, somebody, everybody, each, either, etc.) are *always* singular.	*Each* of the men did *their* homework.	*Each* of the men did *his* homework.
(iv) make certain that in a complex sentence you know exactly to which word the pronoun refers.		Miss Evans is one of those *instructors* who never forgets *their* students' names.

III. Pronoun reference

Pronouns are used to substitute for, or take the place of, nouns. Using them frees us from the boring and unwieldly repetition of nouns. Without pronouns we would have to write the following, for example:

> Tom is a doctor. Tom lives in London, Ontario. Many patients feel that Tom is the best doctor that these patients have ever had.

Since we can use pronouns to substitute for specific nouns, however, we can avoid the rigidity and childishness that using them brings:

> Tom is a doctor *who* lives in London, Ontario. Many patients feel that *he* is the best doctor *they* have ever had.

When using pronouns, be careful to observe the following two rules:
(a) there must be a specific noun to which that pronoun refers.
(b) there must be only one noun to which the pronoun could possibly refer.

Look at the confusion which the lack of a specific noun to refer to causes in the following sentences:

> My uncle, an old college friend, and Doctor Peter Smith came for a visit yesterday. *He* is from Montreal.

[This sentence causes confusion by not clearly defining which person the "He" refers to. In this case, the second sentence would have to be changed to "*Dr. Smith* is from Montreal."]

> *They* don't know what they're doing in Ottawa.

274

[Who does "they" refer to? the Cabinet? the civil service? Members of Parliament? the Ottawa tourists? The sentence would have to be changed to replace the first "they" with a specific noun; e.g. *"Our members of parliament* don't know what they are doing in Ottawa."]

> Runaway inflation, increasing unemployment, and a mounting trade deficit are three major problems our country faces. *This* often causes people to turn to dictators.

[The failure to have one specific noun to which "this" refers causes the reader confusion. To convey a clear meaning the second sentence would have to be changed to read: *"These economic difficulties* often cause people to turn to dictators."]

IV. Modifiers

Modifiers *i.e.* words or groups of words that "modify" or alter the meanings of other words) attach themselves to the appropriate word closest to them in a sentence. Thus, unless you are very careful in placing modifiers, they may change the meaning of the wrong word and cause your reader to misunderstand your meaning, become confused, or end up laughing at what you intended to be a serious point.

Note how the change in the positioning of the following modifiers changes the meaning of the sentences:

He handed the book to the customer with a leather binding. [*This would be a rather strange looking customer.*]

He handed the book with the leather cover to the customer.

She took a loaf of bread from the refrigerator that Aunt Bessie had made. [*Aunt Bessie, we must suppose, had a job in a factory that made refrigerators.*]

She took a loaf of bread that Aunt Bessie had made from the refrigerator. [*Here Aunt Bessie has changed jobs to become a cook.*]

I only asked for one ticket. [*Everyone else, apparently, purchased two or more tickets.*]

I asked for only one ticket. [*The writer was going Dutch treat.*]

He lived in the house built by his great-grand-father for ten years. [*Either Great-grand-father apparently didn't want to take up permanent residence, or else he was a very slow worker.*]

He lived for ten years in the house built by his great-grand-father.

| Walking down the street, a skyscraper came into view. [*An advance in bionics has apparently been made.*] | Walking down the street, I saw a skyscraper come into view. |

Such problems arise from the fact that *we* know precisely what *we* mean when we write the sentence, but forget that others will not know what we mean unless we put our modifiers in exactly the right place. We know that Aunt Bessie never worked in a factory, so it doesn't occur to us that someone else could think that she did. We're just trying to get down on the paper that Aunt Bessie makes her own bread: doesn't everybody know that she does? The answer, of course, is no, not unless *you tell them.*

Make your modifiers say what you mean by placing them with the word that you want them to modify.

If modifiers are a problem in your writing, the easiest way to spot "misplaced" modifiers is either a) to read your own work aloud (preferably a day or so after you wrote it) or b) to have someone else read it aloud for you while you read to yourself over his shoulder. By putting yourself in the role of a stranger coming to the work for the first time, you will recognize the confusion or the change of meaning that results from "misplaced" modifiers.

REMEMBER: Always ask yourself as you write and reread your work, "What will my reader take this passage to mean?"

V. Verb tense consistency

Whenever you write, you must make certain that you always present the reader with one consistent point in time from which to view your material. In the following example the writer mistakenly presents two points of time (one present, one past):

> In *The Edible Woman,* Marion *intends* to marry Peter until she *discovers* he *is* trying to dominate her. When she *realized* what he *was* doing, she *refused* to marry him.

In the first sentence, the writer views the book as existing in the present tense; therefore, he presents the action taking place in the book as occuring in the present tense. Since the writer may have read the book sometime in the past, he suddenly begins, in the second sentence, to write about the action of the book as if it happened in the past instead of maintaining a consistent point of time in the present. The writer should have determined in advance which point of time (i.e. verb tense) would be used throughout his essay.

Not all cases of changing the tense of your verb are as obvious as the above example.

> How many times have you had to hit the brakes because someone else *decides* he *wants* to pull out onto the road?

The incident has become so vivid in the writer's mind that he has gone back into a past experience midway through the sentence and the immediacy of the situation has caused him to switch tenses. Nevertheless, although the switch in time was a natural occurrence for the author, who knew exactly what the situation was that he was describing, it still strikes the reader as awkward and disturbing, and distracts him from the "meat" of the argument. If the author had written

> How many times have you had to hit the brakes because someone else *decided* that he *wanted* to pull out onto the road?

he would have taken the reader through a complete and unified experience.

A short guide to punctuation

Many people are confused by punctuation because they mistakenly think that they are dealing with some abstract set of rules that they do not know. In actual fact, nothing could be further from the truth.

Whenever you use punctuation in your written communication, all that you are really trying to do is to convey to your reader the "structure" of your meaning that, when speaking, you supply by pauses, inflections, tone of voice, and so on. If you were talking to someone, the differences between the two following sentences would be immediately understood by your listener:

> John, is the cause of the problem here?
> *and*
> John is the cause of the problem here.

When you are writing to someone, on the other hand, you use punctuation marks to make your meaning clear to your reader: if you intend the first meaning, you substitute a comma for the pause following "John" and a question mark for the rise in your voice at the end of the sentence; you do not use these punctuation marks if you intend the second meaning.

Therefore, when you try to decide what punctuation to use in a passage, you are only thinking about how to symbolize or represent on the page what you do all the time when you speak. For the most part, successful use of punctuation simply means conveying your meaning accurately by paying attention to how you would say the passage aloud, and translating that emphasis into a symbol.

In the following chapter, we have tried to summarize how each punctuation mark symbolizes a pause or an inflection or some other oral device. If you encounter any situation in which you are still in doubt about the correct symbol to use (i.e. about the punctuation that is appropriate to your meaning), we have included a guide to the "rules" of punctuation that have been abstracted from everyday usage to help you choose correctly.

I. The comma (,)

The comma is used to represent short pauses that are used in speaking to give emphasis or to maintain the clarity of an idea within the sentence.

There are basically ten situations in which you would pause in such a way when speaking and, hence, for which you should use the comma when writing.

1. *In lists*

When you speak, you pause between the *words (or groups of words)* in *a list (or series):*

> I went out to buy *margarine* (pause) *tobacco,* (pause) and *coffee.*
> What walks *on four legs in the morning* (pause) *on two legs at noon* (pause) and *on three legs in the evening?*
> I believe *that he worked hard* (pause) *that he played hard* (pause) and *that he lived a good life.*

When you write the same sentence, you insert commas to represent these pauses:

> I went out to buy *margarine, tobacco* and *coffee.*
> What walks *on four legs in the morning, on two legs at noon,* and *on three legs in the evening?*
> I believe *that he worked hard, that he played hard,* and *that he lived a good life.*

RULE #1: Insert commas between the words (or groups of words) in a list (or series).

2. *Between adjectives in a series*

When you use only one adjective to modify a noun, you do not pause between them when you speak, and therefore you should not use a comma when you write:

> the faithful friend

However, when two (or more) adjectives in a series describe the same noun, you naturally pause between the adjectives:

> the faithful (pause) kind friend

When you write, this pause must be represented by a comma:

> the faithful, kind friend

N.B.

In the above example, the adjectives in the series modify the same noun, "friend", independently. In other words, they do not depend on or change the meaning of each other. Thus you could reverse the order of the adjectives without destroying the meaning of the passage:

the kind, faithful friend

If you encounter a situation in which reversing the order of the modifiers destroys the meaning of the passage, do *not* use commas between the modifiers: for example

the very faithful friend

cannot be reversed to "the faithful very friend". Therefore you should not insert a comma between "very" and "faithful".

RULE #2: Insert commas between adjectives in a series when they modify (independently) the same noun.

3. *Before the words "and", "but", "for", "or" and "nor"*
Whenever you orally connect two main ideas by using "and", "but", "for", "or" and "nor", you pause before you say this connecting word to draw attention to the transition between the two ideas. You should normally insert a comma to symbolize this pause when you write:

The thin man ate his dinner, *and* the fat man ate his heart out.
He ended his speech, *for* he found that his audience had left.
He needed an ace, *but* he drew a two.

N.B.
Do not use a comma before any of these connecting words when the subject of the second main idea is omitted because it is the same as the subject of the first:

He needed an ace *but* drew a two.

RULE # 3: Insert a comma before the words "and", "but", "for", "or" and "nor" when they join two main ideas that have separate subjects.

4. *To set off non-essential information in a sentence*
If you add information to a sentence that is not essential for your listener to understand the main idea of the sentence, you invariably pause before and after that added information. Commas are inserted when such passages are written to symoblize these pauses.

280

4A. Apposition

If a word or expression is placed beside another in the sentence that gives more information about that other word or expression and has the same grammatical construction (e.g. both are nouns), that word or expression is said to be *in apposition* to the other. Since words or expressions used in apposition do not add information essential to the understanding of the sentence, they are set off orally with pauses, and in writing with commas:

> A post-secondary institution, the college deals with mature students.
> The college, a post-secondary institution, deals with mature students.
> Jim found himself going to college, a post-secondary institution.

RULE #4A: Use commas to set off words or expression used in apposition.

4B. Non-essential phrases and clauses
Clauses

If you use clauses beginning with "who", "whom", "which" or "that" (i.e. relative clauses) to add information that is descriptive but not essential to your audience's understanding of the main idea of a sentence, represent the oral pauses with commas that set off the clause:

> John, who won the hundred yard dash, is my best friend.

Although the information in the "who" clause adds an interesting detail, it is not essential to the main idea of the sentence, "John is my best friend". Note how you would normally pause before "who" and after "dash" if you were saying this sentence to someone.

N.B.

If, on the other hand, the sentence were to read,

> The boy who won the hundred yard dash is my best friend.

the "who" clause has become essential to the basic meaning of the main idea because the boy is not named or given any other form of identification; without the information in the "who" clause the audience has no way of knowing which specific boy is referred to. Note that if you were saying this sentence aloud, you would not pause before "who" or after "dash".

Phrases

The same rule applies to verbal phrases. When the phrase contains non-essential information, commas are used to set it off from the rest of the sentence (as pauses would if you were speaking):

> John, wearing a silly grin, wiped the cream pie from his face.

If the information contained in the phrase is essential to the main idea of the sentence commas are *not* used (just as you would not pause when speaking):

> The boy wearing the red cap is my cousin.

RULE # 4B: If a verbal phrase or a relative clause is vital to answering the question "which one or ones", then it is *essential* to the meaning of the sentence and *does not* require commas to set it off.
If a verbal phrase or a relative clause is not vital to answering the question "which one or ones", then it is non-essential and *should be set off* from the rest of the sentence by commas.

5. *Interrupters (of the sentence)*
If you interrupt the natural flow of a sentence by inserting a word, phrase or clause that is out of its normal position in the sentence, you pause when you are speaking to set off or give emphasis to the interrupter. In the written form of the sentence, this pause is represented by a comma.

> I decided, therefore, to go (The "natural flow" of this sentence would be "Therefore I decided to go").
> He fell, alas, on the field of battle.
> Charles, in order to pass the course, stayed up all weekend.
> The Royal Canadian Navy, when it was charged with guarding the convoys crossing the North Atlantic, painted one of the most glorious episodes in its history.

RULE #5: Use commas to set off interrupters from the rest of the sentence.

6. *Contrasting phrases in a sentence*
When speaking, you would always pause to give emphasis to information introduced by the word "not" when that information contrasts with the rest of the sentence. Therefore, when you write you should insert commas *before* and *after* such phrases.

> The car, not the bike, swerved off the road.
> Both partners in a marriage, not just the wife, should be responsible for doing housework.

282

RULE #6: Insert commas before and after phrases introduced by "not" when those phrases contrast with the rest of the sentence.

7. *After "yes", "no", "oh", "well", etc.*

If you begin a sentence with "yes", "no", "oh", "well" or a similar word when speaking, you naturally pause after these words. Use a comma to represent that pause.

> Well, that's that.
> No, I refuse to get involved with that kind of nonsense.
> Yes, I can go this weekend.

RULE #7: Insert a comma after "yes", "no", "oh", "well" and similar words when they introduce a sentence.

8. *To set off a person's name*

Whenever you talk to someone directly and call that person by name, you set off the name by pausing. Commas are used when writing to represent this effect.

> Martha, I have loved you madly all of my life.
> Why don't you drop dead, John?
> Frankly, Charlotte, I don't give a damn.

RULE #8: Use commas to set off the name of a person directly addressed.

9. *To avoid confusion*

If you listen carefully when you speak to someone, you will see that you make brief pauses in your speech simply to prevent your listener from confusing your meaning. Note, for example, how the pauses in the following sentences give the "listener" the key to the meaning of each:

> To win (pause) Mary Nelson will have to try harder.
> To win Mary (pause) Nelson will have to try harder.

These pauses are represented by commas whenever they are necessary to avoid confusion for your reader.

> Call me Gary when you arrive.
> Call me, Gary, when you arrive.

RULE #9: Use commas when necessary to avoid misunderstanding.

10. *To set off dates and places*

You use commas to symbolize the pauses that you normally make between the elements of dates and places.

> On October 13, 1812, the Americans attacked Queenston Heights, Ontario.
> I moved to 197 Clarence St., Brantford, Ontario, on April 12, 1979.

II. The dash (—)

Just as the comma is used to show a reader where we would pause in a sentence if we were speaking, so too is the dash. In fact, the only time that a dash should be used is to replace the comma.

You might at first think that such duplication is unnecessary, but the dash is used whenever we want to add a little extra dramatic effect to the pause.

> I dashed forward to knock the gun from his hand — but I was too late.
> History provides us with one overwhelming lesson — the silliness of man.

1. When you suddenly change the direction of the thought of a sentence, you might want to reflect the drama of that change by using a dash:

> My father was a man of infinite kindness — but he died the cruellest of deaths.

2. You might want to replace the commas with dashes in order to give extra emphasis to explanatory phrases, words in apposition, and so on:

> That young man — his own son — struck the old man.

3. You might want to use the dash to give emphasis to the final words of a sentence when they sum up the preceding ideas:

> The backpack came complete with cooking equipment, sleeping bag, cook stove, and nylon tent — a complete outfit.

III. The semicolon (;)

When you have two complete sentences that are closely connected in meaning, you can stress this connection by using the semicolon to replace the period:

> The perfect spot was down by the river; I knew that from the time I was a child.
> Watch out for him; he's got a mean temper.

Whenever a semicolon is used in such situations, it is only reflecting the type of pauses that are made in oral communication; someone speaking tries to draw the listener's attention to the connection between the ideas of the sentences by pausing slightly longer than for a comma but not as long as for a period. As a matter of fact, it is the misinterpretation of this shortened pause between two sentences that causes people to write comma splices and run-on sentences (see p. 267). For this reason, the semicolon is often the best punctuation to use to correct those errors.

One of the most common difficulties that inexperienced writers encounter is the omission of the semicolon before transitional words other than conjunctions. You should be careful to use the semicolon between two complete sentences (main clauses) when the second sentence begins with one of the following adverbal connectives:

so	consequently	then
yet	henceforth	namely
thus	furthermore	for instance
hence	nevertheless	that is
however	otherwise	for example
moreover	therefore	

Note that a comma is used to reflect the pause after such transitional words, except the very short ones (so, yet, thus):

> I was late; therefore, I had to do without breakfast.
> I know just how you feel; however, I still cannot agree.
> I did not have my car rust-proofed when I bought it; consequently, the car is now worthless.

N.B.

Be careful not to use a semicolon in front of any of the adverbals listed above when they act as interrupters in the middle of a sentence (main clause):

> I know, however, just how you feel.

IV. The colon (:)

Although the colon does not reflect a unique type of oral pause, it is not difficult to use because its purposes are so specialized.

1. *To introduce a long list*

If your list is relatively short and simple, try to incorporate it into your sentence and avoid the use of the colon.

> My greatest pleasures are a quiet lake, a snow capped mountain, and the smell of pine trees.

If, on the other hand, your list is long and detailed you should introduce your list with a *complete sentence* and a colon.

> There are ten first class dining rooms in Vancouver:
> My father would not allow me to have a motorcycle for the following reasons:
> Avoid situations such as the following:

N.B.
Be careful not to end your introduction with "such as".

2. *To introduce a long quotation*

If the quotation is relatively short, try to incorporate it into your sentence.

> "From each according to his ability, to each according to his need" was the basic doctrine of Marx and his followers.

If, on the other hand, the quotation is longer than one sentence, you should introduce it with a complete sentence and a colon.

> Susanna Moodie, in her novel *Roughing it in the Bush,* described her joy on first seeing Quebec City in unrestrained prose: Canadians, rejoice in your beautiful city! Rejoice and be worthy of her — for few, very few, of the sons of men can point to such a spot as Quebec...

V. The question mark (?)

The question mark is used to convey to your reader the inflection (the rise in your voice) that you use orally when you ask a direct question.

> Are you going to the pub?

Remember that a quotation that contains a direct question is read with the same inflection as was used by the speaker quoted.

Thus we use a question mark within the quotation marks.

John asked, "Are you going to the pub?"

However, when a sentence contains an *indirect question,* you do *not* raise your voice and hence do *not* use the question mark.

John asked if I was going to the pub.

VI. The exclamation mark (!)

An exclamation mark is only used to point out to the reader the emphasis you would place on a statement which expresses surprise, shock or some other sudden emotion. Be careful not to overuse it.

Get out of the way!

VII. Quotation marks (" ")

Quotation marks are another instance of punctuation marks which do not reflect a distinct pause or other change in your speech patterns. Once again, however, the very specialized use of the quotation mark makes their correct use relatively easy.

1. *Direct quotations*
Use quotation marks to enclose the exact words that someone has spoken or written.

The old timer asked, "Who was that masked man?"
"Who", the old timer asked, "was that masked man?"

You do not use quotation marks around *indirect* quotations.

The old timer asked who the masked man was.

2. *Extended quotations*

If the passage that you are quoting is longer than *five* lines, you should use a completely different technique to show your reader that you are giving an exact quotation. For the entire passage quoted, use a second margin approximately ½" further in than each original margin, single space the entire passage and *do not* use quotation marks.

The following article, printed on July 1, 1867, illustrates the enthusiasm of the founders of our nation:

> Upon the occasion of the birth of this great nation, stretching from sea to sea, from the temperate climes of the South to the frigid climes of the Arctic waste...

3. *The position of other punctuation when used with quotation marks*

   (i) Place periods and commas *inside* quotation marks:

> "Come here," he shouted.
> The reply came back, "Never."

   (ii) Place colons and semicolons after the closing quotation mark.

> The policeman shouted, "Hands up"; however, the burglar fled.

   (iii) When you use question marks and exclamation points with quotation marks, observe the following rules:

      (a) If the question or exclamation is found *only* within the quotation, the question or exclamation mark goes *inside* the quotation marks.

> "Why are you so late?" John demanded.
> Mary replied, "What's it to you?"

      (b) If the question or exclamation takes in the entire sentence, the question or exclamation mark goes *outside* the quotation marks.

> Did John say, "I am leaving for Saskatoon tomorrow"?

VIII. Punctuation of titles

1. Whenever you refer to the titles of any of the following, use quotation marks around the title:

   (a) A chapter of a book (eg. "The Advance of Democracy" in *A History of the Modern World*).

   (b) An article from a newspaper or magazine (eg. "Motherhood Alone: A Choice and a Struggle" in *The Globe and Mail*).

   (c) An entry from an encyclopedia (eg. "Shakespeare" in *Encyclopedia Britannica*).

   (d) A single episode from a T.V. series or a single song from a record album (eg. "Arrival" from the T.V. series *The Prisoner*).

   (e) The title of a short story or a poem (eg. "Daffodils" from *The Norton Anthology*).

2. Whenever you refer to the titles of longer works such as books, plays, films, T.V. or radio series, newspapers, magazines, and encyclopedias —*underline the title* to indicate that it would be italicized as in the examples above.

IX. The apostrophe (')

1. *To denote possession*

The concept of possession often presents difficulties for inexperienced writers because the apostrophe itself is not heard when we speak. In fact, the failure to use the apostrophe for possession is perhaps the most common error in writing.

The concept of possession itself, however, is not difficult to learn and with a little practice in identifying specific examples of possession in your work, you should be able to avoid misusing or omitting the apostrophe.

"Possession" simply means that you are showing that one thing "belongs to" another (eg. "John's hat" means "the hat belonging to John").

You should not have too much difficulty with the idea of possession when it applies to a person owning something (eg. John's hat), but the problem becomes a little more difficult when you approach the idea that things and abstract ideas can "possess" characteristics or other things:

> The colour of (or belonging to) a rock is the roc*k's* colour.
> The troubles of (belonging to) life are lif*e's* troubles.
> The homework assigned to (belonging to) the class is the clas*s* homework.

You may have to be careful not to go to the other extreme of placing an apostrophe after all words that end in "s". If you are in doubt apply the "belonging to" test:

> Reverse the order of the words (e.g. from "The country's borders" to "The borders—the country") and insert the words "belong to" between them (e.g. "The borders belonging to the country").

If the meaning of the words remains the same you know that you have a case of possession and should use the apostrophe.

The rules by which you determine the position of the apostrophe in the possessing word are the following:

(i) If the "possessing word" ends in any letter other than "s", add 's

> John's hat
> horse's stall

women*'s* coats
ma*n's* shirts

(note that both singular and plural words ending in a letter other than "s" add 's).
(ii) If the possessing word ends in "s", add only the apostrophe

class*'* homework
horse*s'* stalls
dog*s'* lives

(note that it doesn't matter whether the word is singular or plural; as long as the word ends in "s", only add the apostrophe).
(iii) If two or more people (or things) possess the same thing, only the last noun is given the apostrophe.

Fred and Joan's car (they jointly own the car)

If two people or more people (or things) possess two of the same things, both receive apostrophes.

Fred's and Joan's cars

2. *In contractions*

When one or more letters are left out of a word, the apostrophe replaces the omitted letter or letters.

Don't [Do not] do that.
Let's [Let us] go.
I couldn't [could not] do that.
I'll [I shall] go.

Hence a word of warning is in order. Sometimes people confuse contracted words with possessive pronouns.

REMEMBER: You're [You are] doing well.
Your coat has been stolen.
It's [It is] not too late.
Its fur was matted.
They're [They are] coming over later.
Their jobs were boring.
Who's [Who is] coming to dinner?
Whose [possessive] lipstick is on your collar?

3. *Plural forms of letters, figures and signs*

Watch your *P's* and *Q's.*
All of the *6's* and *12's* go in this column.

Words that commonly cause difficulty and confusion

There are a number of words that are often mistakenly interchanged or confused by people when they speak and write. Sometimes the mistake can bring a ridiculous meaning to the sentence that completely destroys the seriousness of the message that the writer intended the reader to receive:

"They found his body in the middle of the dessert" brings up an image in the reader's mind of a 6′4″ detective found dead in a giant bowl of jello, a good scene from a Woody Allen movie, perhaps, but definitely not the tragic *desert* scene that the writer intended to depict.

The following section is intended to give you a quick reference to check the most commonly confused words whenever you have the slightest doubt over whether you have used the right word or not.

It is a good idea to read this entire section over a few times anyway. All too often people assume that they know the correct word or the correct form of a word when in fact they have been making an error for years.

ACCEPT—EXCEPT

ACCEPT—means to receive something or to agree with something.
> e.g."I accepted the certificate from the Dean."
> "I accept that concept".

EXCEPT—means "other than" or "but"
> e.g. "Everyone except Joan had to rewrite the test."

ACCESS—EXCESS

ACCESS—means "coming toward" or "a way to approach something" or "permission to approach something".
> e.g. "I had access to the library".
> "The only access to the mansion was through a guarded gate".

EXCESS—means "an extreme", "too much".
> e.g."His head felt like a race course for the Austrian cavalry because he had drunk to excess the night before."

ALSO—Also is not confused with any other word, but it is commonly overused and abused. It is always best to try to find another word to replace "also". Never use "also" at the beginning of a sentence.

AFFECT—EFFECT

AFFECT—means to cause change or to influence sometime.

> e.g."Smoking affects your breathing."

EFFECT—as a *verb*, means to result in, or to produce a result, when used as a verb.

> e.g.The Prime Minister was unable to effect his legislation.

EFFECT—as a *noun* means the result of something.

> e.g. Troubled breathing is the *effect* of excessive smoking.
>
> Note: "Effect" is most commonly used as a noun.
>
> Note: Except in a few obsolute or technical cases *"affect"* is not used as a noun.

ALREADY—ALL READY

ALREADY—means "previously".

> e.g. "We were already there."

ALL READY—means that everyone or everything is prepared to do something.

> e.g. We were all ready to go.

AMONG—BETWEEN

AMONG—means to be in the midst *of more than two things*, or to divide something for *more than two people*.

> e.g. The five of you will have to decide among yourselves.

BETWEEN—means to be located or to happen so as to separate *two things*; or to divide something for *two people*.

> e.g. I was caught between the devil and the deep blue sea.
>
> I divided the last of the wine between my girl friend and her brother.

AMOUNT—NUMBER

AMOUNT—means the *quantity* of something.

> e.g. The amount of snow that fell last night was incredible.

NUMBER—means a *collection* of persons or things.

> e.g. A number of people came to our house on Christmas Eve.
>
> Note: Errors usually occur in the use of these words when a writer confuses a collection (i.e. a group of people or things) with a quantity, and puts down, for example, "The amount of people who favor abortion is changing."
>
> The correct wording recognizes that the people involved are individuals gathered

into a collection, not a lump of undifferen-
tiated flesh: "The number of people...."

ARE—OUR

ARE—is a form of the verb "to be"
e.g. We *are* going to the store.
OUR—is the possessive form of the pronoun "we".
e.g. Our house burned down.
The confusion of these two words results from the
pronounciation of "our" in some Canadian dialects. If
you are in any doubt about whether you have made
the error when you reread your paper, see whether
you can reword the phrase to read "...belonging to
us; if you can, use "our".

A WHILE—A LOT

No one confuses these expressions, but they certainly are
overused. Both are "colloquial" phrases and are not appropriate
in many formal situations in expository writing. *Avoid* them if
at all possible, but if you must use them, at least note that they
are both spelled as two words.

CAN—MAY

CAN—means *to be able*.
e.g. A cheetah can run at 80 miles per hour.
MAY—means *to have permission*.
e.g. May I go to the washroom? [The only time you
should ask, "Can I go to the bathroom?" is after
being treated by a doctor for bowel problems.]

CHOICE—CHOOSE—CHOSE

CHOICE—is a *noun* which means selection or choosing, or option.
e.g. What choice did I have?
CHOOSE—is a verb which means to select. The "oo" is pronounced the same as the "oo" in "loop".
e.g. Choose the loop, not the pill.
CHOSE—is a verb, the *past* tense of the verb to choose. The "o" in
"chose" is pronounced the same way as the "o" in
"elope"
e.g. They chose to elope.

COARSE—COURSE

COARSE—means rough.
e.g. This sweater is made of coarse wool.
COURSE—means a plan of action or direction.
e.g. of course this course is the course to a brilliant
future.

DESERT—DESSERT

DESERT—as a *noun*, means a place where there is little rainfall.
e.g. Cacti grow in the desert.

DESERT—as a *verb*, means to abandon.

      e.g. He deserted his family.

DESSERT—means those delicious, fattening goodies at the end of a meal.

      e.g. No more dessert for me, thanks. I'm obese already.

DEVICE—DEVISE

DEVICE—(the "ice" is pronounced the same as the frozen substance, ice).

      —a *noun*, means a tool, a scheme, an invention, etc.

      e.g. That device will never fly, Orville.

DEVISE—(The "ise" is pronounced the same as the "ies" in "lies")

      e.g. You had better devise some good lies to account for the pies.

EMIGRATE—IMMIGRATE

EMIGRATE—means to *leave* a country.

      e.g. He emigrated from Canada to avoid paying his taxes.

IMMIGRATE—means to *come* to a country.

      e.g. He immigrated to Canada to find a better life.

EMINENT—IMMINENT—EMANATE

EMINENT—means important, distinguished.

      e.g. She is an eminent lawyer.

IMMINENT—means "about to happen".

      e.g. From the darkness of the clouds we knew a cloudburst was imminent.

EMANATE—means to originate from, to come from.

      e.g. Daylight emanates from the sun.

FEWER—LESS

FEWER—is used to refer to a collection of things that can be counted.

      e.g. Fewer people watch the late movie than watch the National.

LESS—is used to refer to the amount of a material or thing.

      e.g. Less time was lost when a stoplight replaced the stop sign.

      Remember: Fewer people ski when there is less snow than usual.

I—ME

I—is the subjective form of the first person pronoun.

    e.g. When I forgot the punchline, I became the joke.

ME—is the objective form of the first person pronoun.

    e.g. When he hit me with the pie, the joke was on me.

ITS—IT'S

Iᴛꜱ—is the possessive form of the pronoun 'it'. Remember *none* of the personal possessive pronouns (my, your, his, her, our, their) use an apostrophe; therefore, "its" is no exception.

e.g. Its tail drooped between its legs.

Iᴛ'ꜱ—is the contracted form of "it is".

e.g. It's about time for supper, isn't it?

KNOW—NO

Kɴᴏᴡ—means "to be aware of"

e.g. I know when to use "know"

Nᴏ—means "not in any way".

e.g. "No, no," she cried, "you must not hang my daddy."

LATER—LATTER

Lᴀᴛᴇʀ—means "subsequently". The "a" in later is pronounced the same way as the "a" in "play".

e.g. Stephanie can come out to play later.

Lᴀᴛᴛᴇʀ—means the last mentioned thing out of two things mentioned.

The "a" sound of latter is pronounced the same way as the "a" sound in "ladder".

e.g. John and Bert helped us elope. The latter brought the ladder.

LAY—LIE

Lᴀʏ—in the *present* tense, means to put something somewhere.

e.g. Lay the book on the table.

Lɪᴇ—means to assume a position as opposed to being placed in a position.

e.g. Lie down, please; it's time to go to sleep.

The problem: the past tense of the verb "to lie" is "lay".

e.g. John lay in bed thinking, "Shall I just lie here and hope that I laid the book on the table?"

Remember: You lie down each night.

You lay something down on a table.

You lay in bed last night.

You laid your coat down yesterday.

[There is no such word as "layed".]

LESS—LEAST

Lᴇꜱꜱ—the "comparative" form of little; it means "not so large," etc. Less is often used with adjectives and adverbs to create a "negative" comparative.

e.g. likely....less likely

beautiful....less beautiful

sure....less sure

LEAST—the "superlative" form of little; it means "smallest in size, quantity, etc." Least is often used with adjectives and adverbs to create a kind of "negative superlative".

    e.g. certain....least certain

          long....least long

Do not make the mistake of thinking that adding an "-er" or "-est" suffix to the end of a word accompanied by less or least adds emphasis: it simply reduces your phrase to nonsense. *NEVER* write such things as "least likliest" or "less fiercer".

LETS—LET'S

LETS—means "allows".

    e.g. She always lets him go early.

LET'S—is the contracted form of "let us".

    e.g. Let's go to the show.

LIKE—AS—AS IF

LIKE—when used to compare one thing to another, is always a preposition. The group of words that it introduces *never* contains an independent verb.

    e.g. I wish I were like him.

        He was out like a light.

As—when used to compare one thing to another, is always a conjunction, i.e. it joins two clauses (groups of words that each contains a subject and a verb).

    e.g. *He is* the same age *as* I am.

    Remember: the verb used after "as" is often left out or "understood": if you are in doubt as to whether you should use "like" or "as" see if you can use a form of the verb of the sentence after the word that will follow the "like" or "as"; if you can, use "as".

    e.g. I am the same age as—Joan (is). *Therefore*, "I am the same age *as* Joan" *is correct*.

    Remember: Winston tastes good, *as* a cigarette should. You will often find that when your first impulse was to use "like" as a conjunction, the words you really wanted were "as if".

    e.g. He lay there as if he were dead.

LOOSE—LOSE—LOSS

LOOSE—(the "s" is pronounced in the same way as the "s" in "moose") as an adjective, means "not tight", and as a verb, means "to untie".

    e.g. Who let the moose loose?

        Is the skin of a moose loose?

LOSE—(the "s" is pronounced in the same way as the "z" in "booze") means "to mislay".

    e.g. Did you lose the booze in the ooze?

Loss — (rhymes with "toss") means something lost.

e.g. The loss of the toss cost my boss a dime.

The confusion between these words simply results from not knowing which spelling goes with which sounds: remember one and you have them all.

MORE — MOST — ER — EST

MORE — is the "comparative" form of much; it means "greater in quantity or quality".

e.g. I have had more to drink than I should.

More haste makes more waste.

"More" is often used together with an adjective or adverb to create a "comparative" form for that word.

e.g. likely. . . . more likely

certain. . . . more certain

MOST — is the "superlative" form of much; it means "greatest in quantity or quality".

e.g. I love you most of all.

She had the most money of all of us.

"Most" is often used together with an adjective or an adverb to create a "superlative" form for that word.

e.g. certain. . . . most certain

quickly. . . . most quickly.

-ER — is a "suffix" added to the end of many adjectives and adverbs to create the "comparative" forms of those words.

e.g. great. . . . greater

large. . . . larger

late. . . . later

-EST — is a "suffix" added to the end of many adjectives and adverbs to create the "superlative" forms of those words.

e.g. sure. . . . surest

full. . . . fullest

late. . . . latest

People are often confused over which of these alternatives to use when they want to create comparatives and superlatives, but there is a relatively simple guideline to use that regularly works: **If the word that you want to make into a comparative or superlative form has** *three or more* **syllables, use** *more* **or** *most*.

e.g. su-per-cil-i-ous. . . . most supercilious

ri-dic-u-lous. . . . most ridiculous.

(Any dictionary will give you the number of syllables in a word by breaking the word into its component syllables as we have done here.)

NEVER use both -er or -est and "more" or "most" with the same word: *never* write—e.g. "most fiercest", "more faster", etc.

PASSED—PAST

PASSED—is the past tense of the verb "to pass"; it means "went by."

e.g. We passed the bus.

PAST—means that something happened earlier.

e.g. That's all in the past, now.

PERSECUTE—PROSECUTE

PERSECUTE—means "to oppress, to harass, to cause someone trouble."

e.g. Hitler persecuted the Jews.

PROSECUTE—means "to put on trial, to try to prove charges against someone in court."

e.g. Trespassers will be prosecuted.

Of course, you could always try to persecute trespassers, but you would probably be prosecuted for doing so.

PERSONAL—PERSONNEL

PERSONAL—means "private". e.g. These are my personal belongings.

PERSONNEL—means "the staff that works for a firm, college, etc.

e.g. The personnel in this store are a pain.

Watch out for personnel directors who advertise for personal positions.

PRACTISE—PRACTICE

PRACTISE—is the *verb*, and means "to do, to do repeatedly in order to learn a skill, etc."

e.g. He must have practised in order to do that badly.

PRACTICE—is the *noun*, and means "a custom, a repetition of a skill in order to learn it well, etc."

e.g. It is a good practice to check all buttons and zippers.

Make it a practice not to practise your drums after midnight.

PRINCIPAL—PRINCIPLE

PRINCIPAL—as an adjective, means "the most important".

e.g. "the principal cause"

—as a noun, means "the person in charge of a school."

e.g. The principal is your pal.

PRINCIPLE—is only used as a *noun*: it means "fundamental truth or rule of conduct."

e.g. The main principle behind our action is to get the principal fired.

STATIONARY—STATIONERY
STATIONARY—means "standing still."
    e.g. The bus remained stationary.
STATIONERY—means "paper for writing"
    Remember: If you remain stationary too long in front of a stationery store, you might be arrested for loitering.

THEIR—THERE—THEY'RE
THEIR—is the possessive form of "they".
    e.g. They forgot *their heir* when they left their money to charity.
THERE—is an adverb, used in such constructions as "here and there", "over there", and "there are..."
THEY'RE—is the contracted form of "they are".

TO—TOO
To—is used as a preposition, e.g. "to the store", "to town", etc.
    —is part of an infinitive, e.g. "to go", "to run", "to fall", etc.
Too—is an adverb. It means i) likewise or also, and ii) more than enough.
    e.g. I, too, had had too much to drink.

WERE—WE'RE—WHERE
WERE—is the plural form of the past tense of the verb "to be."
    e.g. We were later than we thought.
WE'RE—is the contracted form of "we are."
    e.g. We're in hot water now.
WHERE—is used to ask about the location of someone or something.
    e.g. Where on earth are you dragging me now, Rover?
Make certain that you know where to use were and where to use we're (know which spelling goes with which sound).

WEATHER—WETHER—WHETHER
WEATHER—means "the rain, snow, sleet, etc."
WETHER—is a castrated ram.
WHETHER—is used in such constructions as "Whether you're ready or not, I'm going."
    —A weather man knows whether it will rain or shine.
    —Whether the weather be sunny or bland, I hope you don't meet a wether man.

WHO—WHOM
WHO—is the *subjective* form of the pronoun.
    e.g. Who is coming to the party?
WHOM—is the objective form of the pronoun.
    e.g. Whom do you prefer?

For difficult situations refer to pronouns in the "Common Errors" section of this book.

WHO'S — WHOSE

WHO'S — is the contracted form of "who is".

 e.g. Who's going to Pub night?

WHOSE — is the possessive form of the pronoun "who".

 e.g. Whose hat is this?

  Remember: *none* of the possessive forms of pronouns uses an apostrophe: my, your, his, her, its, our, their and whose.

WORSE — WORST

WORSE — is the "comparative" form of "bad".

 e.g. His condition is worse than it was yesterday.

WORST — is the "superlative" form of bad.

 e.g. Out of all of those lazy bums, he is the worst.

YOUR — YOU'RE

YOUR — is the possessive form of "you".

 e.g. Here's your hat; what's your hurry?

YOU'RE — is the contracted form of "you are".

 e.g. "You're here because you're here because...."

Spelling

In the following chart you will find the major rules for spelling. Most errors in spelling, however, occur in situations not covered by any rule: the writer of a word may pronounce that word in such a way that when he goes to spell the word he writes down what he "hears" and makes a spelling error (e.g. "prejudist" for "prejudiced"); he may even assume that he knows the correct spelling for a word, only to discover later that he has been using the wrong spelling for years.

These points, together with the complexity of the rules themselves, should make the writer aware of one overwhelming fact: a dictionary should be used with great frequency. The authors of this book have often thought that they could easily win the prize for the world's worst spellers; yet very few things leave our desks with spelling mistakes in them. The way we do this is very simple: we *know* that we are terrible spellers; therefore we keep a dictionary open in front of us whenever we write anything.

One word of warning about using the dictionary may be in order. Make certain that you read the meaning of the word when you check for spelling: many words sound similar and are near each other in the dictionary, but mean very different things. There is a world of difference between "cognative" and "cognitive", for example.

Remember: good spelling is the result of long practise.

Some Hints to Help Improve Spelling

1. Correct misspelt words using a dictionary. Write the word in several different sentences if you really want to drive the correct spelling home.
2. Check the pronunciation of words. Pronunciation is a good guide to English spelling more often than people think. *Note:* pronounce the word *carefully*.
3. Check the meaning of words. If you know what a word means, you will tend not to confuse the spelling.
4. Check the make up of words. *Most* spelling errors stem from faulty word-building (e.g. addition of prefixes and suffixes).
5. Whenever possible, use memory devices. They may sound childish at times, but they work:
   e.g. "i before e except after c."
      "The principal is my pal."
   Make up your own "memory devices".
6. Remember: *all* spelling rules have exceptions to them.
7. Never take a chance on spelling an unknown word correctly. WHEN IN DOUBT, USE A DICTIONARY.

1. RULE	EXAMPLES	EXCEPTIONS
i before e except after c	achieve, chief, niece, belief, grief, siege, brief, fiend, yield, shield, etc. After c: ceiling, deceive, receive, conceive, perceive, etc. Note: in all of these words "ie" is pronounced as the "ee" in "eerie".	neither either sleight foreign sovereign surfeit counterfeit forfeit height sheik weird leisure seize
when the "ie" or "ei" are pronounced as "ee" as in "eerie".		
e before i when "ei" is pronounced as in "eight" (a "long" a)	neigh, neighbour, reign, sleigh, eight, etc.	

2. PLURAL FORMS	EXAMPLES	EXCEPTIONS
For most nouns, add s to the singular to form the plural.	boy boys hat hats street streets avenue avenues	
For nouns ending in -ch, -sh, -s, -x, or -z, form the plural by adding -es to the singular.	rich riches brush brushes gas gases tax taxes waltz waltzes	
For nouns ending in a consonant followed by o (e.g. -ho), add -es.	echo echoes tomato tomatoes hero heroes tornado tornadoes	Musical terms ending in a consonant + o: piano pianos alto altos Note: photo photos

For most nouns ending in -f, simply add -s.	hoof	hoofs	calf — calves
	grief	griefs	elf — elves
	proof	proofs	half — halves
	belief	beliefs	knife — knives
	roof	roofs	life — lives
			shelf — shelves
			wife — wives

Many words introduced into English from Latin and Greek have retained their original plural forms.	Latin:		Some foreign words have acquired English plurals:	
	datum	data		
	medium	media		
	bacterium	bacteria		
	Greek:		forum	forums
	thesis	theses	maximum	maximums
	crisis	crises	geranium	geraniums
	analysis	analyses		
	parenthesis	parentheses		
	criterion	criteria		
	phenomenon	phenomena		

Some plural forms are irregular	man	men
	woman	women
	child	children
	ox	oxen
	sheep	sheep
	fish	fish

3. PREFIXES

	EXAMPLES	*EXCEPTIONS*
(Prefixes are syllables added to the beginnings of words to change their meanings dis-, mis-, etc.) For a prefix ending with the same letter as the first letter of the word to which it is to be joined, e.g. "dis-" and "similar"), keep *both* consonants.	dissimilar misspell unnecessary unnerve overrun disservice dissatisfied	For adjoining vowels in such prefix/word situations, note: co-operate re-enter

4. SUFFIXES	EXAMPLES	EXCEPTIONS
(Suffixes are syllables added to the end of words to change their meanings.) A final silent e always makes the vowel (a,e,i,o,u) before it says its name.	mat → mate man → mane met → mete sit → site dot → dote hop → hope cut → cute shut → shute	
A final silent e is *dropped* before a suffix *beginning with a vowel*. e.g. -able, -ed, -ing, -ion, -ish	fire → firing live → livable endure → endurance hesitate → hesitation style → stylish	age → ageing / sliceable slice → outrageous rage → marriageable marriage Note: In all of these words the e is retained to keep the c and g "soft" (say the words aloud, and compare the sounds to the "hard" c and g in "garbled" and "current".
A final silent e is *retained* before a suffix beginning with a *consonant* (all letters other than vowels). e.g. -ful, -less, -ment, -ness	arrange → arrangement love → lovely state → statement bore → boredom	nine → ninth true → truly argue → argument + all cases of -ly able → ably whole → wholly
A final silent e is retained in a few cases where dropping it would cause confusion.	singe → singeing dye → dyeing	
For words of one syllable, (e.g. hit) that end with a single vowel followed by a single consonant, *double* that consonant before a suffix	sit → si*tt*ing hop → ho*pp*ing swim → swi*mm*ing swim → swi*mm*er	Note: This rule does *not* apply to one syllable words ending in two consonants (e.g. *start*) or to one syllable words ending in

Rule	Word	Suffixed	Word	Suffixed
...beginning with a *vowel* e.g. -able / -ed / -ing / -ion / -ish			two vowels followed by a consonant (e.g. *sail*). start sail mail chagrin refer	starting sailing mailed chagrined reference
For words of *more than* one syllable (e.g. pre-fer) that end in a single consonant followed by a single vowel and which stress the *last* syllable, *double* the final consonant before a suffix beginning with a vowel. (e.g. -able, -ed, -ing, -ish). Such words as "pre-FER" have the greatest emphasis placed on the last syllable.	prefer begin permit forget fulfil	preferred beginning permitted forgettable fulfilled		
When the stress is placed on a syllable *other than* the last one, the final consonant is *not* doubled (e.g. for words such as "NAR-row" and "ex-HIB-it" where the most emphasis is placed on a syllable other than the last one).	transfer transfer prosper	transference transfered prospered		
A final y *after* a *consonant* (e.g. -ty) changes to i before most suffixes.	beauty copy silly busy	beautiful copied silliness business	dry sly Note: y is unchanged before i as in beautifying, and in compound words as in byway, citywide.	dryness slyly
A final y *after* a *vowel* (e.g. "oy") usually remains unchanged before suffixes.	boy employ play coy	boys employment playful coyness	day gay lay pay say	daily gaily laid paid said

For a suffix beginning with the same letter as the last letter of the word to which it is to be joined (e.g. "ing" and "ski") retain *both* letters.

suddenness
skiing
hopefully

eighth

-able/-ible

If the word to which the suffix is to be added is complete in itself (e.g. "drink"), it is usually correct to add -able.

drinkable
eatable
readable

inevitable
delectable
repressable

If that word is *not* complete in itself (e.g. "permiss-"), it is usually correct to use -ible.

possible
permissible
irrepressible

possible
permissible
admissible
repressible

If you are still in doubt, the following guideline may be helpful:

If a word ending in -ation can be made out of the root word, then -able is usually correct.
If a word ending in -ssion can be made out of the root word, then -ible is usually correct.

admire   admiration   admirable
consider   consideration   considerable
permit   permission   permissible
admit   admission   admissible
repress   repression   repressible

Note: perfect   perfection   perfectible

-ANT and -ENT

	EXAMPLES	EXCEPTIONS
The letters t and v are usually followed by -ant.	important relevant	insistent persistent competent
"Hard" c (as in cat) and "hard" g (as in good) take -ant.	significant extravagant	

"Soft" c (as in nice) and "soft" g (as in rage), take -ent.

	EXAMPLES	EXCEPTIONS
	adolescent	pageant
	intelligent	

Often the name for a person requires -ant, and the word describing him requires -ent.

"A dependant is dependent on someone else." — superintendent

-SEDE, -CEED, -CEDE

-sede: "Supersede" is the *only* word in the English language to end in -sede.

-ceed: "proceed", "exceed" and "succeed" are the only words in the English language to end in -ceed.

In *all other cases* the word ending pronounced like the word "seed" is spelled *-cede*.

EXAMPLES	EXCEPTIONS
cede	concede
intercede	accede
precede	secede

-C and -IC

-C

Words ending in hard c (e.g. panic) add k before suffixes beginning with e, i, or y (the k keeps the c "hard").

-IC

Words ending in -ic (e.g. authentic), add al before the suffix -ly.

EXAMPLES	EXCEPTIONS	EXCEPTION
traffic	trafficking	
mimic	mimicked	
panic	panicked	
	panicky	
authentic	authentically	
magic	magically	
public		publicly

ROGUES AND DEMONS: *those problem words that haunt us all.*

-ERY and -ARY

"Station*ery* is made of pap*er*."

"Station*ary* means to st*a*nd still."

"A c*or*pse belongs in a cemet*ery*."

For words which are commonly misspelled because people confuse them with other words, see "Words that commonly cause difficulty and confusion" p. 290.

INDEX